HARRIET TUBMAN

Escaped slave, Civil War spy, scout, and nurse, and champion of women's suffrage, Harriet Tubman is an icon of heroism. Perhaps most famous for leading enslaved people to freedom through the Underground Railroad, Tubman was dubbed "Moses" by followers. But abolition and the close of the Civil War were far from the end of her remarkable career. Tubman continued to fight for black civil rights and campaigned fiercely for women's suffrage throughout the remainder of her life.

In this vivid, concise narrative supplemented by primary documents, Kristen T. Oertel introduces readers to Tubman's extraordinary life, from the trauma of her childhood slavery to her civil rights activism in the late nineteenth century, and in the process reveals a nation's struggle over its most central injustices.

Kristen T. Oertel is the Mary Frances Barnard Associate Professor of nineteenth-century American history at the University of Tulsa. She is the author of *Bleeding Borders: Race, Gender, and Violence in Pre-Civil War Kansas* and co-author with Marilyn Blackwell of *Frontier Feminist: Clarina Howard Nichols and the Politics of Motherhood*.

ROUTLEDGE HISTORICAL AMERICANS

SERIES EDITOR: PAUL FINKELMAN

Routledge Historical Americans is a series of short, vibrant biographies that illuminate the lives of Americans who have had an impact on the world. Each book includes a short overview of the person's life and puts that person into historical context through essential primary documents, written both by the subjects and about them. A series website supports the books, containing extra images and documents, links to further research, and where possible, multi-media sources on the subjects. Perfect for including in any course on American History, the books in the Routledge Historical Americans series show the impact everyday people can have on the course of history.

Harriet Tubman
Slavery, the Civil War, and Civil Rights in the Nineteenth Century

KRISTEN T. OERTEL

Routledge
Taylor & Francis Group

NEW YORK AND LONDON

First published 2016
by Routledge
711 Third Avenue, New York, NY 10017

And by Routledge
2 Park Square, Milton Park, Abingdon, Oxon OX14 4RN

Routledge is an imprint of the Taylor & Francis Group, an informa business

Library of Congress Cataloging-in-Publication Data
Oertel, Kristen Tegtmeier, 1969–
   Harriet Tubman : slavery, the Civil War, and civil rights in the nineteenth century / Kristen T. Oertel.
      pages cm. — (Routledge historical Americans)
   Includes bibliographical references and index.
   1. Tubman, Harriet, 1820?-1913.   2. Slaves—United States—Biography.
3. African American women—Biography.   4. Underground Railroad.   5. Fugitive slaves—United States—History—19th century.   6. Antislavery movements—United States—History—19th century.   I. Title.
   E444.T82O35 2015
   326'.8092—dc23
   [B]
   2015008161

ISBN: 978-0-415-82511-5 (hbk)
ISBN: 978-0-415-82512-2 (pbk)
ISBN: 978-0-203-69449-7 (ebk)

Typeset in Minion and Scala Sans
by Apex CoVantage, LLC

For my students—past, present, and future

CONTENTS

ACKNOWLEDGMENTS

Writing about one of the most famous women in American history was a thrilling but daunting task. On the one hand, I rarely had to explain my subject to anyone who asked; even my second-grade daughter could sketch the outline of Tubman's life, and one of my graduate students gave me a finger puppet version of Tubman purchased at a museum gift shop. On the other hand, so many people know about Tubman that the pressure to tell her story in a fresh and engaging way felt overwhelming at times. Thankfully, after teaching college history courses for over fifteen years, I possessed a heuristic tool that guided me through the process. Before every chapter I asked myself: What image of Tubman do most Americans see, and how can I revise and enrich that picture? Furthermore, what does the reading public need to know about Tubman that they didn't learn in the second grade or at a history museum?

Many people helped me answer these questions, beginning with series editor Paul Finkelman, who invited me to contribute to the collection. He read every chapter carefully and provided insightful comments and citations without being overbearing, constantly reminding me that it "was my book." I benefitted greatly from his encyclopedic knowledge of how the law intersects with slavery, abolition, and the war. I also thank Kimberly Guinta and Genevieve Aoki at Routledge who shepherded me through the proposal and drafting process with efficiency and kindness; I also appreciate their patience as fate waylaid the original timeline.

In the midst of drafting the book, I suffered multiple orthopedic injuries in a severe car accident, and I thank the doctors, nurses, and staff at St. John's Hospital and the Kaiser Rehabilitation Center at Hillcrest Hospital in Tulsa for their excellent care. In addition, the physical and occupational therapists at Excel Physical Therapy worked wonders and kept my spirits high as they inquired about my book and historical topics more generally. More than anything, they reminded me of why I do what I do, and they did all they could to get me back on track.

The faculty writing group at the University of Tulsa—Randall Fuller, Brian Hosmer, Joli Jensen, and Lee Anne Nichols—made sure I stayed on target through the right combination of peer pressure and tough questions. Their commitment to me and to our group kept me focused week after week as I churned out page after page, sometimes not knowing where the next paragraph would go or how a sentence would fit. I would also like to thank the Dean's office at the University of Tulsa for granting me a teaching leave at the beginning of this project so that I could conduct initial research; the Chapman Trust, which funds the Mary F. Barnard Chair that I hold, also deserves my gratitude for providing a generous research and travel fund that enabled me to travel to New York and Maryland for additional research and to meet with other historians who have studied Tubman. Thanks to colleagues and friends Andrew Cohen, Carol Faulkner, and Heather Grandsire for hosting me during these research trips.

During my trip to New York, I had the pleasure of meeting one of Tubman's descendants, Ms. Judith Bryant, the great, great granddaughter of Tubman's brother William H. Stewart, who is buried next to Tubman at Fort Hill cemetery in Auburn. Bryant graciously shared family memories of Tubman as passed down to her from her mother, who was seven when Tubman died, and grandmother, who took care of Tubman in her final years. She lamented the tension between the public's perception of the mythical Tubman and "the truth," which she acknowledged was elusive, but I took her concerns to heart as I wrote the book.

I would not have been granted an interview with Judith Bryant nor would I have been able to write one credible word of the book without the scholarship and generosity of Kate Clifford Larson. From the moment I first contacted Kate until the last minutes of drafting the manuscript, I relied on her historical expertise, scholarly integrity, and benevolent heart. She enthusiastically supported my project from its inception, shared copious amounts of sources, and answered too many questions to count. I followed her footnotes like a roadmap to Tubman's life, and she steered me in the right direction when I fell off course. Finally, she read a draft of the manuscript, even as she was putting the finishing touches on her own book project. Kate epitomizes the best kind of colleague, and her advice has been invaluable.

I benefitted immensely from other colleagues' support and from the work of other historians and scholars of Tubman: biographies by Jean Humez, Catherine Clinton, and Lois Horton all provided excellent resources for my own project, and Humez's inclusion of so many original sources about Tubman was incredibly useful. Quraysh Lansana inspired me with his beautiful poems that gave voice to a woman who left so little of her own for posterity, and Milton Sernett's careful and detailed reflections on the Tubman myth informed my own interpretation of her memory. And though I did not see them often enough, my colleagues in women's and African American history, especially those in the Society of Civil War Historians, motivated me with their conference talks, journal articles, and books that continue to push the boundaries of the American narrative. My colleagues in the history and English departments at the University of Tulsa also sustained my work in numerous ways, particularly during my medical leave, and I count myself lucky to have landed at such a congenial and supportive university. Finally, the research assistance provided by Ryan Donaldson helped me put the finishing touches on the manuscript before submission.

As I look forward to its publication, I appreciate the fact that I have finally written a book that my family and friends might actually read from cover to cover! I hope they will enjoy the fruits of my labor because they, too, tended the tree as it grew. First and foremost, my husband, Bob, and my children, Owen and Lily, deserve my heartfelt gratitude for nursing me back to health after the accident and for shoring up my positive attitude as I faced the frustration of delayed deadlines and a backlog of work. Family members Gary Tegtmeier and Mary Kowalski, Diane Tegtmeier and Jim Gilkeson, Walt and Stephanie Tegtmeier, Billie Oertel, and Kathy Wolter also swept in to Tulsa to help heal me, which enabled my return to normal life much more quickly and easily. Tulsa friends Tangie Ballard, Caryn and Scott Brown, Sangita and Romel Chattergee, Stephanie and Brian Dehart, Shandy and Steve Dotolo, Matthew Drever, Rosana Khan, Tracy and Lee Manly, Sadi Owicz, Candace Melton, Teresa and Warren Ross, and Kim Whiting, along with steadfast pals Stacey Evans, Currie Gasche, Jillian Knutson, Bela Roongta, Debbie Sieck, and Kelley Durbin Williams all buoyed me as I transitioned from Jackson to Tulsa, from injury to health, and from book proposal to finished manuscript. I am also indebted to the faculty and staff at the University School, who nurtured my children's emotional and intellectual growth while I recovered and finished the book. Finally, Nathan Mattox and members of University United Methodist Church, especially the Women's Book Club, all prayed for me when I reached the depths of physical and psychological despair. I faced only a fraction of the pain and trauma experienced by Harriet Tubman, but my trials and, especially, my allies helped me identify with my subject, a woman who triumphed over tragedy but who also bore scars that reminded her of the ongoing struggles that life presents.

PART I

HARRIET TUBMAN

INTRODUCTION

A is an Abolitionist—A man who wants to free
The wretched slave—and give to all
An equal liberty.

B is a Brother with a skin
Of somewhat darker hue,
But in our Heavenly Father's sight,
He is as dear as you.

C is the Cotton-field, to which
This injured brother's driven,
When, as the white-man's slave, he toils,
From early morn till even.

D is the Driver, cold and stern,
Who follows, whip in hand,
To punish those who dare to rest,
Or disobey command . . .[1]

In 1847, two years before Harriet Tubman escaped from her master's plantation, an anonymous writer published "The Anti-Slavery Alphabet," a pamphlet that gained widespread appeal after its introduction at the Philadelphia Antislavery Fair that same year. The "alphabet" conveyed abolitionist sentiment as it introduced nineteenth-century children to the building blocks of literacy, so perhaps it is curious that these letters open a book dedicated to unearthing the life of Harriet Tubman, a woman who never learned to read. Yet "The Anti-Slavery Alphabet" illustrates many of the themes that a study of Tubman can reveal. First, the Tubman myth that occupies the public's imagination originated in children's books. In fact, most adults probably learned about this iconic conductor of the Underground Railroad from one of the more than one hundred children's and youth biographies published about Tubman since the 1950s.[2] Second, the characters of the "alphabet," the abolitionist who "wants to free the wretched slave" and the "brother with a skin of somewhat darker hue," highlight the important connections between slaves and their allies in freedom, linkages that Tubman would cement during her many trips back and forth across the Mason-Dixon line. Finally, the "driver" who whips the slave who "disobeys" conjures up the slave rebel, a role Tubman embodied both before and during the Civil War as she helped dismantle the system that had kept her family enslaved for generations.

The "alphabet" also obscures several important themes, however, that Tubman's biography can help illuminate. The causation of the emancipation process implied by the "alphabet"—that white, male abolitionists would free black "brothers"—ignores the ways in which slaves carved out their own paths to freedom, with and without the help of abolitionists (who were both white and black). Tubman's courageous work on the Underground Railroad opens up a window into a world inhabited by the many slaves who "voted with their feet" and weakened the peculiar institution in the decade before the Civil War by emancipating themselves.[3] The male subjects of the "alphabet" also ignore the women, both enslaved and free, who challenged slavery and patriarchy and who have gained impressive historical traction in recent studies about slavery, abolition, and the Civil War.[4] Tubman's life story encapsulates these historiographic trends; she represents the many women who shattered gender barriers in the context of political and military crises and the many slaves and free blacks who boldly attacked slavery in theory and in practice. And yet ultimately, Tubman is a singular and heroic historical figure who defies categorization, which perhaps explains why we know more about her myth than her history. It is my goal to explore the unique richness of Tubman's story while also considering how her life connects us to the history of slavery, the Civil War, and civil rights in the nineteenth century.

***

Harriet Tubman's parents, Ben Ross and Harriet "Rit" Green, were born in Dorchester County, Maryland, just as the ink on the U.S. Constitution was drying. The country's founding document simultaneously ensconced slavery in U.S. law by defining Ben and Rit as property and each of them as three-fifths of a person, but it also opened up the possibility for slavery's extinction, as it mandated the cessation of the Atlantic slave trade and lifted up "the Blessings of Liberty." In 1822, the year Rit gave birth to her daughter Araminta Ross, later known as Harriet Tubman, the United

States and the institution of slavery had expanded westward, and the cotton economy fueled the beginnings of the Industrial Revolution in the United States. Slavery had also become increasingly sectionalized, thriving in the Deep South and dying a gradual but stubborn death in the upper South and the North.

Forty years later, after Tubman had rescued dozens of slaves, including her elderly parents and the bulk of her extended family, President Abraham Lincoln issued the Emancipation Proclamation, a military order that set the nation on a path toward de jure black freedom. Tubman knew that a piece of paper could not guarantee the freedom of a race of people who had been held captive for centuries, so in 1862 she joined the Union army in South Carolina, where she helped over 700 slaves escape to Union lines and nursed countless soldiers and freedmen back to health. Tubman worked for another kind of freedom thirty years later as she participated in woman's suffrage conventions at the end of the century. She recognized that women, particularly black women, could not claim the freedom she fought so hard to win while they remained second-class citizens. When Tubman died in 1913 at the age of ninety-one, she could relish in the fact that she helped destroy an institution that had thrived in the Americas for hundreds of years, but she also lamented the stubborn legacies of tyranny that persisted in Jim Crow laws in the South and that disfranchised women everywhere.

In essence, Tubman's life reveals the arc of a nation's struggle with its most divisive and ironic feature: how a country, founded in liberty, could perpetuate racial and gender inequalities for centuries. Tubman provides us with a remarkable example of the enduring human spirit that challenged this injustice. Indeed, it was Tubman's faith in God, her family, and her future that motivated her activism, but it was also her ability to connect with an existing and expanding network of like-minded black and white activists that ensured her success. One Civil War reporter described Tubman as a "Black 'She Moses,'" and the title is fitting. She was black and female when white and male ruled the day, but Moses determined to set all of her people free.[5]

NOTES

1. Anonymous (although now attributed to Philadelphia Quakers Hannah and Mary Townshend), "The Anti-Slavery Alphabet" (Philadelphia: Merrihew and Thompson, 1847), reprinted at http://www.gutenberg.org/files/16081/16081-h/16081-h.htm.
2. Milton C. Sernett, *Harriet Tubman: Myth, Memory, and History* (Durham: Duke University Press, 2007), 37.
3. Recent studies that explore African Americans' role in the emancipation process include: Eric Foner, *Gateway to Freedom: The Hidden History of the Underground Railroad* (New York: Norton, 2015); Richard Blackett, *Making Freedom: The Underground Railroad and the Politics of Slavery* (Chapel Hill: The University of North Carolina Press, 2013); Stanley Harrold, *Border*

War: Fighting over Slavery before the Civil War (Chapel Hill: The University of North Carolina Press, 2010); and David Blight, *A Slave No More: Two Men Who Escaped to Freedom* (Boston: Houghton, Mifflin, Harcourt, 2007).

4. Recent studies on enslaved women include: Daina Ramey Berry and Deleso A. Alford, eds., *Enslaved Women in America: An Encyclopedia* (Santa Barbara, CA: ABC-CLIO, 2012); Thavolia Glymph, *Out of the House of Bondage: The Transformation of the Plantation Household* (New York: Cambridge University Press, 2008); Stephanie Camp, *Enslaved Women and Everyday Resistance in the Plantation South* (Chapel Hill: The University of North Carolina Press, 2004); and Jennifer Morgan, *Laboring Women: Reproduction and Gender in New World Slavery* (Philadelphia: University of Pennsylvania Press, 2004).

5. The term "Black 'She Moses'" was coined by a reporter for *The Wisconsin State Journal* in a June 20, 1863, story about the Combahee River raid. See Kate Clifford Larson, *Bound for the Promised Land: Harriet Tubman, Portrait of an American Hero* (New York: One World/ Ballantine, 2004), 365n55.

CHAPTER 1

MINTY

Minty, short for Araminta, was a feisty and headstrong young slave. . . .
When she grew up she became Harriet Tubman, the courageous and
heroic woman who helped hundreds of slaves escape to freedom through
the Underground Railroad.

From *Minty, A Story of Young Harriet Tubman*[1]

Google Harriet Tubman's name with the word "hero," and over 215,000 websites will flood your computer screen in 0.31 seconds. First on the list is the site "MyHero.com," a source that uses "media, art, and technology to celebrate the best of humanity" and that features Tubman as "a shining example of self-determination and faith, fueled by rugged endurance."[2] Another site claims that Tubman's name is "synonymous with bravery and freedom" and reprints a poem that locates the origins of Tubman's heroism:

Harriet Tubman didn't take no stuff
Wasn't scared of nothing neither
Didn't come in this world to be no slave
And didn't stay one either.[3]

The poem and the many websites that note Tubman's heroic qualities often speak of her time as a conductor on the Underground Railroad and her courageous resistance to the institution of slavery. Tubman stands out among the majority of her peers for her ability to escape from slavery's chains *and* to voluntarily return to the South and lead dozens of her friends and family members to freedom.

But Tubman's resistance to the slave regime was hardly unique, and even her return trips into slave territory were not unprecedented. Rather, she joined a rising tide of enslaved and free blacks and white abolitionists who challenged slaveholders' claims to their "property" and had encouraged freedom seekers along the porous border for decades. Furthermore, even those slaves who never left the plantation resisted white attempts to control their lives and their futures. Slave resistance spanned a wide range of behaviors—from small-scale actions like feigning sickness or breaking tools to more overt challenges like running away or poisoning one's master—but most slaves created spaces in which they could assert their humanity, constantly reminding their masters of slavery's instability. Scholars have identified this resistance as a primary factor in causing the downfall of the institution, claiming that "black women and men's struggles against slavery ultimately contributed to their emancipation . . . slaves' persistence in pushing for temporary or permanent forms of freedom strained slave owners, the South, and the nation."[4] Tubman and other slaves who "didn't come in this world to be no slave and didn't stay one either" collectively pierced a thorn in the slaveholder's side, a thorn that festered until the Civil War.

In order to fully comprehend Tubman's heroism and that of the countless other slaves who chose to be thorns and resist the slave regime, we first must construct the scaffolding that kept the institution of slavery in place for centuries. Economics, culture, and law coalesced to maintain the slave system, and the twin ideals of patriarchy and white supremacy dominated social relations in the colonial South. The cotton economy that emerged after Eli Whitney introduced the cotton gin in 1793 expanded the institution in the Deep South and the West and tied the economic future of the country to its success. As the peculiar institution marched westward from Georgia to Texas, planters scrambled to buy more slaves in order to grow more cotton in order to buy more slaves. From birth to death, generation after generation, most black folk in America were enslaved, and the democratic nation they called home conspired to keep them that way. It is against these remarkable odds that Harriet Tubman, or "Minty" as she was first called, emerged as a hero.[5]

***

When Harriet Tubman's grandparents were born in the mid-eighteenth century, slavery was legal in all thirteen colonies, and only a handful of states, including Massachusetts and Vermont, abolished the institution in the immediate wake of the American Revolution. Other states, like New York and Pennsylvania, passed gradual emancipation laws during or after the Revolution, so that by 1820 the overwhelming majority of blacks living above the Mason-Dixon Line were free. Yet even in the free states of New England and the mid-Atlantic, a few aging blacks, born before the passage of the gradual emancipation acts, remained in slavery until the 1840s, as did a few slaves in Illinois, born there during the territorial period. Just below these mid-Atlantic states, in what historians now refer to as the upper or border South, numerous masters voluntarily manumitted their slaves, even as their neighbors tenaciously supported slavery and retained their slaves. Thus, for example, by 1860 most blacks in Delaware were free. By this time about half the blacks in Maryland were free, but of course the other half were slaves. Outside of Delaware slavery remained vibrant and enormously profitable, and the massive expansion of cotton cultivation in the Deep South and Southwest provided a steady market for slaves born in the Chesapeake and the Carolinas who could be sold further south. By this time even southerners called their system a "peculiar institution" because it was geographically isolated and fundamentally contrary to the ethos of the new democratic American republic.[6]

At least three generations of Tubman's ancestors called the Eastern Shore of Maryland home, and slavery's roots ran very deep in the Chesapeake Bay. At the time of Tubman's birth the institution was declining in the upper South, as tobacco cultivation gave way to less labor-intensive crops like corn and wheat, but modern slavery in America originated in the Chesapeake in the early seventeenth century. Thus, slavery had always been a way of life in Virginia and Maryland, and the first federal census of 1790 indicates that 60 percent of the entire U.S. slave population lived in these two states alone. Working as field hands to harvest tobacco and cereal grains and as skilled laborers like carpenters, cooks, and ship caulkers, these slaves and their free black counterparts played a central role in Maryland's economy. And while manumissions increased in the early nineteenth century and the common practice of "hiring out" offered slaves greater mobility and economic freedom, planters and landholders in large part determined the size and shape of the black community on the Eastern Shore. "During the antebellum years black people in Maryland—slave and free—experienced the agony of slavery's slow death, but not the deliverance. The middle ground . . . set close boundaries on the liberty of the ostensibly free, and played havoc with bonds of love, friendship, and family among slaves and between them and free black people."[7]

Harriet Tubman's extended family experienced the ironic pangs of slavery's gradual demise on the Eastern Shore of Maryland in the early nineteenth century. In Dorchester County, where Tubman's parents and grandparents lived, the population of slaves stood at 4,566 in 1810, down from 5,337 in 1790, but slaves still composed roughly 40 percent of the county's population.[8] Tubman's mother, "Rit" Green, was owned by Mary

Pattison, who inherited Rit in 1797 and who brought Rit with her to her new home when she married Joseph Brodess in 1800. Mary gave birth to a son, Edward, in 1801, but her husband Joseph died the next year, and the young, widowed mother remarried in 1803. Mary's second husband, Anthony Thompson, owned Tubman's father, Ben Ross, and so it was this union of the Thompson and Brodess estates that brought Rit and Ben together. Records indicate that they married around 1808 (although slaves were not permitted to legally marry) and immediately started their family, which would eventually grow to include nine children. Thompson paid a midwife on March 15, 1822, presumably for her assistance with Rit's fifth labor and delivery, when Araminta, or "Minty" as they first called Harriet, joined her four older brothers and sisters on the Thompson plantation. Later that year, Thompson's stepson, Edward Brodess (Mary's son from her first marriage), inherited Rit, Minty, and her other children from Thompson after turning 21. However, Brodess and his stepfather locked horns over his inheritance, and it is likely that Rit and her children remained on the Thompson plantation at least until Brodess married Eliza Ann Keene in 1824.[9]

Tubman remembered very little about her early childhood, but the experiences she did recall were typical of most enslaved children. In an interview later in life, Tubman said that her mother left her and her younger siblings at home every day while Rit "cooked up to the big house." Tubman was only about five years old, but her mother put her in charge of her baby brother, whom she held "by the bottom of his dress" and swung "all around, his feet in the dress and his little head and arms touching the floor, because I was too small to hold him higher." She recollected that her mother often returned home late at night and that to soothe the cranky baby, she would "cut a fat chunk of pork and toast it on the coals and put it in his mouth."[10] Many young slave children were left alone while their parents worked in the fields or as house servants. Thomas Jefferson even instructed that slave "children till 10 years old . . . serve as nurses," on his plantation, and while elderly slaves might supervise these child nurses from time to time, it is likely that children were raising children on a regular basis on many plantations.[11] The dangers associated with unsupervised child care did not trump the value of their parents tending crops or cooking for the master's family.

Thus, basic physical safety often eluded enslaved children not only because they were sometimes left alone, but also because they were subjected to violent treatment by their masters. For example, Delia Garlic was only a young teen when her owner disapproved of her childcare skills and brutally punished her; Garlic's mistress grabbed a nearby hot iron and " 'ran it all down' her arm and hand, and 'took off all de flesh when she done it.'" Corporal punishment was commonplace in a slave regime, and masters did not shield children from the violence they used to enforce slave discipline. One overseer whipped a slave girl for "shirking" her duties and defended his actions by saying, "If I hadn't punished her so hard she would have done the same thing again to-morrow, and half the people on the plantation would have followed her example."[12] Overseers and masters knew that fear of violent punishment motivated slaves to work, and they instilled that fear early in children's lives.

Tubman was no different; scars on the back of her neck reminded her of one of her first jobs as a slave, when she was hired out at age seven or eight to serve as a nurse and maid for a woman Tubman later referred to as "Miss Susan." Since Minty had "never seen the inside of a house better than a cabin in the negro quarters, [and] was put to house-work without being told how to do anything," she made mistakes and paid for them with her stinging flesh. Miss Susan kept a whip above the fireplace mantel and wielded it when she believed Minty had not dusted the parlor furniture and floors sufficiently. Young Minty cried out in pain and Susan's sister, Emily, intervened to save the girl from more beatings; she instructed Minty how to sweep and dust while preventing the dust from resettling, a lesson that undoubtedly saved Tubman from further suffering in the parlor.[13]

But the parlor mantel was not the only location of a whip in Miss Susan's home. The slave mistress "laid upon her bed with a whip under her pillow" and slept, while Minty rocked and tended to Miss Susan's "cross, sick child" throughout the night. If the baby fussed or cried, indicating that Minty had neglected her rocking duties by falling asleep, "then down would come the whip upon the neck and face," thus creating an "enforced habit of wakefulness" in her. Although it is unclear exactly how old Minty was when she worked for Susan, most biographers estimate that she was between seven and ten, indicating that she had to endure sleepless nights and physical abuse on a regular basis as a very young girl. Dusting by day and rocking by night, Minty, like many other slave children, understood the drudgery of slave labor from an early age.[14]

As evidenced by Minty's experiences, the institution of slavery relied on violence to maintain it, and while planters preached paternalism and claimed they cared for their slaves like their own children, even the most enlightened masters used varying degrees of corporal punishment and the constant threat of violence as tools of social control. The "ability to physically correct one's dependents was a defining feature of patriarchal privilege" in the Chesapeake, and rarely were the "exact limits of disciplinary violence" ever defined in legal statutes.[15] Slave masters *and* mistresses like Miss Susan began instructing their charges on the intricacies of slave discipline when they were children. Perhaps the South's most famous planter, Thomas Jefferson, understood that productivity required submission to the work regimen and that enslaved children must learn habits of obedience for a profit to be made. Jefferson employed a "dozen little boys from 10 to 16 years of age" in his nail factory at Monticello, and he knew that his overseer, Gabriel Lilly, whipped "the small ones" if they fell short of his expectations as workers. And although Jefferson instructed his son-in-law to tell Lilly that the whip "must not be resorted to but in extremities," he also told him that "[the boys] require a vigour of discipline to make them do reasonable work." In Jefferson's carefully calibrated world, enslaved children would rarely be whipped, but when the nail boys balked at waking up early on a cold winter's day and arrived late to the nail forge, Lilly beat them for truancy and Jefferson endorsed the practice.[16]

In addition to using the whip sparingly with children, some manuals consulted by planters and overseers also suggested restraint when it came to physically beating or whipping female slaves. However, exceptions existed just as they did with Jefferson's nail boys; if enslaved women acted in "stout and mannish" ways or defied authority, then masters could "beat [them] downe" with impunity.[17] For example, when an enslaved woman named Sophia ran away repeatedly from her Arkansas plantation, her master, Isaac Spencer, flogged her mercilessly for her offense. One witness described Spencer as looking "calm and deliberate" as he whipped Sophia "using a cowhide with a plaited buckskin lash about fifteen inches long" and then "salted her back" with a cob, after which Sophia looked "deranged." Sophia's habitual opposition to Spencer's rules garnered a severe and unequivocal response that left her in a state of confusion and intense pain, even though he knew that Sophia escaped with a harmless goal in mind: to see her children who lived on a nearby plantation.[18] Clearly masters and overseers often disregarded age, gender, and family concerns when it came to slave discipline.

Perhaps the most revolting example of slave owners' lack of consideration for gender or physical condition is when masters dug holes in the ground before whipping pregnant female slaves. One slave remembered that her sister and grandmother were in the cotton fields of Arkansas when her sister, who was pregnant at the time, began to lag behind; after the overseer's commands failed to increase the woman's work pace, he dug a hole in the ground in preparation for a whipping.[19] Another former slave testified to this practice on his plantation: "A woman who gives offense in the field, and is large in a family way, is compelled to lie down over a hole made to receive her corpulency, and is flogged with a whip or beat with a paddle, which has holes in it; at every stroke comes a blister."[20] In a slave regime pregnant bellies, and the future field hands that grew inside them, would be protected even though the enslaved mother suffered with each stripe that marked her naked back. Gender and age mattered little if a recalcitrant slave threatened the foundation of one's control, and planters asserted their mastery with violence on an equal opportunity basis.

Whipping was the most common form of physical punishment, but slave owners employed more horrific methods of discipline as well. One master hammered nails through a barrel, shut a slave inside it, and then rolled the barrel down the hill. Another master hung a rebellious slave by his thumbs from a beam, while another placed a large stick underneath a slave's knees, made him squat down, and then tied his hands to each end of the stick before whipping him.[21] And while extreme punishments like dismemberment and castration fell out of favor by the late eighteenth century and legislatures passed laws against them, regulations did not necessarily prevent masters from breaking the rules and returning to old practices. Planters sometimes lost their tempers and violently retaliated against their rebellious slaves, like one Virginia planter who castrated and dismembered a runaway slave in 1773.[22]

By the mid-nineteenth century castration was outlawed in most states, but a few cases flew in the face of these regulations. In 1850 the Tennessee master Gabriel Worley believed that the only way he could control his "turbulent and insolent" slave was to castrate him. Worley cited the offending slave's propensity for running away and "harassment" as justification for the castration and exhibited no moral qualms about committing the act, other than to ensure that the "gentler sex" would not witness it. Worley "banished all the female family members from the premises, and with the assistance of his son and a 'certain razor' 'did strike, cut off, and disable the organs of generation' of Josiah," his slave. Worley was convicted of "mayhem" and sentenced to jail, which indicates that the community no longer approved of castration as a form of punishment, but his slave, Josiah, still suffered from his master's blatant disregard of the legal code.[23]

One need look no further than the runaway ads themselves to find evidence that masters continued to maim their slaves, even in the nineteenth century. Descriptions of slaves who were missing toes and ears and displayed "disfigured appendages" emerge from the pages of southern newspapers. The ads also featured examples of slaves who bore scars due to burning and branding, in addition to the ubiquitous example of slaves who were "very much marked with the whip" on their backs and sides.[24] Abolitionists began using these ads to highlight the brutality of the system, reprinting ads that described slaves with "gunshot wounds, cropped ears, whipping scars, and cuts from knives or axes." But masters depended on physical evidence of past behavior to determine a slave's worth; at slave auctions they would inspect slaves' bodies and "read" their scars "like a deck of tarot cards," cataloguing each one's size, shape, and approximate age to determine whether a particular slave was more or less rebellious than another who sported different scars.[25]

Although many slaves, including Harriet Tubman, carried scars from their abuse at the hands of their owners and employers, the scar that most profoundly shaped Tubman's life was the one on her head that marked the time a heavy weight cracked her skull. Historian Kate Larson claims that this injury "changed the course of her life, not only through the physical disability it caused, but also because it sparked physiological changes that redefined the way Tubman viewed the world."[26] Tubman was in her early teens when the fateful incident occurred and thus was old enough to be hired out to work as a field hand on a local plantation. One of her fellow workers, a male slave, left the field without permission and went to a nearby store but was quickly pursued by his overseer, who likely forced Tubman to accompany him. When the overseer found the disobedient slave at the store, "he swore he should be whipped, and called on Harriet, among others, to help tie him. She refused, and as the man ran away, she placed herself in the door to stop pursuit. The overseer caught up a two-pound weight from the counter and threw it at the fugitive, but it fell short and struck Harriet a stunning blow on the head." Bleeding profusely and slipping in and out of consciousness, Tubman convalesced for two days at a nearby house but was forced to return to her plantation soon afterward. She told an interviewer that after returning to the fields, she worked with "blood an' sweat rollin down my face till I couldn't see."[27]

The injury caused extremely painful and frequent headaches for the rest of Tubman's life, and perhaps most importantly, initiated a lifelong struggle with seizures. Tubman probably suffered from a type of epilepsy because "the bright lights, colorful auras, disembodied voices, states of tremendous anxiety and fear alternating with exceptional hyperactivity and fearlessness, and dreamlike trances while appearing to be conscious . . . are classic symptoms of temporal lobe epilepsy." The daily burden of combating these symptoms, especially the periodic narcolepsy that so many of Tubman's contemporaries mentioned, and the chronic headaches she experienced, would eventually lead her to seek out a doctor at Massachusetts General Hospital who performed brain surgery to alleviate her suffering. But the surgery, which Tubman claimed did provide her with some relief, was not performed until the late 1890s, meaning that for most of her life she not only endured the physical abuse associated with her enslavement, but also experienced the pain and suffering that accompanied her injury.[28]

Yet Tubman's brain injury manifested itself in more positive ways as well, and perhaps explains why she developed and maintained an intense and visceral faith in God and in the guidance and protection she believed came directly from spiritual visions. Tubman grew up immersed in a spiritual world that blended indigenous African and Christian forms of worship, since it is believed that her maternal grandmother, Modesty, was born in Africa, and the Eastern Shore was home to a number of ethnic Africans, particularly from the Akan region of West Africa's Gold Coast.[29] Many African religious beliefs involved spirit possession or divining, religious practices that historians and anthropologists have documented in slave societies throughout the Americas. Historian Michael Gomez notes that "spirit possession was a fine art in many African societies," and James Sweet demonstrates that African slave diviners "literally received a spirit from the other world, giving the spirit a human form" and that these spirits often "entered their hosts through their heads."[30] Although it is impossible to know whether Tubman believed that her head injury opened up a direct line of communication with the spiritual world, she developed an intimate relationship with God and prayed often for guidance when making important decisions. When asked how she mustered the courage to repeatedly put herself in danger during her many trips on the Underground Railroad, Tubman always replied, "Why don't I tell you ... t'wan't *me*, 'twas *de Lord*! I always *tole* him, 'I trust to you. I don't know where to go or what to do, but I expect you to lead me,' an' he always did."[31]

Tubman's belief that God communicated with her directly could have been shaped by African spiritual practices, but we also know that her family attended a local Methodist church and was exposed to Episcopal, Baptist, and Catholic influences as well. Dr. Anthony Thompson, the son of Tubman's first master and stepbrother to her owner, Edward Brodess, preached at a Methodist church in Dorchester County, and Tubman and her family sometimes attended his services. Her parents "claimed Thompson was just 'pretending to preach' and was nothing but 'a wolf in sheep's clothing,'" but Tubman undoubtedly absorbed some of the lessons he conveyed during his sermons, though "obey your master" was likely not one of them. It is probable that she also attended two local black churches, the Bazzel Methodist Episcopal Church, located just southeast of the Brodess plantation, and Scott's Chapel, another Methodist church; regardless, Tubman confronted the tenets of evangelical Protestantism on a regular basis in addition to any African cultural practices that her neighbors and relatives maintained.[32]

The spread of evangelical Christianity during the early nineteenth century, often referred to as the Second Great Awakening, shaped the southern black community in profound ways. Methodist and Baptist churches sprung up throughout the South and attracted thousands of new members because their simple message of salvation through grace and their more emotional style of worship appealed to uneducated white and black audiences. John Thompson, a slave from Maryland, described his conversion to Methodism after years of finding his mistress's Episcopalian worship obtuse and boring. Thompson said that an itinerant Methodist minister travelled near his plantation and "preached in a manner so plain that the way faring man, though a fool, could not err therein. . . . It opened the prison doors to them that were bound and let the captive go free." Thompson remembered that "nearly every slave he knew" converted to Methodism after hearing this preacher and described how the word spread from plantation to plantation.[33] Black membership in evangelical churches exploded as a result of this new approach to worship. For example, one Methodist conference in Mississippi experienced a dramatic increase in conversions, going from roughly 1,500 black members in 1837 to over 12,000 in 1860, almost all of whom were enslaved.[34]

In addition to using itinerant ministers who traveled to rural areas and thus exposed more slaves to evangelical styles of worship, Baptist and Methodist churches also allowed black preachers to carry their message to the slave quarters. Baptists and Methodists "stressed ability to communicate and enthusiasm for the Gospel" rather than a strict understanding of theological doctrine, which enabled uneducated free blacks and slaves to serve as preachers in their communities. Enslaved blacks much preferred their own preachers over white ones, some travelling ten miles or more each way just to hear a black preacher, so when these denominations began supporting them, the conversions among slaves only increased. Black preacher Henry Adams, who pastored the first independent black church in Louisville, Kentucky, reportedly converted over 10,000 people during his lifetime.[35]

In addition to individual conversions, large camp meetings served as conduits for thousands of slave conversions, as worshippers shouted and danced when the spirit moved them, embracing a more physical and emotional style of worship that mimicked African forms of worship.[36] Tubman likely attended at least one camp meeting, for they occurred regularly on the Eastern Shore, and she also witnessed black preachers, perhaps even the free black female ministers Zilpha Elaw and Jarena Lee, who preached at a number of camp meetings on the Eastern Shore and in Baltimore churches between 1820 and 1850. In 1824 Lee spoke in Denton, Maryland, less than thirty miles from Tubman's home. Lee remembered that "many slaves walked twenty, thirty, or more miles to come to meetings, knowing they had to return the same number of miles to be ready to work the next day." William Cornish, a slave who lived on the Eastern Shore, said his master would allow him to travel as far as Baltimore to participate in camp meetings, and another slave, Jacob Johnson, travelled in a canoe from Calvert County to Dorchester County to attend a meeting with his master's permission. Some masters tried to decrease the mobility of blacks on Sundays, but because slaves had travelled to faraway churches and meetings since the Revolutionary era and some camp meetings were hosted by plantation masters themselves, it was difficult to challenge the ritual.[37]

Masters who hosted camp meetings were among the many whites who, like slaves and free blacks, were swept up in the spiritual fires of the Second Great Awakening. Some Chesapeake planters who converted to evangelical Christianity began to question the morality of slavery, even to the point of manumitting their slaves. Indeed, the Methodist and Baptist churches in Virginia experienced tensions among its white members over the slavery question from the 1780s until the dawn of the Civil War. In Southampton County, Virginia, congregants at the Black Creek Baptist church "declared slavery 'Unrighteous,'" and its minister, David Barrow, and a number of his parishioners freed all of their slaves. Furthermore, Barrow participated in a Baptist convention in 1790 that issued a remarkable statement opposing slavery, referring to the institution as a "violent deprivation of the rights of nature" and vowing to "extirpate the horrid evil from the land."[38] Thirty-five years later, another minister from Black Creek church announced that he "would not administer the ordinances of the Gospel to the church any longer—because a Part of the church were slave holders."[39] It seems that the growing belief that slavery was a sin took hold among some southern whites, even slaveholding ones, and they chose to take the doctrine of "free will" to its logical conclusion, in the process freeing their slaves and their own souls from sin.

But even the doctrine of "free will" and the pressure among evangelicals to manumit slaves did not change most slaveholders' minds, and in fact, proslavery doctrine found the seeds of its most enduring defense in evangelical interpretations of the Bible. Historian Douglas Ambrose argues that "the notion of the hierarchical, paternalistic, Christian household that characterized evangelical discussions of slavery by 1810 remained a constant feature of the southern defense of the social order there." A story in an 1807 issue of the *Virginia Religious Magazine* called "A Sabbath Evening, at Mr. Jervas's" illustrates this style of paternalism. The fictional Mr. Jervas extols the virtues of educating one's slaves in Christianity and reassured his audience that such teachings would not "inspire them with high notions of liberty," but rather was "the readiest way to incline them to act as they ought." Mr. Jervas further defined the perfect paternalist relationship: "The duties of masters and servants are reciprocal. It is the servant's duty to honor and obey his master, and serve him with fidelity. It is the master's duty to protect, feed, and clothe his servant, and give him such instruction as is necessary for his salvation."[40] In their attempts to convince slaveholders to attend to their slaves' souls, men like the fictional Jervas ensured the planter class that perfect obedience would result if slaves found religion. Evangelical Christianity could deliver slaves' and their masters' souls while also offering justification for slavery and its attendant system of social control.

The split in white interpretations of the Bible and the meaning of evangelical Christianity culminated in the mid-1840s when the Methodist, Baptist, and Presbyterian churches divided into southern and northern branches. Southern church leaders cited their northern brethren's "unconstitutional" actions regarding slavery as a fundamental reason for the split, though the process was not taken lightly. Mississippi Methodist minister John G. Jones described his painful experience with the "great schism" of 1844 and 1845: "The mind of the church was filled with this unprecedented disaster. To this writer, it was the darkest day he had ever seen. . . . It is a fearful thing to rend the body of Christ." But however "fearful" it was to break apart the "body of Christ," southern church leaders refused to maintain a connection with northern churches that increasingly preached anti-slavery doctrine. Black and white evangelicals who embraced the idea that slavery was a sin promoted a liberation theology that referenced the Old Testament and Moses freeing the slaves. They looked to the Biblical past to inspire future dreams of freedom—that slavery would be abolished and the kingdom of heaven on earth would reign when "the last would be first and the first would be last."[41]

Tubman's dreams of freedom could have been spiritually inspired, and she believed that her dreams and visions allowed her to foresee the future. Tubman told her biographer Sarah Bradford that while still enslaved, "she used to dream of flying over fields and towns, and rivers and mountains, looking down upon them 'like a bird,' and reaching at last a great fence, or sometimes a river, over which she would try to fly." She later believed these visions predicted her escape from slavery, particularly because as she reached "the fence" or river that blocked her way to freedom, and just as "'it 'peared like I wouldn't hab de strength . . . dare would be ladies all drest in white ober dere, and dey would put out dere arms and pull me 'cross.'" Tubman claimed that the women in her dreams who "pulled her across" to freedom were the very Quaker women who helped ensure her success on the Underground Railroad.[42]

Tubman noted that her father also possessed the power to see the future and believed she had inherited this talent from him, but the notion of flying to escape oppression pervaded several African cultures, particularly those who hailed from the Bight of Biafra like the Igbo, and it is likely that she interpreted her dreams through this historical and cultural lens. Folktales recorded in a number of slave narratives contain examples of "flying Africans" who harnessed indigenous magical powers to transport themselves back to Africa. One former slave remembered that his mother "use tuh tell me bout slaves jis bring obuh from Africa wut hab duh supreme magic powuh. . . . Ef dey belieb in dis magic, dey could scape an fly back tuh Africa." What historians have discovered is that while Africans certainly weren't physically flying off their plantations, they might have been running away or committing suicide, thus escaping their enslavement. Many African cultures held the belief that "at death one returned to the land of one's birth," so suicide would literally carry a slave back to his or her home country, hence the notion of flying back to Africa.[43]

"Flying Africans" who pursued freedom via suicide exercised an extreme form of slave resistance, but historians have recently documented that slave suicide was not all that uncommon. The practice emerged during the Middle Passage, when slaves chose self-destruction over a brutal existence in the hold of a filthy slave ship and an uncertain future on the other side of the Atlantic. Historian Terri L. Snyder argues that "captive Africans' self-destruction was common enough to warrant the use of the earliest technologies for suicide prevention," like installing nets on the decks of ships to prevent slaves from throwing themselves overboard and using speculums to force feed slaves who attempted to starve to death. One merchant who sold speculums to slave ship captains claimed that "slaves were frequently so sulky, as to shut their mouths against all sustenance, and this with a determination to die; and it was necessary their mouths should be forced open to throw in nutriment, that they who had purchased them might incur no loss by their death."[44] Slaves recognized the value of their bodies and their labor to their masters, and they used suicide as a means to deny slaveholders of that value and to assert their agency as human beings, even if it meant extinguishing their own lives.

While some slaves escaped their fate by "flying away" and committing suicide, Tubman used her dreams of flying as a roadmap to seize her freedom by running away, perhaps the most common form of overt slave resistance. But like contemplating suicide, slaves often viewed their escape from the plantation as a life-or-death choice, both in the sense that perpetual enslavement meant "social death" and running away sometimes posed mortal dangers. Frederick Douglass cast the decision as such in his autobiography: "In coming to a fixed determination to run away, we did more than Patrick Henry, when he resolved upon liberty or death. With us it was a doubtful liberty at most, and almost certain death if we failed. For my part, I should prefer death to hopeless bondage."[45] Douglass, Tubman, and countless others made the choice to seek freedom and in doing so, defied the slave system that was constructed to keep them in bondage. Exact numbers are impossible to calculate, but historians argue that "the inability to control runaways left slave owners in a quandary. . . . No matter how diligent, punitive, or lenient . . . they remained unable to halt the stream of slaves that left their plantations and farms." Indeed, some scholars claim that runaways posed the single "most perplexing and intractable problem" for slaveholders and repeatedly cast freedom seekers as "rebels on the plantation."[46]

Given Tubman's history of resistance to her enslavement, her graduation to full-scale slave rebel and conductor on the Underground Railroad is not that surprising. Beginning with several incidents that occurred when she was just a child, Tubman made it clear that she would not always follow orders or accept her degraded status as defined by the white power structure. At the tender age of just six, Tubman's master forced her to leave the relative safety of her mother's home and travel ten miles to live with the family of James Cook. Cook paid Tubman's master for her labor in exchange for teaching her the trade of weaving from Cook's wife, undoubtedly with the goal of hiring her as a full-time weaver. But the young Tubman refused to learn how to weave, even though she clearly possessed the requisite intelligence, because "she hated her mistress, and did not want to live at [her] home, as she would have done as a weaver."[47]

A year or two later, when Tubman worked as a nurse and maid at "Miss Susan's," she again exhibited courage and defiance in the face of white authority. Tubman took advantage of a marital spat between Susan and her husband, and while the couple argued she took a lump of sugar out of the sugar bowl. Miss Susan caught Minty in the act, however, and "De nex' minute she had de raw hide down," ready to beat the child for "stealing" the sugar. To escape Susan's violent wrath, Minty bolted out the door and remembered that her owners "came after me, but I jes' flew, and dey didn't catch me. I run, an' run, an' I run, I passed many a house, but I didn't dar' to stop, for dey all knew my Missus an' dey would send me back."[48] Like many slaves, even at a young age Minty knew that by avoiding a whipping fueled by an angry reaction, she might get a less intense beating later, after the punisher had cooled off and collected his or her senses. She used her power to escape and resist Miss Susan's beatings, and while she likely paid for it later (she remembered, "I knowed what was comin'"), she asserted what little independence she had to guarantee that the beating occurred on her timetable, not Miss Susan's.

Minty's strength to resist her masters grew with age, and she understood as a teenager that opposing the slave system was often dangerous and potentially deadly. Perhaps the closest Tubman ever came to death was when she suffered that blow to the head as a teenager after refusing to help an overseer recover a runaway slave who had sought protection at a local general store. Remember the scene: the overseer instructed Minty to tie down the runaway, but she rebuffed him. As her rebellious peer fled the store, Minty stood in front of the doorway to ensure his successful departure, which put her in the direct line of fire of the overseer's violent wrath. Instead of hitting its intended target, the paper weight thrown by the overseer struck Minty on the head, causing her to pass out and bleed profusely. But maybe the overseer actually meant to hit Minty. Didn't she defy his orders to help capture the slave? Weren't overseers and masters prone to reactionary violence when faced with recalcitrant slaves?

The ways in which Minty resisted her bondage as a child and adolescent reflect a larger culture of resistance fostered by slaves across the spectrum—from overt forms of opposition like running away and suicide to a covert peccadillo like stealing a lump of sugar or "accidentally" spilling a drink on a dinner guest. Daily resistance was most often covert (unless slaves were caught in the act) and often involved property crimes. They broke tools, set fires to barns and crops, abused livestock, and took their masters' food and clothing. One Louisiana farmer "caught two of his slaves, Harry and Roberson, tying the rear legs of his pigs together, throwing the end of the rope over a tree, pulling the animals into the air, and swinging them as they squealed in pain. Two of the pigs, the owner lamented, were badly crippled."[49] These pigs found themselves strung up for entertainment, but most pigs ended up on people's tables, and stealing livestock, particularly small animals like chickens, was one way slaves expressed their discontent with the inadequate and inferior rations they received from their owners.

Some slaves preferred to deprive their masters of their labor rather than their property, as young Minty did when she refused to learn to weave. Slaves chopped cotton slowly or harvested sugarcane carelessly so as to make it less valuable, and at times they feigned illness or hid out for portions of the day to avoid work or punishment. One slave mistress wondered why progress on her farm moved at a snail's pace even though her slaves seemed "to be busy all the time," and work slowdowns and sabotage were likely to blame. Finally, slaves could mitigate their drudgery with alcohol, which was technically illegal in the quarters except when the masters distributed it, and many masters complained about drunken slaves who, for obvious reasons, made inefficient workers.[50]

Other forms of overt slave resistance, like arson and poisoning, posed more direct threats to masters than drunken or careless workers. Maryland planters had struggled with the crime of arson since the earliest days of settlement, and they punished slave offenders swiftly and publicly. One slave convicted of arson in 1729 had "his right hand severed" and then after hanging him, his body was "quartered and distributed throughout the countryside." In 1751 Maryland law deemed slave arson a capital offense and broadened the crime's definition to include the "wilful burning" *or attempted* burning of not only main dwelling houses but also out buildings like barns, grain storage bins, or tobacco houses. In 1819 Virginia further expanded its arson laws and defined accessories to arson as capital offenders and named the property protected by these laws to be any dwelling, barn, stable, or crop that a slave burned. Yet slaves continued to use arson as a form of resistance, as one master discovered in 1845 when his slave,

Jane, took hot coals from a fire and placed them on quilt squares under his bed. Slave arsonists like Jane destroyed valuable property and perhaps most importantly, made it clear that slaves could strike at their masters' pocketbooks and threaten their personal safety.[51]

Slave rebels also posed direct threats to their masters by poisoning them, and white fears of being poisoned by their slaves were a "feature of southern life throughout the age of slavery." Slaves used their knowledge of plants and herbs to sicken and kill their masters, often by inducing symptoms that mimicked common maladies like dysentery, which made the crime easy to conceal. Masters responded to the practice of poisoning by passing strict laws against it, and in the mid-eighteenth century both South Carolina and Virginia made it a capital offense to teach another slave about poisoning and prohibited slaves from working with apothecaries.[52] Like in many arson cases, slave women were often subject to poisoning accusations because of their positions in the kitchen and as healers and midwives. Diarist Mary Boykin Chestnutt recounted a story about a slave master, Dr. Keitt, who discovered that his female servant had been trying to poison him by putting a noxious white powder in his tea every morning. The *South Carolina Gazette* reported that a slave woman had poisoned her mistress's baby, likely by feeding it milk and food laced with poison.[53]

Cases of slaves murdering their masters or their masters' children were extremely rare, however. More often, enslaved women, including Harriet Tubman, healed the sick and dying on their plantations with herbal remedies, some of which were likely passed down from their African foremothers and forefathers. Although we can't know for sure how Tubman learned about the healing properties of certain plants and herbs, she would eventually employ this knowledge during her years as a conductor on the Underground Railroad, when she had to administer opium to infants to quiet them during dangerous escapes, and when she served in the field as a Union nurse, treating dysentery with herbal tea.[54] Just as Union officers sought out Tubman because of her reputation as a talented nurse, many planters, especially in rural areas, often relied on slave "root doctors" and healers to keep their slaves healthy in the quarters and to treat their own families' maladies in the Big House. Yet the dependence on slave medicine placed masters in a precarious position; on the one hand, they saved money and time by not hiring white doctors to attend to their slaves, but on the other, they empowered slave healers by investing them with control over medicinal practices and flirted with the possibility that slaves could turn on them and poison rather than heal their families and their property.[55]

Enslaved women practiced these overt forms of resistance at similar or even higher rates than men, but they ran away from their plantations less frequently than their male counterparts, making Tubman stand out among her female peers in this respect.[56] According to a database of runaway slave advertisements from newspapers in five southern states (Virginia, North and South Carolina, Tennessee, and Louisiana), women made up roughly 20 percent of all advertised runaways between 1790 and 1860.[57] These figures do not include women who absconded for short periods of time, because these small escapes typically did not merit an advertisement, but they do indicate that men in their twenties were much more likely than women to escape their plantations with the goal of leaving them permanently. Women's family concerns, especially their biological ties to children, made them less likely to abscond from their masters. Historians have been careful to qualify, however, that "slave women desired freedom as much as slave men and were often as assertive and aggressive on the plantation as male slaves," but "the task of uprooting and carrying children in flight 'was onerous, time-consuming, and exhaustive.'"[58] Some women with children, even pregnant women, countered these statistics, and ran away from their plantations, sometimes leaving behind their children, an indication of just how desperately they sought freedom.

Harriet Tubman challenged the statistical norms and defied the odds: in a field of resistance that was dominated by men, she was a woman who ran away; when running away alone or in pairs was safer and potentially more successful, she lead groups of slaves to abscond together; and when most freedom seekers never dared to return to their place of enslavement, Tubman risked her life again and again by returning to the South to carry more slaves "'cross the river" to freedom. Tubman realized her dreams of flying across the border to free lands, and after a life of resistance to slavery—from the young girl who ate from the forbidden sugar bowl to the teenager who took a blow to the head rather than assist in the capture of her fellow slave— she took her final steps toward freedom on the Underground Railroad. Her peers would call her Moses and we might call her a hero, but Harriet was merely living out her childhood dreams.

Notes

1. Alan Schroeder and Jerry Pinkney, *Minty: A Story of Young Harriet Tubman* (New York: Penguin Putnam, 2000), back cover.
2. Mission Statement, http://myhero.com/about/01-mission.asp and comment submitted by Amatul Hannan, http://www.myhero.com/go/hero.asp?hero=harrietTubman.
3. Eloise Greenfield, "Harriet Tubman," http://www.anisfield-wolf.org/2013/03/harriet-tubman-american-hero.
4. Gabor S. Borritt, ed., *Slavery, Resistance, and Freedom* (New York: Oxford University Press, 2007), xiv, xv–xvi.
5. Ira Berlin, *Generations of Captivity: A History of African-American Slaves* (Cambridge, MA: Harvard University Press, 2003), 167–169.

6. Berlin, *Generations of Captivity*, 103–105.

7. Barbara Jeanne Fields, *Slavery and Freedom on the Middle Ground: Maryland during the Nineteenth Century* (New Haven: Yale University Press, 1985), 24, 38.

8. Kate Clifford Larson, *Bound for the Promised Land: Harriet Tubman, Portrait of an American Hero* (New York: Ballantine, 2004), 13.

9. Larson, *Bound for the Promised Land*, 8–10, 16–19.

10. Emma Telford interview, qtd. in Larson, *Bound for the Promised Land*, 20–21, 310 n13.

11. Wilma King, *Stolen Childhood: Slave Youth in Nineteenth Century America* (Bloomington: Indiana University Press, 2011), 74.

12. King, *Stolen Childhood*, 84, 219.

13. Sarah H. Bradford, *Scenes in the Life of Harriet Tubman* (Auburn, NY: W.J. Moses, 1869), 10–12.

14. Bradford, *Scenes*, 13.

15. Terri L. Snyder, "'To Seeke for Justice': Gender, Servitude, and Household Government in the Early Modern Chesapeake," in Douglas Bradburn and John C. Coombs, eds., *Early Modern Virginia: Reconsidering the Old Dominion* (Charlottesville: University of Virginia Press, 2011), 138.

16. Henry Wiencek, "Master of Monticello," *Smithsonian* 43, No. 6 (October 2012): 40–97.

17. Snyder, "'To Seeke for Justice,'" 138–139.

18. Kelly Houston Jones, "'A Rough, Saucy Set Of Hands To Manage': Slave Resistance in Arkansas," *Arkansas Historical Quarterly* 71, No.1 (2012): 6–7.

19. Jones, "'A Rough, Saucy Set,'" 15–16. The whipping apparently never occurred this time, however, because the pregnant woman's mother threatened the overseer and prevented the punishment.

20. Testimony of Moses Grandy, qtd. in Venetria K. Patton, *Women in Chains: The Legacy of Slavery in Black Women's Fiction* (Albany: State University of New York Press, 2000), 7. See also Jacqueline Jones, *Labor of Love, Labor of Sorrow: Black Women, Work, and the Family, from Slavery to the Present* (New York: Basic Books, 1985) for examples of the practice of whipping pregnant female slaves.

21. Glenn McNair, *Criminal Injustice: Slaves and Free Blacks in Georgia's Criminal Justice System* (Charlottesville: University of Virginia Press, 2009), 143–144.

22. Philip D. Morgan, "Slave Life in Piedmont Virginia," in Lois Green Carr, Philip D. Morgan, and Jean B. Russo, eds., *Colonial Chesapeake Society* (Chapel Hill: University of North Carolina Press, 1988), 469n64.

23. Diane Miller Sommerville, *Rape and Race in the Nineteenth-Century South* (Chapel Hill: University of North Carolina Press, 2004), 77.

24. David J. Libby, *Slavery and Frontier Mississippi, 1720–1835* (Oxford: University Press of Mississippi, 2004), 54.

25. Dea H. Boster, *African American Slavery and Disability: Bodies, Property, and Power in the Antebellum South, 1830–1860* (New York: Routledge, 2013), 47, 84.

26. Larson, *Bound for the Promised Land*, 41–42.

27. Bradford, *Scenes*, 74; Telford, "Harriet," 6, qtd. in Larson, *Bound for the Promised Land*, 317n39.

28. Larson, *Bound for the Promised Land*, 43, 281–282.

29. Larson, *Bound for the Promised Land*, 10–11; Lois E. Horton, *Harriet Tubman and the Fight for Freedom: A Brief History with Documents* (New York: Bedford/St. Martin's, 2013), 6, 9.

30. Michael Gomez, *Exchanging Our Country Marks: The Transformation of African Identities in the Colonial and Antebellum South* (Chapel Hill: University of North Carolina Press, 1998), 253; James Sweet, *Recreating Africa: Culture, Kinship, and Religion in the Afro-Portuguese World* (Chapel Hill: University of North Carolina Press, 2003), 139, 142.

31. Qtd. in Bradford, *Scenes*, 35.

32. Larson, *Bound for the Promised Land*, 45–47.

33. Barry Hankins, *The Second Great Awakening and the Transcendentalists* (Westport, CT: Greenwood Press, 2004), 71.

34. Randy J. Sparks, "'To Rend the Body of Christ': Proslavery Ideology and Religious Schism from a Mississippi Perspective," in John R. McKivigan and Mitchell Snay, eds., *Religion and the Antebellum Debate Over Slavery* (Athens: University of Georgia Press, 1998), 288.

35. Hankins, *The Second Great Awakening*, 71–72; Bridget Ford, "Black Spiritual Defiance and the Politics of Slavery in Antebellum Louisville," *The Journal of Southern History* 78, No. 1 (February 2012): 70.

36. Albert Raboteau, *Slave Religion: The "Invisible Institution" in the Antebellum South* (New York: Oxford University Press, 1978, 2004), 61–62.

37. Larson, *Bound for the Promised Land*, 49–50.

38. Qtd. in Patrick H. Breen, "Contested Communion: The Limits of White Solidarity in Nat Turner's Virginia," *Journal of the Early Republic* 27, No. 4 (Winter 2007): 685. See also Randolph Ferguson Scully, "'I Come Here Before You Did and I Shall Not Go Away': Race, Gender, and Evangelical Community on the Eve of Nat Turner's Rebellion," *Journal of the Early Republic* 27, No. 4 (Winter 2007): 661–684.

39. Breen, "Contested Communion," 690.

40. Douglas Ambrose, "Of Stations and Relations: Proslavery Christianity in Early National Virginia," in McKivigan and Snay, eds., *Religion and the Antebellum Debate Over Slavery*, 54–55.

41. Mitchell Snay, *Gospel of Disunion: Religion and Separatism in the Antebellum South* (Chapel Hill: University of North Carolina Press, 1997), 134–138; Randy Sparks, "'To Rend the Body of Christ,'" 273.

42. Bradford, *Scenes*, 79.

43. Gomez, *Exchanging our Country Marks*, 117, 120. Gomez finds that in Virginia "between 1710 and 1760 [the Igbo] constituted some 38 percent of its total importation of African captives" (115). It is likely, then, given that most slaves in the Chesapeake region were received at Virginia ports that Tubman's grandparents grew up among Igbo slaves if they were not related to the Igbo themselves.

44. Terri L. Snyder, "Suicide, Slavery, and Memory in North America," *The Journal of American History* 39 (June 2010): 39–41. Quote is from Thomas Clarkson, *The History of the Rise, Progress, and Accomplishment of the Abolition of the African Slave Trade by the British Parliament* (2 vols., London, 1808), I, 377. For other studies that consider slave suicide, particularly during the Middle Passage, see Marcus Rediker, *The Slave Ship: A Human History* (New York: Penguin, 2008); Eric Robert Taylor, *If We Must Die: Shipboard Insurrections in the Era of the Atlantic Slave Trade* (Baton Rouge: Louisiana State University Press, 2006); and Stephanie E. Smallwood, *Saltwater Slavery: A Middle Passage from Africa to American Diaspora* (Cambridge, MA: Harvard University Press, 2007).

45. Frederick Douglass, *Narrative of the Life of Frederick Douglass* (New York: Bedford/St. Martin's, 1845, 2003), 95.

46. John Hope Franklin and Loren Schweninger, eds., *Runaway Slaves: Rebels on the Plantation* (New York: Oxford University Press, 1999), 261, 293.

47. Bradford, *Scenes*, 73–74.

48. Sarah H. Bradford, *Harriet, the Moses of Her People* (New York: J.J. Little & Co., 1901), 135–136.

49. Franklin and Schweninger, *Runaway Slaves*, 2.

50. Franklin and Schweninger, *Runaway Slaves*, 3; Diane Mutti Burke, *On Slavery's Border: Missouri's Small Slaveholding Households* (Athens: University of Georgia Press, 2011), 166.

51. Thomas D. Morris, *Southern Slavery and the Law: 1619–1860* (Chapel Hill: University of North Carolina Press, 1996), 330–332; Harriet C. Frazier, *Slavery and Crime in Missouri, 1773–1865* (Jefferson, NC: McFarland and Co., 2009), 157–158.

52. Peter McCandless, *Slavery, Disease, and Suffering in the Southern Low Country* (Cambridge: Cambridge University Press, 2011), 176.

53. Deborah Gray White, *Ar'n't I a Woman: Female Slaves in the Plantation South* (New York: Norton, 1999), 79.

54. Bradford, *Scenes*, 38.
55. McCandless, *Slavery, Disease, and Suffering*, 177.
56. Carol Berkin, *First Generations: Women in Colonial America* (New York: MacMillan, 1997), 126.
57. Franklin and Schweninger, *Runaway Slaves*, 328–332.
58. Franklin and Schweninger, *Runaway Slaves*, 212. See also Betty Wood, *Women's Work, Men's Work: The Informal Slave Economies of Lowcountry Georgia* (Athens: University of Georgia Press, 1995), 110.

CHAPTER 2

MOSES

On this path of becoming
Shrouded by hoot owl

White snake and nosy deer
Callous feet muster creek . . .

Amidst rusty leaves **Moses hushes**
them up the mountain half her body

Lost in river the other in stars
Her hands a basket her face grit

A young man guiding wife and child
through purple water looks over

His shoulder at the broken ones
in back ghosts rattling their bones

"Purgatory" by Quraysh Ali Lansana[1]

Quraysh Lansana breathes life into Harriet Tubman in his poetry collection, *They Shall Run: Harriet Tubman Poems*. In the poem "Paregoric," he envisions what Tubman might have been thinking when she administered opium to a fussy baby during one of her daring escapes; in "Hole" he surmises how angry she must have been when she risked re-enslavement by returning to Maryland to reunite with her husband, only to find him with another woman. Lansana also identifies Tubman as so many of her contemporaries did: "Moses hushes them up the mountain, half her body lost the river, the other in stars." Images of runaway slaves crossing rivers with "Moses" leading the charge abound in memories of Tubman. Comparisons to the biblical Moses began early in Tubman's career as an Underground

Railroad (UGRR) conductor and have persisted in this century, as evidenced by Lansana's 2004 poem. Another famous figure on the UGRR, William Still, a free black man who lived in Philadelphia, referred to Tubman as "Moses" when describing one of her many successful escapes from Maryland. He remembered that "she had faithfully gone down into Egypt, and had delivered these six bondmen by her own heroism." He further remarked that "in point of courage, shrewdness and disinterested exertions to rescue her fellow-men, by making personal visits to Maryland among the slaves, [Moses] was without her equal."[2]

The moniker "Moses" is Tubman's most enduring identity for good reason. Between 1849 and 1860, she made approximately thirteen trips back into slavery to rescue dozens of slaves and provided crucial information to scores of others so that they could make their own escapes from the Eastern Shore of Maryland.[3] And during the Civil War, she and Colonel James Montgomery led a raid up the Combahee River that resulted in over 700 slaves escaping to Union lines.[4] In her capacity as Moses, in her ability to skillfully and successfully lead people out of bondage, she earned her reputation as the consummate engineer of the Underground Railroad, and it is likely that she approved of the name. For Tubman never defined herself as exceptional or attributed her success to her own ingenuity or bravery; rather, she believed God protected her and her charges. Thomas Garrett, a white ally on the UGRR, wrote in 1868 that Tubman "declared to me that she felt no more fear of being arrested by her former master, or any other person . . . for she said she never ventured only where God sent her, and her faith in a Supreme Power truly was great."[5] Her unflinching faith in God motivated every trip, every step, every whisper, as Moses led her people across the river to the Promised Land.

**

Unlike the biblical Moses, however, Harriet Tubman had more than God's help in her mission to free her people. She tapped into a network of enslaved and free African Americans and white abolitionists that connected slave communities with free towns and cities, and contrary to childhood myths, this network involved very few underground tunnels and actual railroads. Instead, average black and white citizens who opposed slavery facilitated slaves' escape to freedom, offering them food, shelter, clothing, and information to ensure their safe travels northward. According to biographer Kate Larson, Tubman relied especially on the black community "that provided the protection, communication, and sustenance she required during the darkest and most dangerous days of fighting for freedom."[6] In addition to her black allies, Tubman also referenced the white women from her "flying dreams," the Quakers in Delaware and Pennsylvania who protected her and her charges in times of need. In fact, the interracial nature of the system has led one author to argue that the Underground Railroad was "the country's first racially integrated civil rights movement, in which whites and blacks worked together ... ultimately succeeding together in one of the most ambitious political undertakings in American history."[7]

Although it is impossible to measure how many slaves permanently escaped or to determine exactly when and where routes on the Underground Railroad existed, several scholars now argue that its effectiveness at destabilizing the slave power cannot be ignored. Historian Eric Foner argues that "the fugitive slave issue played a crucial role in precipitating the Civil War" because "the actions of fugitive slaves exemplified the political importance of slave resistance as a whole and raised questions central to antebellum politics." Particularly in the border regions, in states like Tubman's native Maryland and in Kentucky and Missouri, slaves, free blacks, and white abolitionists conducted what historian Stanley Harrold has dubbed a "war of attrition," using violence and determination to effect "a series of mass slave escapes [that] encouraged insecurity among masters," ultimately causing political leaders in the Border South to seek "federal action to stop escapes." Beginning with the Fugitive Slave Law in 1850 and ending with a plea for a federal slave code in 1860, slaveholders appealed to the federal government and argued that it must protect its citizens' property rights, including their rights in slaves. When southerners felt the U.S. government failed to uphold their rights, especially after the "Black Republican" Abraham Lincoln was elected, they bolted from the Union. Harrold asserts that the conflict over fugitive slaves "in the borderlands had been the most enduring, emotional, and violent of the issues driving the sections apart." In addition, historian Richard Blackett notes that "the actions of the slaves who found countless and ingenious ways" to escape their enslavement "had a profound if not always appreciated influence on the debate over slavery's future."[8]

Regardless of whether the UGRR and the fugitive slave problem played a major or minor role in precipitating the Civil War, freedom seekers systematically challenged the institution of slavery and caused slaveholders great emotional and financial distress for decades prior to the war. Tubman's own experience provides just one example of how runaways embodied the phrase "troublesome property."[9] Tubman escaped twice from her owner, Eliza Brodess, the first time with her brothers Ben and Henry, and the second time, on her own. Like Tubman and her brothers, many slaves left their plantations for short periods of time and returned on their own volition, which was, in fact, the most common type of runaway problem that masters faced. While Brodess waited two weeks to advertise the first escape, hoping that Minty and her brothers would return, she undoubtedly fretted about where her property had gone and worried about how the other slaves on her plantation and in the extended community would perceive their escape. Masters understood that a blatant and public rejection of slavery's foundation, the white control of black bodies, fundamentally weakened the institution; in short, runaways revealed the weak links in the master's chains. Slaveholders recognized this vulnerability and did all they could to intimidate and control freedom seekers; stricter slave codes, violent retribution, and the threat of sale to the Deep South all conspired to keep slaves on the plantation. But as Tubman's case demonstrates, sometimes masters' attempts to control their property could backfire, and in fact it was the threat of sale, the idea of being torn away from her family and friends, that set Harriet and so many others on a path to freedom.

The conditions leading up to Tubman's first escape in 1849 characterize a number of runaways' origins. Tubman's master, Edward Brodess, passed away in March of 1849, and a master's death always brought uncertainty to the slave community. Death resulted in probate courts and the calling in of debts, which often meant that a master's heirs had to sell off slaves to satisfy creditors. In addition, settling an estate almost always involved dividing property, and unless masters made specific bequests of slaves to specific relatives, the deceased's slaves were inevitably sold at auction, with the proceeds divided among the heirs. But even before Brodess died, Tubman feared that she would soon be sold because her master had been "bringing people to look at me, and trying to sell me." Reports of her impending sale circulated the plantation, and Minty "heard that some of us was going . . . with the chain-gang down to the cotton and rice fields, and they said I was going, and my brothers, and sisters." Tubman remembered that she "groaned and prayed for ole master," asking, "Lord, change dat man's heart!" She hoped that God would respond to her prayers and that she would not be sold, but the rumors and prospective buyers kept trickling in to the slave cabins month after month. Finally in March, after hearing that she would be sold down South, she changed the tone of her prayer and God answered it, but not in the way she had anticipated. She pleaded, "Oh Lord, if you ain't never going to change that man's heart, kill him, Lord, and take him out of the way."[10] Brodess died on March 7th, leaving Minty and her siblings vulnerable to creditors and slave traders.

Tubman had more reasons to dread being sold away from the Eastern Shore than having to leave her brothers and sisters. Approximately five years earlier, Minty Ross became Harriet Tubman after marrying John Tubman, a free black who worked in or around Peter's Neck, just north of the Thompson plantation where Minty had been hired out. It was not uncommon for free blacks and slaves to marry on the Eastern Shore, although such arrangements meant tying the family's future to the enslaved parent's status.

Under Maryland law, any children born to an enslaved woman would be slaves for life. Thus John and Harriet's children would be slaves, even though their father was a free man. John must have loved Harriet to risk knowing that his wife and future children would remain in chains, even as he undoubtedly worked hard to save money to buy her freedom. Perhaps Harriet and John planned to earn enough money to free her before starting their family with this knowledge in mind. Harriet's master had hired her out for a number of years to her father's master, Dr. Anthony Thompson; she hauled timber with her father, Ben, and plowed fields for other masters in the area using the two oxen she purchased with money she had saved from other jobs.[11] Now maybe she and John hoped to use these oxen to work together to earn her freedom.

But the Tubmans' dreams shattered when Edward Brodess died in March, and his widow, Eliza, began selling their slaves to satisfy his debts. First Brodess tried to sell Tubman's niece Harriet (likely named after Rit, Tubman's mother), and Harriet's 2-year-old daughter, Mary Ann, but the scheduled auction never occurred. Then Brodess turned to another of Tubman's nieces, Kessiah, and advertised for her sale at auction in August of 1849. But legal problems arose from Kessiah's potential sale, so Brodess again attempted to sell Tubman's niece Harriet, and her daughter Mary Ann. On June 17, 1850, Thomas Willis purchased the two slaves for $375.[12] Kessiah's mother, Linah, who was Tubman's sister, had been sold away from the Eastern Shore almost two decades earlier, along with Soph, another of Tubman's sisters. Tubman "had already seen two older sisters taken away as part of a chain gang, and they had gone no one knew whither; she had seen the agonized expression on their faces as they turned to take a last look at their 'Old Cabin Home'; and had watched them from the top of the fence, as they went off weeping and lamenting, till they were hidden from her sight forever."[13] Tubman refused to repeat their fate, and in the wake of Kessiah's attempted sale, she determined to seek her freedom sometime in the fall of 1849. Two of her younger brothers, Ben, aged 26, and Henry, aged 19, also decided to join their 27-year-old sister on that first trip.

Records indicate that John Tubman tried to persuade his wife not to flee the region, although his reasons for doing so remain unclear. Perhaps he thought the worst would never happen or maybe, as a free-born man, he could not fully understand the fear engendered by the possibility of being wrenched from one's home and family or the anxiety that Tubman experienced when picturing her life on a faraway cotton plantation. She told her biographer, Sarah Bradford, that in the weeks before her departure, "she never closed her eyes that she did not imagine she saw the horsemen coming, and heard the screams of women and children, as they were being dragged away to a far worse slavery than that they were enduring there."[14] If

John Tubman struggled to grasp the extent of his wife's fears, certainly he worried about the prospects of her success; he knew that the deck was stacked against Harriet because bloodhounds and slave catchers stood ready to pursue runaways as soon as word of their escape spread throughout the Eastern Shore.

Her brothers undoubtedly had the bloodhounds in mind when soon after the siblings escaped, Ben and Henry became "appalled by the dangers before and behind them" and "dragged" their reluctant sister back to the Thompson plantation. A newspaper advertisement broadcast an award for the group's capture on October 3rd, and their owner, Eliza Brodess, claimed the trio had run away on September 17th. Thus we know that they were on the run for at least two weeks, probably hiding out in the dense forests or taking shelter with sympathetic slaves or free blacks. Brodess anticipated their eventual goal, asking the *Delaware Gazette* to copy her runaway ad and run it in their paper, but no evidence exists that they made it out of Maryland. One account notes that Tubman's brothers "disagreed with her about directions," so perhaps they remained in or near the Eastern Shore before returning to Dorchester County. What we do not know is exactly when they returned, if they received punishments for their rebelliousness, or when Tubman determined to leave again on her own.[15]

Tubman's exact departure date or escape route during her second trip are also unclear, but the best research indicates that she likely departed from Dr. Anthony Thompson's plantation, Poplar Neck, located on the Choptank River just north of the village of the same name. Her mother, Rit, lived on this plantation, according to the 1850 census, and Tubman remembers wanting to say goodbye to Rit before leaving but knowing that she couldn't reveal her plans. Rit had already mourned the loss of three daughters to the slave coffles of the interstate slave trade, and Tubman knew that she would greet the knowledge of another's departure with "cries and groans." So to provide her mother with a clue, she went to the "Big House" and found her friend Mary, whom she believed would understand her veiled secret and keep it close. Just as she and Mary ventured outside to find some privacy, Dr. Thompson rode up the path on his horse, but Tubman was determined to communicate her plans. Using a method she would rely upon repeatedly during her subsequent trips to freedom, she sang a song that carried her message:

> I'm sorry I'm going to leave you
> Farewell, oh farewell;
> But I'll meet you in the morning,
> Farewell, oh farewell.
> I'll meet you in the morning,

I'm bound for the promised land,
On the other side of Jordan,
Bound for the promised land.[16]

Thompson watched her sing and perhaps suspected that she was up to something, especially since she had just run away a few weeks earlier. But remarkably, he continued toward the house as Tubman exited the gate to his property for the last time.

Leaving at dusk and travelling through the night, she used the North Star and the Underground Railroad to guide her movement from the Eastern Shore to her final destination, Philadelphia. Tubman told a friend later in life that she had confided in a white woman before her departure, probably a local Quaker, who gave Tubman directions to the first safe house on her route and provided her with names of people who would assist her and receive her at the second safe house. This Quaker ally likely directed Tubman to the Levertons, a Quaker family known for their participation in the UGRR in Dorchester County. The Levertons lived very near the Thompson estate, so Tubman could have easily walked to their home in one night after leaving Poplar Neck. The woman of the house received Tubman and immediately handed her a broom and instructed her to sweep the front walk, making it look like she was a servant going about her normal daily tasks. When the woman's son returned home that night, he reportedly hid Tubman in the back of his wagon and drove her to the second safe house, from which she was passed on to the next "station" until reaching Philadelphia. According to biographer Kate Larson, "several of the area's most active Quaker abolitionists lived within a mile of [Dr.] Thompson's new home" in Poplar Neck; in addition, a small free black community existed nearby, and Tubman undoubtedly found refuge amidst these white and black allies in Maryland and beyond.[17]

What has become known is the Underground Railroad was firmly established by the time of Tubman's escape. Although its origins, routes, and overall effectiveness are the subject of ongoing debate, recent scholarship establishes its existence in dozens of states, from expected locations like Delaware and upstate New York to lesser known routes as far south as Florida and as far west as Kansas and Texas.[18] In all of these places the UGRR provided an unprecedented opportunity for whites and blacks to interact in defense of a shared goal: to end slavery. The people who populated the UGRR firmly believed that they could enact their goal of abolition by depriving the institution of slavery of its most important resource, the slaves themselves. As author Fergus Bordewich argues, "In the underground, blacks and whites discovered each other for the first time as allies in a common struggle, learning to rely on each other not as master on slave, or child on parent, but as fellow soldiers in a war that most Americans did not yet even know had begun." This interracial phalanx served as the "driving wedge" of the abolitionist movement, putting into practice what antislavery speeches and pamphlets had only preached about for decades.[19]

Quakers populated both the lecture halls that broadcast abolitionist ideas and the Underground Railroad that put this philosophy into practice. In the seventeenth century, the founder of Quakerism, Englishman George Fox, believed that Christ revealed his teachings by communicating directly with his followers through the "Inner Light" or simply, "the Light," and Tubman would have understood this approach. Fox wrote, "The Lord did lead me gently along, and did let me see his love, which was endless and eternal and surpasseth all the knowledge that men have in the natural state . . ." Fox and the other members of the Religious Society of Friends (Quakers were also known collectively as "Friends") argued that all people possessed the Inner Light, even women and slaves, and by the mid-eighteenth century, many Quakers began speaking out against slavery and marking it as a sin. Quakers in Pennsylvania protested slavery as early as 1688, and by 1784 American Quakers prohibited their members from owning slaves and proceeded to establish antislavery societies in dozens of communities across the country.[20]

Quakerism is often associated with Pennsylvania and northern states like Ohio, but even in the South Quakers rejected slavery as an institution. In 1815 a group of Friends near Knoxville formed the Tennessee Manumission Society, which mandated that each member hang the following sign in their homes: "Freedom is the natural right of all men; I therefore acknowledge myself a member of the Tennessee Society for Promoting the Manumission of Slaves."[21] Similarly, the Virginia Manumission Society was founded by Quakers in 1791 and its Yearly Meeting submitted a letter to the state legislature arguing that slavery was "an evil in our country—an evil which has been of long continuance, and is now of increasing magnitude." Quaker women in Virginia also registered concern in a veiled reference to interracial sex, claiming that their "female descendants" would be threatened by the "increasing evils of slavery." Next door in Tubman's home state of Maryland, Friends organized protest meetings against the Missouri Compromise in 1820, and Baltimore citizens like Quaker Elisha Tyson led the charge in favor of liberalizing manumission laws and enhancing freedmen's rights.[22]

An active and sustained Quaker presence in these southern border states served as an important foundation for abolitionist activity that eventually linked these Quakers with their black and white peers of all faiths in northern border states like Delaware, Pennsylvania, and Ohio. Free blacks in Cincinnati, for example, joined forces with Levi Coffin, a Quaker originally from North Carolina, and together formed an "inter-racial cooperative" that funneled fugitives through this important border and river town.[23] Furthermore, two of the most important Supreme Court cases involving fugitive slaves in the 1840s originated in border states, and both of these cases served as precedence for the 1850 Fugitive Slave Law; in Vaughn v. Williams (1845) and Jones v. Van Zandt (1847) slaves from Missouri and Kentucky, respectively, escaped to Indiana and Ohio where they found white allies who facilitated their quest for freedom.[24] These porous and contentious borders, stretching from Maryland to Missouri, witnessed an increasing amount of fugitive slave activity as the antebellum period drew to a close and provided slaves from the South with an escape route lined with willing partners like William Still and Lucretia Mott.

Hoping to stem the tide of freedom seekers to northern states, southerners constructed a legal apparatus to recover runaway slaves, first in the U.S. Constitution and then in the infamous Fugitive Slave Act of 1850. Article IV, Section 2, of the U.S. Constitution mandated the return of "person[s] held to Service or Labour in one State" if they escaped to another state. The clause "assumed masters could cross state lines to 'claim' escapees without help or interference from the local authorities." However, a number of "cross-border incursions" in border states like Pennsylvania and Virginia soon made it clear that masters needed the government's help to secure their property. In 1788 disputes over the status of ex-slave John Davis embroiled the Governors of Virginia and Pennsylvania, Davis's former master, and the Pennsylvania Abolition Society in a protracted and violent legal conflict. Davis, whose Virginia master had travelled with him to rural Pennsylvania, claimed his freedom based on Pennsylvania's recent abolition law; his master, however, argued he was still a slave by birth in Virginia, and three bounty hunters crossed the border into Pennsylvania and kidnapped Davis to assert his master's property rights. The Governor of Pennsylvania, in turn, attempted to extradite the bounty hunters and free Davis, but the Governor of Virginia refused and wrote to President Washington, "urging federal action to facilitate delivery of fugitives from justice." The President consulted Congress on the matter, and not surprisingly, several Virginia Congressmen defended the bounty hunters, "claiming the Pennsylvania government had permitted the 'negro club' to commit 'robberies . . . on the innocent citizens of Virginia.'" These debates led to the creation and passage of the Fugitive Slave Law of 1793, which allowed masters to recover alleged fugitive slaves even if they ventured into free states.[25]

As the 1849 advertisement for the return of "Minty" indicated, Harriet Tubman's master hoped that the legal apparatus put in place by the Fugitive Slave Law would compel her fellow citizens in Maryland and in neighboring Delaware to identify and return Minty and her two brothers. Eliza Brodess offered $100 for Tubman's capture "if taken out of the State, and $50 . . . if taken in the State," and instructed the authorities to "lodge" the runaways at one of three local jails. While we don't know if the slave catchers ever got close to Minty and her brothers, Brodess trusted the proslavery legal system in the Eastern Shore, and perhaps she attributed Minty's initial return to the effectiveness of her ad or the fear inspired by the slave patrol or their barking dogs. We do know, however, that Tubman would eventually escape slavery's grips and evade the slave catchers repeatedly throughout the 1850s, and she and other slaves exasperated their owners and took advantage of their proximity to the border between slave and free territory.[26]

Thus it is not surprising that border-state legislators like Senator Thomas Pratt of Maryland and Senator James Mason of Virginia led the charge to strengthen the Fugitive Slave Law in the late 1840s. Pratt claimed that his home state lost $80,000 annually because of escaped slaves and argued, "Of all the subjects doing harm at the South, and providing excitement, the escape of fugitive slaves is doing the most harm, because it has been felt more practically, than any other of the causes of complaint." Similarly, the Virginia House of Delegates registered its concern over the fugitive slave problem in February 1849, and noted the potential for conflict if Congress did not take action: "The territory of the nonslaveholding states will be invaded in sudden and rapid incursions by those who have been robbed of their property," inciting "petty border warfare." The *Lexington Observer* linked three of the most vulnerable border states together—Kentucky, Virginia, and Maryland—and asserted that citizens in these states needed "U.S. appointees" to help them protect their slave property. The siege mentality harbored by many southern slaveholders who blamed the "negro clubs," "negro stealers," and other agents of the Underground Railroad for their slaves' resistance, combined to create pressure on the federal government to put teeth into the Fugitive Slave Law, the most controversial component of legislation later referred to as the Compromise of 1850.[27]

The consummate border-state slaveholder and statesman, Kentucky Senator Henry Clay, and his colleague Daniel Webster initiated the compromise, and Clay believed that it represented "an amicable arrangement of all questions in controversy between the free and the slave States, growing out of the subject of slavery." Problems emerged after northerners and southerners locked horns about how to settle the western and southwestern territories gained from Mexico after the Mexican War. The final bill contained the following provisions: California was admitted to the Union as a free state; New Mexico and Utah Territories were organized without any prohibition on slavery, and slavery was allowed in both places; the New Mexico and Texas border was adjusted in favor of Texas; Congress granted Texas millions of dollars in federal bonds to pay off the state's pre-statehood debts; the domestic slave trade (but not slavery) was outlawed in Washington, D.C.; and finally, the newly retooled Fugitive Slave Act strengthened the federal government's role in the recovery of runaway slaves. Clay referred to the compromise as an "amicable arrangement" because the North gained a free California and the abolition of the slave trade in D.C., while the South enjoyed the potential for slavery in New Mexico and Utah, as well as the promised enforcement of the Fugitive Slave Act. But in actuality, the bill only stoked the fires of sectionalism, particularly because tensions arose over the fugitive slave issue.[28]

The exact outlines of the Fugitive Slave Act reinforced the provisions first laid out in 1793 and added new protections for slaveholders. The bill created a system of U.S. commissioners who were responsible for hearing cases on fugitive slaves, issuing arrest warrants, calling out the army and state militias to enforce the law, and granting "certificates for returning [slaves] to their masters." A simple affidavit submitted by a master could serve as the only evidence of ownership and would initiate legal proceedings for a slave's return. Most egregiously, according to abolitionists, commissioners received $10 for each certificate granting return, but only $5 for denying a return (presumably because less paperwork was involved in the latter case). Unlike the 1793 law, those slaves who claimed to be free were denied the right to a trial or to testify on their own behalf, jury trials were specifically banned, and in defiance of the U.S. Constitution, the law suspended the right of habeas corpus for alleged slaves. Federal marshals could be fined $1,000 (about $30,000 today) if they allowed a fugitive to be rescued from their custody. Men and women who assisted fugitives could also be charged a $1,000 fine and in addition were subject to a $1,000 penalty paid to the owner of the slave. They could also be sentenced up to six months in jail for helping to rescue a slave. As historian Joan Waugh notes, "This bill was going to bring no end of trouble from up North."[29]

Indeed, trouble began brewing even before the bill passed, as groups of free blacks and abolitionists organized to resist any provisions that required unwilling U.S. citizens to serve as slave catchers. Frustrated by the debates going on in Congress, white abolitionist Gerrit Smith called a "Fugitive Slave Convention" in August of 1850 that convened in the small town of Cazenovia, New York, where over 2,000 people gathered in an apple orchard to affirm their commitment to abolition. What distinguished the convention was the diversity of its attendants—one newspaper claimed that "persons of every sect in religion, of every party in politics, and every shade of complexion" attended—and the radical philosophy articulated by Smith's "Letter to American Slaves from those who have fled from American slavery."[30] Attendees included Frederick Douglass, the Reverend Samuel May, the Reverend Jermain Loguen, and recently freed slaves like Emily and Mary Edmonson, all of whom seemed to play a role in helping Smith craft the infamous "Letter," which urged slaves to break their chains and escape from slavery. Smith, who would be elected to Congress in 1852, shocked the nation with his unabashed call to arms, telling American slaves that "by the rules of war, you have the fullest liberty to plunder, burn, and kill, as you may have occasion to do to promote your escape." Furthermore, Smith promised white support for freedom seekers, warning slave catchers that "Defeat—disgrace—and it may be death—will be [your] only reward for pursuing [your] prey into this *abolitionized* portion of our country."[31] The Cazenovia convention represented a biracial commitment to helping the fugitive slaves who heeded Smith's radical call, and when the Fugitive Slave Law passed a month later, resistance to it was already underway as antislavery citizens and state legislatures posed challenges to protecting slave property.

While Gerrit Smith and Frederick Douglass were voicing the will of fugitive slaves and their allies at Cazenovia, Harriet Tubman was making plans to rescue her family and friends from the Eastern Shore, aware that the dangers she faced as a runaway had just increased when the Fugitive Slave Act passed in September of 1850. This knowledge did not deter her, however, because Tubman would not rest until her family surrounded her. She remembered feeling isolated in Philadelphia and longing to reconnect with her home people: "I was a stranger in a strange land; and my home, after all, was down in Maryland; because my father, my mother, my brothers, and sisters, and friends were there. But I was free, and they should be free. I would make a home in the North and bring them there, God helping me."[32] She vowed to begin the process of reconstituting her family in the winter of 1850 when she received word that Eliza Brodess intended to put her niece Kessiah and Kessiah's two young children on the auction block again. Tubman left Philadelphia and established a temporary base of operations in Baltimore, where she stayed with her brother-in-law Tom Tubman, who worked on the city's docks, along with other free blacks and hired slaves, many of whom originally hailed from Dorchester County. Baltimore in the 1850s had a thriving black community that included 25,000 free blacks and 3,000 slaves who supported dozens of black churches and thirty mutual aid societies. This network of extended family and friends helped Harriet and Kessiah's free husband, John Bowley, create a plan to rescue Kessiah and her two children, James Alfred (6) and baby Araminta, during the auction in December.[33]

Like Harriet's husband, John Tubman, John Bowley married Kessiah knowing that the worst could happen—that his wife and children could be sold away from him. But it was not unheard of for free spouses to purchase their partners' or children's freedom, and perhaps Bowley had prepared for such a day or at the very least, knew how to approach the process with help from willing allies in the community. On auction day John Brodess, Eliza Brodess's son, served in his mother's stead during the sale and accepted a bid from a potential buyer, but when the auctioneer called for the buyer after a dinner break, he discovered a ruse. John Bowley had managed to fool the auctioneer and win the bid, but instead of showing up to pay for and collect his "property," he secreted his wife and children at a nearby house until he could transfer them to Baltimore and Harriet's waiting arms. Tubman received them, hid them with friends while they recovered from their perilous journey, and then carried them to Philadelphia a few days later.[34]

Tubman returned to Baltimore in the early spring of 1851 to help her youngest brother, Moses, secure his freedom. Little is known about Moses's escape, other than that he, along with his three older brothers (Robert, Ben, and Henry), had absconded earlier that winter and were living in the woods to "escape the dreaded 'chain gang.'" Moses's brothers were offered a job with a local lumber man and emerged with a labor contract that protected them from sale for at least another year. Moses, however, "was not included in this arrangement," for some reason and thus remained in the woods, suffering from frost bite, until his sister "from her own place of concealment, entered into communication with him" and brought him to safety. They left Dorchester County and used Harriet's connections in Baltimore and Philadelphia to successfully evade capture. From Philadelphia they then travelled further north to safety, although no record exists of Moses's permanent residence after his escape.[35]

We know a bit more about Tubman's emotional trip to the Eastern Shore in the fall of 1851 because she told several interviewers about this infamous homecoming. Tubman always vowed to return and bring back her husband, John, to live with her, although it remains puzzling why John never moved to Philadelphia on his own accord given that he was a free man. It is likely that Harriet did not provide him with information about her specific location out of necessity—she needed to protect herself and her allies in Philadelphia. Maybe she waited until a permanent plan for their free life together could be developed, and in the meantime she worked tirelessly to save money, enough to buy John a new suit of clothes with which to start this new life. Perhaps she intended to pose as his slave and knew that he needed a respectable suit to look the part of a successful free black man travelling with his property. Or maybe she thought that a new set of clothes would help convince her skeptical husband that living in a free state was worth the price of leaving his job, family, and friends in Maryland.

Regardless of her plans, they were dashed soon after her arrival in Dorchester County that fall, when she learned that John Tubman had married a free black woman named Caroline. Filled with jealousy and betrayal, she considered confronting John and his new wife but decided to funnel her rage elsewhere. She acknowledged "how foolish it was just for temper to make mischief," and claimed that if John "could do without her, she could do without him."[36] Tubman refused to waste a dangerous trip back to the Eastern Shore, however, so she redirected her energy from retrieving her husband to helping a group of slaves from the area reach freedom in Philadelphia.

John Tubman might have spurned the prospect of living in a free state because he knew the line between freedom and slavery grew increasingly blurry after 1850; with the new Fugitive Slave Act, African Americans like John Tubman who had been born free were increasingly vulnerable to greedy and duplicitous slave catchers even in northern cities. In an effort to protect the free black citizens residing in their states, nine states had already passed personal liberty laws by 1850: these laws stipulated rights for accused runaways, like ensuring habeas corpus, and enacted kidnapping penalties for officials and citizens who pursued alleged fugitive slaves. After 1850, these nine northern states adopted new and/or strengthened personal liberty laws, eight additional states enacted personal liberty legislation, and some states (like Wisconsin) even deemed the Fugitive Slave Law unconstitutional. State-defined liberty laws counterpoised federal law protecting slavery, leaving many local judges and citizens in a quandary of confusing and conflicting messages about how to address the fugitive slave question.[37]

Men and women on the Underground Railroad and antislavery citizens across the North exhibited little confusion, however, and only ratcheted up their commitment to abolition. Free blacks in particular worked tirelessly to ensure their own safety and that of their enslaved brethren. African American abolitionists like William Still and Robert Purvis gathered in Philadelphia soon after the Fugitive Slave Act passed and pledged to "resist to the death any attempt to enforce [the Act] upon our persons." The Pennsylvania Society for the Abolition of Slavery formed the General Vigilance Committee to protect free blacks and runaways, and it chose Still as its secretary and then chairman. Still and his many black and white colleagues assisted hundreds of escaping slaves as they passed through Pennsylvania, embodying the Philadelphia Female Anti-Slavery Society's vow "to disobey the [fugitive] law" and reject "all laws which have been or may be enacted to sustain the system of American Slavery."[38] Furthermore, the Philadelphia Vigilance Committee raised money to defend the abolitionists who helped William Parker and others escape slave catchers in a deadly shootout in Christiana, Pennsylvania, in September 1851. Referencing the Christiana incident, Lucretia Mott affirmed her commitment to the cause, claiming that "the opposition and violence we have to encounter only show the necessity of more active and extended anti-slavery effort."[39]

Mott, a founding member of the American Anti-Slavery Society, played an active role in the UGRR and was crucial to the success of the larger abolition movement. Like her Quaker forbearers, Mott preached "the primacy of the inner light," a light that motivated her radical activism and in turn elicited "oratorical challenge, public derision, and even mob violence." Together with William Still, a free black, and white abolitionist Passmore Williamson, Mott helped an enslaved woman named Jane Johnson secure her freedom in 1855. Mott accompanied Johnson to a hearing in Philadelphia where she testified on behalf of Williamson, who had been accused by Johnson's master of kidnapping his property; Johnson asserted that she had not, in fact, been kidnapped, but instead chose to leave her master who had willingly brought her into free territory. After her defiant statement, Johnson exited the courtroom quickly while her master fumed at her testimony. Mott and three other local abolitionists whisked Johnson into a carriage waiting outside the courthouse and flew to Mott's house, where Johnson burst through the front door and then darted out the back, boarding the carriage again after it circled the block in an attempt to avoid detection. Jane Johnson, with Mott's help, successfully evaded her master's attempts to reclaim her, and like many slaves in that infamous decade, found freedom on the UGRR.[40]

The activism of abolitionists like Mott made Philadelphia and Boston safer for freedom seekers than other northern cities with less organized antislavery communities, but Tubman and her charges understood that to fully secure their freedom, they needed to cross the border into Canada. Tubman recalled, "I wouldn't trust Uncle Sam wid my people no longer; I brought 'em all clar off to Canada," because the only place they would be safe was "under the paw of the British Lion," since Great Britain had abolished slavery in 1834.[41] Tubman viewed Queen Victoria's dominion as a sanctuary and extended her practice of traversing borders northward. In this light we can view her border crossing in both a national and transnational sense, as Tubman took advantage of England's legal protections against extraditing fugitive slaves.[42] She expressed knowledge of and confidence in the Queen's protection by singing these lyrics when entering Canada:

> Oh I heard Queen Victoria say,
> That if we would forsake,
> Our native land of slavery,
> And come across de lake;
> Dat she was standing on de shore,
> Wid arms extended wide,

To give us all a peaceful home,
  Beyond de rolling tide;

Farewell, ole Master, don't think hard of me,
I'm traveling on to Canada, where all de slaves are free.[43]

  Given Tubman's referral to the United States as "Uncle Sam," perhaps the "ole Master" she mentions in the song is her home country, the "native land of slavery." She asks for America's forgiveness as she rejects the United States and settles in a land where "all de slaves are free." The Queen's dominion beckoned, and Tubman transplanted the "land of Canaan" from New York to Canada.

  Beginning with a documented trip in December of 1850, Tubman typically carried fugitives from Philadelphia to Albany and then on to Rochester, New York, before finally arriving in St. Catharines, West Canada (present-day Ontario). Tubman followed this route a number of times, using her connections on the Underground Railroad to move dozens of people from the upper South to Canada. Yet we often lack the exact names or precise movements involved in each of Tubman's trips because their clandestine nature belied documentation. Thomas Garrett later told Tubman's biographer that during the 1850s he had "not felt at liberty to keep any written word of Harriet's or my own labors," because "the laws [were] very severe where any proof could be made of anyone aiding slaves on their way to freedom." We know from post-war records, however, that Tubman connected with a number of well-known conductors, like Garrett, Frederick Douglass, and William Still on a regular basis.[44]

  Garrett was one of Tubman's most important allies, and his strategic location in Wilmington, Delaware, served their common mission well. Situated on the west bank of the Delaware River, between Baltimore and Philadelphia, Wilmington was home to more free blacks than slaves and supported a "very strong population of black UGRR workers," some of whom attended the African Union Methodist Church. Garrett owned a mercantile shop in downtown Wilmington, where he set up a successful iron and hardware business that enabled him to save thousands of dollars to assist runaways. According to one of his biographers, Wilmington, Delaware, "was an ideal and practical location for Thomas Garrett to both raise a family and carry out the command he believed was given to him by the Almighty: to assist the runaway slave to freedom." A dedicated Quaker like his peers in Philadelphia, Garrett followed the Inner Light to do God's will, which led him to work with Tubman.[45]

  Garrett acknowledged how much Tubman's faith motivated her success, remarking that he had "never met with any person, of any color, who had more confidence in the voice of God, as spoken direct to her soul." Tubman's spirituality guided her through Garrett's station many times, even when Garrett himself wondered if he had the means to help her. Often outfitting Tubman and members of her party with essentials for their escape like shoes and clothes, Garrett remembered that one time Tubman showed up at his door and he said, "Harriet, I am glad to see thee! I suppose thee wants a pair of new shoes." Harriet replied, "I want more than that . . . God tells me you have money for me." Garrett asked how much, and after pondering the question she replied, "About twenty-three dollars." Garrett stood in disbelief because he had just received twenty-four dollars "and some odd cents" from Eliza Wigham, a member of the Antislavery Society of Edinburgh in Scotland, who had instructed Garrett to pass along the collection to Tubman. Garrett responded, "To say the least, there was something remarkable in these facts, whether clairvoyance, or the divine impression on her mind from the source of all power, I cannot tell."[46]

Call it fate or the divine, Tubman cheated the odds during her long trips from slavery to freedom. During one trip in the winter of 1851, when Tubman took eleven freedom seekers from Maryland to Canada, she used the transnational route that she traversed repeatedly for the next decade. The final U.S. destination on this route was Rochester, where Frederick Douglass housed them and ensured they boarded the train for St. Catharines, Canada.[47] Douglass wrote that this party "was the largest number I ever had at any one time, and I had some difficulty providing so many with food and shelter." But he also remembered that the freedom seekers were "content with very plain food, and a strip of carpet on the floor for a bed," and they endured the cramped and meager conditions with grace until Douglass could raise enough money to send them across the border.[48]

Tubman remained with the group in St. Catharines during that brutally cold winter of 1851–1852, but returned to Philadelphia in the spring to begin preparations for more trips back to Dorchester and Caroline Counties in Maryland. Evidence indicates that she brought out a group of eight slaves from the Eastern Shore in the fall of 1852, although none of the members of this particular party have been identified. In contrast, and thanks to records kept by Philadelphia conductor William Still, we know Tubman rescued three of her brothers and three other Dorchester County slaves in the winter of 1854. Still wrote, "'Moses' arrives with six passengers," on December 29, 1854, and recorded descriptions of each member of Tubman's group: Benjamin, Henry, and Robert Ross, three of Tubman's brothers who were owned by Dr. Anthony Thompson; Jane Kane, who was engaged to Ben Ross; and Peter Jackson and John Chase, men who might have worked with the Ross brothers in nearby Caroline County. After their arrival in Philadelphia, the Ross brothers promptly changed their last names to Stewart to protect their identities. Tubman's brother Henry reluctantly left behind his wife, Harriet Ann, and their two young children, and Robert also left his wife, Mary, and their two boys, along with a newborn baby girl named Harriet. But undoubtedly they believed that Tubman would return for their wives and children in the future, since she was committed to reconstituting her entire family in freedom, including her sister Rachel and the Ross family's elderly parents, Rit and Ben.[49]

The successful rescue of three of her brothers in 1854, particularly Ben and Henry, who had attempted to escape with Harriet the first time in 1849, must have brought Tubman great satisfaction, especially given that the national debate over slavery grew increasingly tense after the passage of the Kansas-Nebraska Act in May of 1854. The controversial bill extended the doctrine of popular sovereignty (and the possibility of slavery) to the Kansas and Nebraska Territories, and critics argued that it negated the Missouri Compromise of 1820, which had prohibited slavery from expanding north and west of the southern boundary of Missouri. Opponents of the bill organized protests throughout the country, most famously in the small town of Ripon, Wisconsin, where a group of "Anti-Nebraska" citizens met in a schoolhouse and formed the nascent Republican Party. The Republican Party, "no prefix! no suffix; just plain Republican," as *New York Tribune* editor Horace Greeley urged, spread across the upper Midwest and the rest of the North like wildfire. Just two years later in the 1856 presidential election, the new party, under the slogan "Free Soil, Free Labor, and Free Men," carried eleven northern states and almost won the election; by 1860 the Republicans would garner enough party adherents to elect the President of the United States.[50]

The earliest Republican platforms advocated for the repeal of the Kansas-Nebraska Act and affirmed a commitment to preventing slavery's expansion in the western territories, especially in Kansas, where settlers were already rushing to provide the necessary votes to make Kansas a free state under the doctrine of popular sovereignty.[51] Emigration companies organized throughout New England and the upper Midwest and sent antislavery citizens and supplies to Kansas Territory to counter the proslavery influence pouring in from across the border in Missouri. The clash of ideologies carried over to the ballot box, as tensions over fraudulent voting practices led to violent intimidation and eventually bloodshed, garnering the region the infamous name "Bleeding Kansas."

No one knows how closely Tubman followed the events in Kansas, although most newspapers throughout the country carried stories about the conflict on a daily basis during the spring of 1856, especially after proslavery thugs destroyed the free-state town of Lawrence and South Carolina Representative Preston Brooks brutally caned Massachusetts Senator Charles Sumner after he delivered his famous speech, "The Crime Against

Kansas." Certainly Tubman learned of Bleeding Kansas's most famous resident, John Brown, around this time because news that he murdered five proslavery men near Pottawatomie Creek in Kansas Territory horrified slaveholders and antislavery citizens alike. Brown's ability to escape the authorities after committing the Pottawatomie murders "nurtured the legend of his seemingly superhuman heroism," according to one biographer.[52]

Maybe Brown's "superhuman heroism," which in part stemmed from his ability to initially evade capture and his undying commitment to free the slaves, endeared Brown to Tubman, and we know they both shared a passionate belief that slavery was a sin against God. They met for the first time in April of 1858, during one of Brown's trips back East to raise money and arms for antislavery settlers in Kansas and to begin planning his fated raid on Harpers Ferry. Brown's friend, black abolitionist Reverend Jermain Loguen, introduced them in St. Catharines where Brown hoped to recruit willing fellow soldiers in his war against slavery. Tubman apparently embraced his plan and encouraged her fellow fugitives to support him, and Brown immediately recognized how Tubman's intimate knowledge of the black abolitionist network that connected the southern and northern border states could facilitate his plans in Virginia. Brown expressed the utmost confidence in Tubman's abilities to help lead a rebellion, claiming that she "could command an army as successfully as she had led her small parties of fugitives."[53]

Their mutual respect and admiration seemed instantaneous, leading one biographer to claim that Brown was "perhaps the one white person Tubman most admired." Similarly, Brown praised Tubman and wrote to his son that Harriet was "the most of *man* naturally; that I *ever* met with," and he referred to her repeatedly as "General Tubman." Meant as compliments, Brown recognized Tubman's consummate leadership skills and steadfast courage as masculine, but identified these manly qualities as assets. In an age when being "strong-minded" was viewed as "the very antithesis of what social norms defined as woman's appropriate persona," Tubman exhibited not only a strong mind but a rebellious spirit that challenged both gender and racial conventions about women and blacks.[54] But Brown embraced these apparent transgressions, perhaps because he too defied social norms for proper, restrained manhood and pacifist Christian resistance to slavery. A century after the Civil War, Brown would be lauded as the "blackest white man anyone had ever known," while Tubman remained the "most manly" woman Brown had ever met. Both Tubman and Brown traversed ideological and geographical boundaries to accomplish their God-inspired purpose to fight slavery to the death.[55]

Brown crossed national and regional boundaries, travelling throughout Canada, New England, and the upper Midwest raising money and support for his abolitionist agenda, and he returned to Bleeding Kansas after meeting Tubman to practice what he preached, perhaps even inspired by Tubman's example. In December of 1858, Brown and fellow free-state man George B. Gill led a party of twenty antislavery men to Vernon County, Missouri, to rescue slave Jim Daniels, his pregnant wife, and their two children from their master Harvey Hicklan. Brown's party quickly and easily liberated the Daniels family plus another slave and appropriated Hicklan's horses and wagons, which Brown believed rightly belonged to Daniels because his labor had purchased them. The party then travelled to a neighboring farm and busted into the family's home, threatened the slave owner, and freed his five slaves. The entire group fled north towards Topeka, Kansas, where they sought shelter with a local antislavery family. Before arriving in Topeka, however, proslavery patrols caught up with the group but were surprised to find that Brown had armed all the slaves and instructed them to shoot if threatened; the slave catchers were thus outnumbered and hightailed it back to Missouri, giving the conflict the misnomer of "Battle of the Spurs." Brown's group of Missouri fugitives eventually numbered twelve, because Jim Daniels's wife gave birth to a baby boy (appropriately named John Brown) during the 1,000 mile trek to Canada. Quakers in Springdale, Iowa, hid them in a boxcar that took the party to Chicago, where Allan Pinkerton, the railroad detective (and future body guard of Abraham Lincoln) put them in another railroad car to Detroit.[56] Just as Tubman had done so many times, Brown successfully ferried his party to safety across the Canadian border.

The risks of travelling with a large party that included young children and trekking such a long distance did not deter Brown, much like Tubman's parents' advanced ages and feeble health did not hijack her commitment to liberating them. In what was probably one of her most daring rescues, Tubman crept back into Dorchester County after hearing that her father might be arrested for harboring fugitive slaves. Ben and Rit were both in their 70s, and Tubman knew that she would have to make arrangements to accommodate their inability to walk great lengths. So she secured a makeshift wagon with "a board on the axle to sit on, another board swung with ropes, fastened to the axle, to rest their feet on," and they fled to Wilmington. Thomas Garrett received them and sent them on to William Still's in Philadelphia, from where they travelled to New York City and Rochester. Maria Porter, secretary of the Rochester Ladies' Anti-Slavery Society, harbored them for two weeks until they found safe passage to St. Catharines. It must have brought Ben and Rit great joy to arrive in a city that already housed a number of their children, grandchildren, and great-grandchildren, but their daughter, Harriet, could not rest until the entire family was reunited. So she promptly returned to the Eastern Shore in an unsuccessful attempt to rescue her sister Rachel and Rachel's two children.[57]

Tubman remained near Maryland during the summer and early fall of 1857, and she passed along vital information to almost forty local slaves who stole their own freedom in October and dozens more who escaped later that fall and early winter. Slaveholders on the Eastern Shore sounded the alarm after twenty-eight slaves escaped in just one night from multiple plantations, including fifteen slaves from Samuel Pattison's estate. One Maryland paper referred to the escapes as a "Negro Stampede," and local slave catchers mobilized to try and stop the exodus. They blamed local free blacks for the problem, linking them to the "'negro worshipers' of the North," and anyone in the region who was suspected of harboring runaways risked vigilante justice, like tarring and feathering, and even lynching. But nothing seemed to stop the stream of runaways, so that by 1859, the national press reported that "stampedes of slaves" had fled the Eastern Shore.[58]

Unfortunately for Tubman, however, the tightened slave patrols and threat of white vigilantism deterred her from rescuing her sister Rachel, forcing her to return to upstate New York, Boston, and then Canada to raise funds until she could plan another successful foray back into Maryland. The fugitive community in St. Catharines, including her aging parents, suffered from a lack of adequate housing, employment, food, and clothing, and Tubman soon turned her attentions to remedying these problems. Travelling throughout New York and Boston, she met with people like Gerrit Smith, William Seward, Wendell Phillips, and Franklin Sanborn. Smith and Sanborn were members of John Brown's "Secret Six," the inner circle of men who helped Brown plan his Harpers Ferry raid, and Tubman could have met them as a result of her interest in Brown's raid. But her primary goal, it seems, was to find a more stable and comfortable home for her family, and William Seward answered this call.[59]

At the time Seward owned property in upstate New York in the small town of Auburn, where the family lived together when he wasn't in Washington serving in the U.S. Senate. It may have been Lucretia Mott who introduced Tubman to Mott's sister, Martha Coffin Wright, who lived in Auburn and kept close company with William Seward's wife, Frances Miller Seward, and Frances's sister, Lazette Miller Worden.[60] Frances Seward and her son, William H. Seward, Jr., might very well have brokered the deal that resulted in William, Sr., selling Tubman a seven-acre farm, which included a house, a barn, and several outbuildings, for the market price of $1,200. Furthermore, Seward allowed Tubman, even though she was a woman and a fugitive slave and thus not a citizen capable of owning property, to finance the sale; she put down only $25 and paid $10 plus interest every three months to mortgage the property. The Sewards were well known for their stewardship to African Americans and immigrants, but Senator Seward also might have seen Tubman as a political asset as he prepared to run for

President in 1860. Protecting a family of fugitives would certainly raise his political capital among the region's antislavery elite. Regardless, Tubman moved her parents and brother John Stewart (who had changed his name from Robert Ross) to Auburn, where they would remain in relative safety until the political fallout from Brown's Harpers Ferry Raid would send them all fleeing back to Canada for guaranteed protection.[61]

Tubman and John Brown met several times in 1858 and 1859, and it is clear that Brown very much wanted Tubman's help as he waged his war against slavery. When organizing a convention in Chatham, Canada (across the border from Detroit), Brown hoped that Tubman would join him in his endeavor to encourage black recruits to support his mission. When Tubman did not meet him on the train to Chatham, he urged a friend to seek her out: "I did not find my friend Harriet as I expected. . . . May I trouble you to see her at once; & if she is well: by all means have her come on immediately." Franklin Sanborn remembered that Tubman was in Brown's "confidence in 1858–59, and he had a great regard for her, which he expressed to me. She aided him in his plans, and expected to do so still further, when his career was closed by that wonderful campaign in Virginia." Brown sought Tubman's advice regarding the timing of the raid, and records indicate that she suggested July 4th as a symbolic and ideal date. But Brown struggled to gather enough recruits that spring and summer of 1859, forcing him to delay the attack until later in the fall.[62]

When Brown's forces finally descended upon the small federal armory at Harpers Ferry, Tubman was not among them, although it appears that Brown searched for her in earnest earlier that fall. It is likely that illness prevented her participation, but it is also possible that she, like Frederick Douglass, decided that the risks outweighed the likelihood of success. On the day of the raid Tubman sensed Brown's misfortune, telling a friend that "something was wrong . . . that it must be Captain Brown who was in trouble." The next day newspapers confirmed her worst fears as they broadcast the events at Harpers Ferry.[63] When the Virginia government executed Brown for treason in December, Tubman mourned the loss of her comrade, but she also drew strength from his courage and his faith. She told her friend Edna Cheney, "Its clar to me, it wasn't John Brown that died on that gallows. When I think how he gave up his life for our people, and how he never flinched, but was so brave to the end; its clar to me it wasn't mortal man, it was God in him." She recognized that Brown's "failure" led not only to his martyrdom but also that his actions stoked the embers of sectionalism, bringing the nation closer to war and slavery closer to extinction. Brown did "more in dying, than 100 men would in living," Tubman said, and she also believed that "God is a prayer-hearing God, [and] I feel that his time is drawing near."[64]

Indeed, Brown's raid increased paranoia among slaveholders, an anxious fire that needed little fuel after a decade of intense antislavery activism and slave resistance. Some southerners, especially from vulnerable border states like Maryland and Virginia, began calling for secession in the wake of Harpers Ferry. In November the editor of the Baltimore *Sun* argued that disunion would be better than living under "a government, the majority of whose subjects or citizens regard John Brown as a martyr and a Christian hero," while James De Bow's *Review* argued that "our Northern Brethren has shed Southern Blood on Southern soil! There is—there can be no peace!"[65] Fear of another Brown's raid, combined with increasing concern over fugitive slaves and an ever-expanding UGRR network of black and white abolitionist allies, pushed southerners to their limit. When posting runaway ads, tightening slave patrols, and using federal troops to help recover runaways failed to work, slaveholders turned to secession as the best solution to the problem of their "troublesome property." In 1859 the rumored (and likely exaggerated) price for Tubman's capture stood at $12,000 (about $300,000 today), but neither reward money nor the increased proslavery vigilance after Brown's raid facilitated her capture or slowed Tubman's activism. Instead, Moses trusted that God would protect her and would answer her people's prayers.[66]

Notes

1. Quraysh Ali Lansana, *They Shall Run: Harriet Tubman Poems* (Chicago: Third World Press, 2004), 17, 11.
2. William Still, *The Underground Railroad: Authentic Narratives and First-Hand Accounts* (New York: Dover Publications, 2007; first published by Porter & Coates, 1872), 157.
3. Kate Clifford Larson, *Bound for the Promised Land: Harriet Tubman, Portrait of an American Hero* (New York: Ballantine, 2004), xvii, 144. Larson's careful calculations estimate that Tubman "personally brought away about seventy former slaves," but she also gave instructions to "approximately fifty more slaves who found their way to freedom independently." She also claims that Sarah Bradford's often-repeated figures of 19 trips and 300 slaves were "flagrantly exaggerated" (xvii).
4. Larson, *Bound for the Promised Land*, 216.
5. Thomas Garrett to Sarah Bradford, June 1868, qtd. in Lois E. Horton, ed., *Harriet Tubman and the Fight for Freedom: A Brief History with Documents* (New York: Bedford, 2013), 140–141.
6. Larson, *Bound for the Promised Land*, xvii.
7. Fergus Bordewich, *Bound for Canaan: The Epic Story of the Underground Railroad, America's First Civil Rights Movement* (New York: Harper Collins, 2005), 5.
8. Eric Foner, *Gateway to Freedom: The Hidden History of the Underground Railroad* (New York: Norton, 2015), 7, 22; Stanley Harrold, *Border War: Fighting over Slavery before the Civil War* (Chapel Hill: The University of North Carolina Press, 2010), 137, 118, 211; and Richard Blackett, *Making Freedom: The Underground Railroad and the Politics of Slavery* (Chapel Hill: The University of North Carolina Press, 2013), 4. For a comprehensive list of the major identifiable figures of the Underground Railroad see Tom Calarco, *People of the Underground Railroad: A Biographical Dictionary* (Westport, CT: Greenwood Press, 2008).
9. Kenneth Stampp first used this term in his iconic book, *The Peculiar Institution: Slavery in the Ante-Bellum South* (New York: Knopf, 1956), 91.

10. Larson, *Bound for the Promised Land*, 73.
11. Larson, *Bound for the Promised Land*, 64.
12. Larson, *Bound for the Promised Land*, 76–77.
13. Larson, *Bound for the Promised Land*, 32. For an account of Tubman's sisters' sale and its impact, see also "Interview with Harriet Tubman," Sydney Howard Gay Papers, Journal 1855–1856, Columbia University Special Collections, copy courtesy of Larson.
14. Sarah H. Bradford, *Scenes in the Life of Harriet Tubman* (Auburn, NY: W.J. Moses, 1869), 15.
15. Bradford, *Scenes*, 16; Larson, *Bound for the Promised Land*, 76–79.
16. Larson, *Bound for the Promised Land*, 80–84.
17. Larson, *Bound for the Promised Land*, 81–83; Catherine Clinton, *Harriet Tubman: The Road to Freedom* (Boston: Back Bay Books, 2004), 36. The Quaker woman was probably either Esther Kelley or Hannah Leverton, because both women lived in the immediate area, but definitive evidence of their direct involvement remains elusive.
18. The most recent scholarly overview of the UGRR is Foner, *Gateway to Freedom*, where he studies the network in New York City specifically and the overall political impact of the UGRR as a whole; see Foner, pp. 11–27 for a brief historiographical overview of the UGRR. See also the first comprehensive study of the UGRR written by Wilbur Siebert, *The Underground Railroad from Slavery to Freedom* (New York: MacMillan, 1898), and its corrective by Larry Gara, *The Liberty Line: The Legend of the Underground Railroad* (Lexington: University of Kentucky Press, 1961).
19. Bordewich, *Bound for Canaan*, 437–438. See also Stanley Harrold, *Subversives: Antislavery Community in Washington, D.C., 1828–1865* (Baton Rouge: Louisiana State University Press, 2003) for evidence of interracial cooperation in the antebellum period; and Blackett, *Making Freedom*, especially pp. 68–89.
20. Thomas D. Hamm, *The Quakers in America* (New York: Columbia University Press, 2003), 15, 34–35. See also Jerry William Frost, ed., *The Quaker Origins of Antislavery* (Norwood Editions, 1980) and Brycchan Cary, *From Peace to Freedom: Quaker Rhetoric and the Birth of American Antislavery, 1657–1761* (New York: Yale University Press, 2012).
21. Ann Hagedorn, *Beyond the River: The Untold Story of the Heroes of the Underground Railroad* (New York: Simon and Schuster, 2002), 19–20.
22. Ryan P. Jordan, *Slavery and the Meetinghouse: The Quakers and the Abolitionist Dilemma, 1820–1865* (Bloomington: Indiana University Press, 2007), 18, 6–7.
23. Nikki Marie Taylor, *Frontiers of Freedom: Cincinnati's Black Community* (Athens, OH: Ohio University Press, 2005), 152.
24. Paul Finkelman, *An Imperfect Union: Slavery, Federalism, and Comity* (Union, NJ: The Lawbook Exchange, 2000), 245–252.
25. Harrold, *Border War*, 21–23. See Paul Finkelman, *Slavery and the Founders: Race and Liberty in the Age of Jefferson*, 3rd ed. (New York: M.E. Sharpe, 2014), 102–132 for a detailed discussion of the Davis case and the 1793 law.
26. *Cambridge* (MD) *Democrat*, 3 October 1849, reprinted in Larson, *Bound for the Promised Land*, 79.
27. Harrold, *Border War*, 141–143, 11–12. For a discussion of the term "negro stealers," and the abolitionist threat perceived by slaveholders see Kristen Oertel, *Bleeding Borders: Race, Gender, and Violence in Pre-Civil War Kansas* (Baton Rouge: Louisiana State University Press, 2009), 33–34 and Oertel, "'Nigger-loving Fanatics' and 'Villains of the Blackest Dye'": Racialized Manhood and the Sectional Debates," in Jonathan Earle and Diane Mutti Burke, eds., *Bleeding Kansas and Bleeding Missouri: The Long Civil War on the Border* (Lawrence: University Press of Kansas, 2013): 65–80.
28. Joan Waugh, *On the Brink of Civil War: The Compromise of 1850 and How It Changed the Course of American History* (Wilmington, DE: Scholarly Resources, 2003), 75, 182–184.
29. Waugh, *On the Brink*, 183–184; Paul Finkelman, "The Appeasement of 1850," in Paul Finkelman and Donald Kennon, eds., *Congress and the Crisis of the 1850s* (Athens, OH: Ohio University Press, 2012), 69–70.

30. Stanley Harrold, *The Rise of Aggressive Abolitionism: Addresses to the Slaves* (Lexington: University of Kentucky Press, 2004), 126–130.

31. Gerrit Smith qtd. in Harrold, *Aggressive Abolitionism*, 192, 221. See also Carol Faulkner, *Lucretia Mott's Heresy: Abolition and Women's Rights in Nineteenth-Century America* (Philadelphia: University of Pennsylvania Press, 2011), 162.

32. Bradford, *Scenes*, 20.

33. Larson, *Bound for the Promised Land*, 89. For Baltimore in the 1850s see Horton, *Harriet Tubman*, 19; Fields, *Slavery and Freedom on the Middle Ground*, 62; and Christopher Phillips, *Freedom's Port: The African American Community of Baltimore* (Urbana: University of Illinois Press, 1997).

34. Larson, *Bound for the Promised Land*, 89–90. John Bowley used a sail canoe to transport his family from the Eastern Shore to Baltimore, a distance of about ninety miles. These vessels mimicked large Native American canoes carved out of multiple trees but added one or two sails to increase speed and maneuverability. See Geoffrey Footner, *Tidewater Triumph: The Development and Worldwide Success of the Chesapeake Bay Pilot Schooner* (Centerville, MD: Tidewater Publishers, 1998). Thank you to Kate Clifford Larson for this reference.

35. Larson, *Bound for the Promised Land*, 90. Quotes from "Interview with Harriet Tubman," Sydney Howard Gay Papers, Journal 1855–1856, Columbia University Special Collections, p. 56.

36. Larson, *Bound for the Promised Land*, 90–91; Horton, *Harriet Tubman*, 20; Jean Humez, *Harriet Tubman: The Life and the Life Stories* (Madison: The University of Wisconsin Press, 2003), 183–184.

37. Shearer David Bowman, *At the Precipice: Americans North and South during the Secession Crisis* (Chapel Hill: University of North Carolina Press, 2010), 52, 57, 63; Finkelman, "The Appeasement of 1850," 69. For Wisconsin's law see Thomas D. Morris, *Free Men All: The Personal Liberty Laws of the North* (Baltimore: Johns Hopkins University Press, 1974), 197–199.

38. William Still, qtd. in Faulkner, *Lucretia Mott's Heresy*, 163; Ian Frederick Finseth, ed., *The Underground Railroad: Authentic Narratives and First-Hand Accounts* (New York: Dover Publications, 2007), vi.

39. Faulkner, *Lucretia Mott's Heresy*, 164–165.

40. Faulkner, *Lucretia Mott's Heresy*, 6–7, 165–166. See also Finkelman, *Imperfect Union*, 255–262 for information about the Passmore Williamson case.

41. Bradford, *Scenes*, 27, 77.

42. Daniel J. Broyld, "Harriet Tubman: Transnationalism and the Land of a Queen in the Late Antebellum," *Meridians: Feminism, Race, and Transnationalism* 12, No. 2 (2014): 78–98.

43. Song qtd. in Bradford, *Scenes*, 33.

44. Thomas Garrett, qtd. in Bradford, *Scenes*, 48–49.

45. James A. McGowan, *Station Master on the Underground Railroad: The Life and Letters of Thomas Garrett* (Jefferson, NC: McFarland, 2005), 37, 39, 43, 97.

46. Bradford, *Scenes*, 48–53.

47. Larson, *Bound for the Promised Land*, 94.

48. Frederick Douglass, *Life and Times of Frederick Douglass from 1817 to 1882* (London: Christian Age Office, 1882), 231–232.

49. Larson, *Bound for the Promised Land*, 96; Still, *The Underground Railroad*, 156–159.

50. Melanie Susan Gustafson, *Women and the Republican Party, 1854–1924* (Urbana: University of Illinois Press, 2001), 1. For a thorough exploration of the Kansas-Nebraska Act, which was technically referred to as the "Act to Organize the Territories of Nebraska and Kansas" or the "Nebraska Bill" at the time, see John R. Wunder and Joann M. Ross, *The Nebraska-Kansas Act of 1854* (Lincoln: The University of Nebraska Press, 2008), 1–2.

51. William E. Gienapp, *The Origins of the Republican Party, 1852–56* (New York: Oxford University Press, 1987), 105, 275. See also Nicole Etcheson, *Bleeding Kansas: Contested Liberty in the Civil War Era* (Lawrence: University Press of Kansas, 2004), 100–107, and Oertel, *Bleeding Borders*, 85–86.

52. David Reynolds, *John Brown, Abolitionist: The Man Who Killed Slavery, Sparked the Civil War, and Seeded Civil Right*s (New York: Random House, 2005), 178.

53. Larson, *Bound for the Promised Land*, 156–160.

54. Larson, *Bound for the Promised Land*, 156–158; Wendy Hamand Venet, *A Strong-Minded Woman: The Life of Mary Livermore* (Amherst: University of Massachusetts Press, 2005), 6.

55. Famous Black Panther Party founder H. Rap Brown said that Brown was the "blackest white man anyone had ever known." See R. Blakeslee Gilpin, *John Brown Still Lives! America's Long Reckoning with Violence, Equality and Change* (Chapel Hill: University of North Carolina Press, 2011), 185.

56. Robert E. McGlone, *John Brown's War Against Slavery* (New York: Cambridge University Press, 2009), 210–212; Etcheson, *Bleeding Kansas*, 202–203; and Kristen Oertel, "Blazing a Path to Freedom: African Americans and Their White Allies in Bleeding Kansas," http://www.black past.org/perspectives/blazing-path-freedom-african-americans-and-their-white-allies-bleeding-kansas.

57. Larson, *Bound for the Promised Land*, 143–144.

58. Larson, *Bound for the Promised Land*, 144–151, 348n84, 348n100.

59. Larson, *Bound for the Promised Land*, 161–166.

60. Humez, *Harriet Tubman*, 26.

61. Larson, *Bound for the Promised Land*, 163–166.

62. Letter from John Brown to William H. Day, 16 April 1858, qtd. in McGlone, *John Brown's War Against Slavery*, 398n49; Bradford, *Scenes*, 54; Larson, *Bound for the Promised Land*, 166.

63. Bradford, *Scenes*, 83.

64. Edna Dow Littlehale Cheney, "Moses," *Freedmen's Record*, March 1865, and Martha Coffin Wright to William Lloyd Garrison II, 10 January 1869, both cited in Larson, *Bound for the Promised Land*, 177. For the effects of Brown's raid see Paul Finkelman, "Manufacturing Martyrdom: The Antislavery Response to John Brown's Raid," in Paul Finkelman, ed., *His Soul Goes Marching On: Responses to John Brown and the Harpers Ferry Raid* (Charlottesville: University Press of Virginia, 1995), 41–66.

65. Qtd. in James Abrahamson, *The Men of Secession and Civil War, 1859–1861* (Wilmington, DE: Scholarly Resources, 2000), 9–10.

66. Thomas Wentworth Higginson wrote to his wife that there was a "reward of twelve thousand dollars offered for her in Maryland." See Higginson to L. Higginson, 17 June 1859, cited in Larson, *Bound for the Promised Land*, 171. Sara Bradford also records the figure of $12,000 for "the woman who enticed them away," referring to Tubman when describing one of her many escapes from Maryland. See Bradford, *Scenes*, 30, 21–22.

CHAPTER 3

GENERAL

They may send the flower of their young men down South, to die of the
fever in the summer, and the ague in the winter. . . . They may send them
one year, two years, three years, till they are tired of sending or till they
use up all the young men. All no use! God's ahead of master Lincoln. God
won't let master Lincoln beat the South 'till he does the right thing. Master
Lincoln, he's a great man, and I am a poor negro; but the negro can tell
master Lincoln how to save the money and the young men. He can do it
by setting the negroes free.

Harriet Tubman, January 1862[1]

By the spring of 1860, Harriet Tubman had said goodbye to one of her
heroes, John Brown, but the name Brown had coined for her, "General," was
just beginning to catch fire among the leaders of the abolitionist movement,
men and women who would eventually recommend Tubman's service in
the Civil War. Perhaps it comes as no surprise given Tubman's active role in
dismantling slavery before the war that "the General" refused to sit on the
sidelines, travelling back to the South to finish the job she had begun more
than a decade earlier when she ferried her first group of slaves to freedom.
This time, however, her southern destination wasn't the border state of
Maryland, a state that remained in the Union; instead Tubman journeyed to
the epicenter of the rebellion, South Carolina, a state that had long embodied the political and economic power of slavery in the United States.

Serving troops stationed in the Department of the South, an area that
would eventually encompass South Carolina, Georgia, and Florida, Tubman began her war work in traditional ways, as a laundress and nurse, but
military officials soon recognized her talents as a spy and scout and used
her in several military capacities. As a Union army scout, spy, and then

soldier, helping to lead a raid that netted over 700 escaped slaves, Tubman's new moniker of "General" gained increasing credibility. Together with Colonel James Montgomery, a Kansas "Jayhawker" and former associate of John Brown's, Tubman helped plan and execute the June 1863 raid up the Combahee River in South Carolina that not only freed hundreds of slaves but also destroyed the nearby rice plantations and garnered supplies for the Union army. Although some disagreed with their tactics of "total war" at the time, Tubman and Montgomery now look prescient, not only in their use of black soldiers in battle but also in waging hard war on the Confederate countryside.[2]

The Union army initially viewed escaped slaves as enemy contraband, then as potential soldiers and key players in the battle to break the Confederacy's resolve and deplete their resources. Military historian Joseph Glatthaar argues, "Blacks alone did not win the war, but timely and extensive support from them contributed significantly and may have made the difference between a Union victory and stalemate or defeat." President Lincoln slowly accepted this logic and eventually characterized blacks' participation in the Union army even more dramatically: "Any different policy in regards to the colored man, deprives us of his help, and this is more than we can bear. . . . This is not a question of sentiment or taste but one of physical force which may be measured and estimated, as horse-power and steam-power are measured and estimated. Keep it, and you can save the Union. Throw it away, and the Union goes with it."[3]

Although it would take the President over a year to publicly acknowledge the strategic importance of enlisting black soldiers, Tubman never doubted the central role blacks would play in their own liberation and viewed her participation in the Civil War as an extension of her work on the Underground Railroad. Biographer Kate Larson notes "that it was Tubman's battles to claim liberty for scores of friends and relatives that marked the beginning of a strategic, political, and even military consciousness that eventually prepared her for a role on the battlefields."[4] But like Tubman's success on the UGRR, her triumphs in the Civil War simultaneously illustrate her exceptional abilities and her dependence on a network of ordinary men and women—enslaved and free, white and black—that supported her quest for freedom. Finally, "General" Tubman's story also demonstrates the ways in which blacks and their allies pressured the nation's leaders to accept emancipation as both a weapon of war and a moral imperative.

* * *

Tubman's wartime activities evolved naturally out of her persistent efforts to free her fellow Eastern Shore slaves, particularly the few family members that remained in the region at the war's commencement. Soon after

Lincoln's election in November of 1860, Tubman resolved to return to Dorchester County to retrieve the last immediate family members left enslaved, her sister Rachel and Rachel's two children. But when Tubman arrived in the area sometime in late November, she discovered that Rachel had recently died, and she maneuvered unsuccessfully to collect Rachel's children, Ben and Angerine. Harriet must have been devastated to learn of her sister's death and frustrated at her inability to carry her niece and nephew to freedom, but she resolved to do what she could and not waste a trip back to the Eastern Shore. So instead of rescuing Ben and Angerine, who could not be extracted from their plantation safely at the time, Tubman helped another local family, the Ennals: Stephen, Stephen's wife Maria, and their three children, the youngest of whom was only 3 months old. The Ennals were joined by a man named John and a "poor woman escaping from Baltimore in a delicate state," so the party numbered seven total "passengers." Pursued almost immediately by slave patrols, Tubman sought safety in the middle of a swamp, lodging her charges on a small island covered with tall grass. The group shivered with cold and fear, and Tubman was forced to drug the infant with laudanum to prevent its cries from alerting slave catchers to their location. Luckily they found Quaker allies who housed them and sent them further north, and the group arrived at Thomas Garrett's station in Wilmington in December. After a nearly month-long journey, Tubman's friends in Auburn announced on December 30th that Tubman had "just pioneered safely" yet another group of slaves from Maryland to upstate New York.[5]

Tubman ushered in the New Year from the relative comfort of Gerrit Smith's home in Peterboro, where she nursed her frostbitten feet and contemplated how to support her family in Auburn and respond to the ever-increasing dangers posed by the secession winter. South Carolina bolted from the Union in December 1860, and by March of 1861 Georgia, Florida, Alabama, Mississippi, Louisiana, and Texas had joined South Carolina to create the Confederate States of America, enshrining slaveholders' rights in their new constitution. Debates over secession raged in the remaining southern states, and outgoing President Buchanan did little to stop the crisis. According to his most recent biographer, "Buchanan continued to lend his ear to cabinet officers who were actively conspiring against the United States" and "pass his plans on to secessionist leaders throughout the South."[6] Congress tried to stop the political bleeding but only by acting in ways that would forever protect slavery.

Both houses of Congress passed a remarkable last-ditch effort to reunite the country, referred to then as the Corwin Amendment, just hours before Lincoln ascended the steps of the Capitol on Inauguration Day. Authored by Ohio Representative Thomas Corwin, the proposed amendment protected slavery in the states where it already existed, articulating what many southerners argued was already implied in the Constitution itself: "No amendment shall be made to the Constitution, which will authorize or give to Congress the power to abolish or interfere within any State, with the domestic institutions thereof, including that of persons held to labor or service by the laws of said State." Ironically, this would-be Thirteenth Amendment stands in direct opposition to the actual Thirteenth Amendment, adopted in 1865, that officially freed the slaves. In 1861, however, Lincoln "dutifully performed the task" of forwarding the Corwin Amendment to each state's Governor in March (though ultimately he did not endorse it), perhaps hoping it would help ensure the loyalty of key border slave states like Maryland. In fact, Maryland and Ohio eventually ratified the Corwin Amendment, but not until after the firing on Fort Sumter in April, when Virginia, North Carolina, Tennessee, and Arkansas joined the Confederacy and the country lost all hope of compromise and avoiding civil war.[7]

Tubman watched the nation disintegrate while trying to keep her family and the freedmen's community intact. Her family increased by one member sometime during the winter of 1861–1862 when Tubman returned to Maryland and "kidnapped" a young girl named Margaret Stewart. The exact details of the event are unclear, but several plausible theories exist that attempt to explain Tubman's motivation for taking Margaret from her childhood home. At the time Margaret was referred to as Tubman's niece, the daughter of one of her brothers, possibly Ben, who had married a free woman with whom he had several children. Margaret claimed to be a twin, and one of Ben's sons, Benjamin, was born around the same time as Margaret (between 1849–1850), which makes it possible that Margaret was, in fact, Ben's daughter. Margaret's daughter, Alice Lucas Brickler, later remembered that "Aunt Harriet ... fell in love with the little girl who was my mother ... [and] secretly and without so much as a by-your-leave, took the little girl with her to her northern home." Perhaps even more curious than her "kidnapping," Margaret did not live with Tubman or Tubman's extended family, but rather was placed in the care of Lazette Worden and Frances Seward at the Seward home where she lived and learned to "speak properly, to read, write, sew, do housework and act as a lady."[8]

Given that Tubman made sure Margaret enjoyed the privileges of living with an elite, white family in Auburn, it is also possible that Margaret is Harriet Tubman's biological daughter, whom she wanted to protect more than ever as the Civil War broke out. Margaret was born around the same time that Harriet travelled frequently between Baltimore and Philadelphia, and perhaps Tubman arranged for her baby to be kept in a Baltimore home, with family or friends, where another baby of roughly the same age would have had a nursing mother available to care for Margaret. Thus young

Margaret viewed her cousin as a biological twin, and Harriet as a "favorite aunt" who stopped by for long visits in between her trips on the Underground Railroad. Margaret also bore a striking resemblance to Harriet, lending credence to the possibility that she was her biological child or at the very least her aunt, but unfortunately, the extant records fail to definitively construct the family tree.[9]

If Tubman was, after all, Margaret's mother, it is not surprising that she kept her parentage a secret. Even if her ex-husband, John Tubman, had fathered the child (which was likely), their marriage dissolved soon after Margaret's birth, and perhaps Harriet didn't want to draw attention to that failed relationship. Or maybe John was not Margaret's father, and Harriet was hiding something even more scandalous. Regardless, Harriet would have needed a local family to care for her daughter while she worked to free the rest of her extended family, and after successfully ferrying all but her sister Rachel and Rachel's children to Auburn and/or St. Catharines in 1860, she was ready to establish a permanent, northern home for Margaret. But after committing the past decade to rescuing fugitive slaves and plotting with rebels like John Brown, the last thing Tubman wanted to do was rest on her laurels and live in the relative comfort of upstate New York. So she ensconced Margaret in a safe and financially secure home and proceeded to engage in the war effort in the best way she knew how: by helping to free more slaves.

The trickle of fugitive slaves that Tubman and others sustained in the years prior to the war quickly turned into a stream of freedom seekers, as runaways looked to the Union army for protection from their Rebel masters. Even before the fighting began in April of 1861, eight enslaved men sought their freedom at Fort Pickens in Florida in March, telling the fort's commander that they believed federal soldiers "were placed here to protect them and grant them their freedom." The commander, compelled by the Fugitive Slave Law to return slaves to their owners, handed the men over to the local sheriff, and most Union officials initially followed this policy; but on May 23, Major General Benjamin Butler liberated fugitives who came to Fortress Monroe in Virginia on the grounds they were "contrabands of war" and could not be returned to their master, a Confederate colonel. Within a few months the War Department would endorse this policy.[10] As the war progressed and army posts received an increasing number of fugitives, historian Ira Berlin claims that "slaves forced Federal soldiers at the lowest level to recognize their importance to the Union's success. . . . In time, it became evident even to the most obtuse Federal commanders that every slave who crossed the Union lines was a double gain: one subtracted from the Confederacy and one added to the Union."[11]

When three slaves wanted to add their strength to the Union at Fortress Monroe, Virginia, Major General Benjamin Butler devised a plan to usurp the Fugitive Slave Law by claiming that he had a legal right to "confiscate" enemy property. He asked if the Rebels shall "be allowed the use of this property against the United States" while "we not be allowed its use in aid of the United States?" Thus, in keeping with President Lincoln's stated war aims to reunite the country "as is," without disrupting slavery in the states where it already existed, the federal army declared runaway slaves as "contrabands of war" and thus subject to their possession. Ironically, by legally denying the slaves' humanity and classifying them as property, the Union believed they could weaken the Confederacy without touching the thorny issue of emancipation.[12]

Benjamin Butler was not the only Union General who took matters of emancipation into his own hands and pressed the government to develop a policy on the contraband issue. Further west in Missouri, General John C. Frémont issued a qualified emancipation proclamation in August of 1861, declaring that all slaves who left their Missouri Rebel masters were free.[13] Runaways in this border state had already taken advantage of the state's porous borders, particularly to the west where Kansas had just entered the Union as a free state in January. Senator James H. Lane of Kansas immediately began organizing these runaway slaves in southeastern Kansas, where they would eventually comprise the First Kansas Colored, mustered into federal service at Fort Scott, Kansas, as "the first regiment of black troops recruited in a Northern state."[14]

Similarly, in Florida and Georgia, states where slaves had already been accustomed to seeking freedom during military conflicts like the Seminole Wars, Major General David Hunter issued his own emancipation order in April of 1862 for slaves living near Fort Pulaski, Georgia, classifying fugitives as freedpeople and devising ways to funnel their energies into the Union war effort. He reinforced this order in May, declaring slaves in parts of coastal South Carolina, Georgia, and Florida as free and ordering the enlistment of "all physically fit black men between ages eighteen and forty-five" in the Union army. Both Frémont's and Hunter's orders elicited praise from abolitionist corners, and other like-minded officers, like General John W. Phelps, then stationed in New Orleans, believed that "the African should be permitted to offer his block for the temple of Freedom."[15]

Neither Hunter nor Frémont received permission to issue these emancipation orders from the War Department, however, and Frémont's order affected a state that was still in the Union. Lincoln rightly worried that these actions would drive Missouri and Kentucky into the Confederacy, and he immediately countermanded them. Still trying to ensure that the border states would remain in the Union, Lincoln walked tentatively and slowly along the road to emancipation, and tried to placate states like Missouri and Kentucky by offering compensated emancipation and discussing colonization plans to New

Mexico Territory and Haiti. In the spring and early summer of 1862 Lincoln urged the four loyal slave states to accept compensated emancipation as a way of ending all slavery in the Union and sending a firm message to the Confederacy that Kentucky and the border slave states would never secede. When this tactic failed, Lincoln began to turn the wheels of uncompensated emancipation.[16]

The increasing number of contraband showing up at Union camps and pressure from radical Republicans in Congress encouraged Lincoln to sign into law the First and Second Confiscation Acts (August 1861 and July 1862, respectively), measures designed to take advantage of the emerging groundswell of military support offered by freedom seekers. The Confiscation Acts articulated Butler's logic of defining runaway slaves as contraband of war, and thus "enemy property" subject to possession, and allowed Union forces to employ contraband as laborers, which enabled all white men to serve on the front lines. The Second Act went further and designated all slaves belonging to persons "engaged in rebellion" as contraband and began laying the groundwork for black enlistment in the armed forces by authorizing Lincoln to use freedmen "in such manner as he may judge best for the public welfare." Another piece of legislation, the Militia Act, followed close on the heels of the Second Confiscation Act and emancipated not only black males who joined the army but also their mothers, wives, and children who entered federal lines and contributed to the Union war effort.[17]

As Lincoln and Congress gradually moved toward enlisting black soldiers and broader emancipation, Harriet Tubman prepared to join the war effort herself, knowing that she could facilitate her people's transition to freedom and further the Union's war aims. Tubman's abolitionist friends William Lloyd Garrison and George L. Stearns likely introduced her to Massachusetts Governor John Andrew, who undoubtedly recognized that her experience with the Underground Railroad would prove useful for wartime activities like spying.[18] In May 1862 Governor Andrew sent her to South Carolina, where Union forces had taken possession of the coastal islands and the "Port Royal Experiment" was just underway. The Port Royal Experiment resettled freedmen and their families on abandoned or seized plantations, and abolitionists travelled to the region, hoping to provide freedmen with education and exposure to the principles and practices of free labor.[19] Tubman joined men and women like Edward S. Philbrick and Harriet Ware in their common quest to "*do something* in this great work that is going on," as Philbrick said, and they also hoped to show the world that "the blacks will work for motives other than the lash."[20]

When Tubman arrived in the region, she immediately began assisting with local efforts to feed, clothe, and care for the thousands of contraband and Union soldiers stationed in the Port Royal district. Tubman remembered that she "first took charge of the Christian Commission house at Beaufort," which served as a supply depot established by the YMCA and provided Union soldiers with food, clothing, and books. But she soon turned to assisting contraband with their economic transition to freedom, setting up a "wash house" that eventually employed dozens of washerwomen. Tubman used a $200 grant from the government to set up the facility, where she taught freedwomen how to use their skills as cooks, seamstresses, and laundresses to serve the Union soldiers and earn a living for themselves and their families.[21]

Like many women involved in the war effort, Tubman began her work in more traditional ways, like cooking, washing, and nursing, providing essential services to the troops. Washing, in particular, had long been "women's work" on the plantations, and the camp women who lived among Union soldiers deloused and disinfected soldiers' uniforms and undergarments, actions that lifted soldier morale and promoted sanitation, vital to controlling the spread of disease. Because they performed "socially significant" work in familiar environments, the black laundresses were not "simply refugees of war, vulnerable females seeking male protection in the army camps. On the contrary, they were a resourceful group of women employing their traditional skills to survive."[22]

Like washing, cooking was viewed as "women's work," but many men also served their regiments as cooks and both male and female cooks were held in high esteem, especially since they were required to be resourceful and flexible in their culinary ventures. Soldiers often captured local fauna, ranging from raccoons to alligators, and the cooks were expected to turn any bounty into dinner for the troops. One army surgeon recorded that in a matter of three days, the local cook had to wrestle an alligator tail, which the officers found "delicious and superior to other fish when cooked," and a five-foot-long king snake, which was skinned and fried for consumption. More traditional food was offered up by one black proprietor of a small "restaurant" located near where the 55th Massachusetts was stationed in North Carolina. After feigning that she had little food to share with the soldiers who knocked on her door, the "nice colored woman . . . ended by getting us a fine breakfast of eggs, breads, flapjacks, coffee, butter and molasses."[23] Another cook, called "Aunt Charlotte" by the soldiers, was lauded by a unit in North Carolina for her culinary skills and was paid $6 a month for her services. The Sanitary Inspector for the Department of North Carolina wrote, "Many a sick and wounded soldier . . . had reason to bless the culinary accomplishments of this venerable contraband cook, and to praise the alacrity with which, in times of their greatest need, she exerted her skill to save them from suffering." The daily Civil War rations of hard tack and salt pork paled in comparison to the baked pies and freshly brewed root beer offered by Tubman and other black women, causing one die-hard racist soldier to write home to his family that "blacks weren't so bad after all," when referring to a "colored" Virginia woman who cooked for him while he recovered from a war wound.[24]

A few women like "Aunt Charlotte" received payment from the army for their services, but most women cooked and cleaned to support themselves because the army could not provide rations for them. Undoubtedly because of her connections to powerful figures like Governor Andrew, Tubman was at first issued rations, but she eventually refused them because she did not want to receive "special treatment" that her fellow ex-slaves did not enjoy. In addition to the wash house she set up for female contraband, Tubman ran an "eating house" in Beaufort, where she sold pies, gingerbread, and root beer. She enlisted a group of contraband to circulate throughout the camps and peddle her goods, and she made enough money to maintain her meager lifestyle and send a few dollars home to her parents.[25] In sum, she quickly established herself as an important resource in the region, which drew the attention of local officers like Major General David Hunter.

Tubman immediately admired Hunter, in part because he had just made a declaration of emancipation for slaves residing within the Department of the South. Although Congress prohibited the enlistment of black troops in the spring and early summer of 1862, Hunter proceeded with his plans to raise a regiment of local black soldiers and sought Tubman's assistance in this process. Hunter's initial approach proved controversial, because he forced some black recruits to join the army at gunpoint instead of waiting for volunteers to fill his ranks. The recently freed slaves were understandably reluctant to sign up for service, given that they had no reason to trust anyone with white skin, particularly men who wielded guns and shouted orders. One volunteer at Port Royal criticized Hunter openly, calling him an "ignorant, obstinate fool," while another explained why his tactics were ineffective: "The confirmation of the report that Hunter is going to draft these people, causes a great deal of feeling [among the blacks]. . . . They will hide, if possible, and it is hard to feel that they have been so treated as to make them as suspicious of a Yankee's word as they have always been of a white man's."[26] Hunter ignored his critics, however, which made Tubman's assistance all the more crucial, given that blacks might trust "General Tubman" when she assured them that the "Yankee Buckra" meant no harm.

In fact, Tubman told Sarah Bradford that "it was almost impossible to win [blacks'] confidence, or to get information from them" if you were white. "But to Harriet they would tell anything; and so it became quite important that she should accompany expeditions going up the rivers, or into unexplored parts of the country, to control and get information from those whom they took with them as guides."[27] Even though Tubman could be trusted, recruitment progressed slowly in the winter of 1862, as blacks waited for the federal government's assurance that the risks they took to seize their freedom would be rewarded in the form of emancipation and protection within Union lines. The full measure of these rewards would not be realized until the Emancipation Proclamation took effect on January 1, 1863.

Tubman likely participated in the celebrations that marked the Emancipation Proclamation, and the Reverend Thomas Wentworth Higginson, former member of John Brown's "Secret Six" whom Tubman had met in 1859, recorded the momentous events that transpired that New Year's Day in his memoir, *Army Life in a Black Regiment*. Higginson, then a colonel in the army, had arrived in the area in November of 1862 to take charge of the 1st South Carolina Volunteers, and Tubman welcomed him to the region in early December when she rode out to Brigadier General Rufus Saxton's headquarters about three miles from Beaufort. No doubt they talked about their mutual friend and comrade in arms, John Brown, who had been martyred for the cause for which they now both fought and would soon celebrate. Although Tubman had predicted freedom for the slaves years before and found the Emancipation Proclamation somewhat anticlimactic, for Higginson, it capped his lifelong commitment to abolitionism and represented a dream come true for the ex-slaves who marched in his unit.[28] One of his soldiers greeted him that morning and said, "I think myself happy this New Year's Day. . . . This day last year I was a servant to a Colonel of Secesh; but now I have the privilege to salute my own Colonel."[29]

Thousands of visitors streamed into "Camp Saxton" to join the celebration: ex-slaves dressed in their Sunday best, black and white soldiers and officers, and the teachers and nurses like Tubman who populated the Port Royal district. The Reverend James H. Fowler opened the festivities at 11:30 a.m. with a simple prayer, which was then followed by a formal reading of the Emancipation Proclamation by Doctor William Brisbane, a former slaveholder who had freed his slaves decades before but who remained a resident of the Sea Islands. An army chaplain then passed out dozens of U.S. flags, and the crowd spontaneously erupted in an emotional rendition of "My Country, 'Tis of Thee":

> There suddenly arose, close beside the platform, a strong, male voice . . . into which two women's voices instantly blended, singing, as if by an impulse, that could no more be repressed than the morning note of the song-sparrow. . . . Firmly and irrepressibly, the quavering voices sang on verse after verse; others of the colored people joined in; some whites on the platform began, but I motioned them to silence. I never saw anything so electric; it made all other words cheap; it seemed the choked voice of a race at last unloosed.[30]

After Higginson and other members of the crowd dabbed their tears away, the program continued with a series of speeches that captured the egalitarian spirit of the day. Two black soldiers, Sergeant Prince Rivers and Corporal Robert Sutton, spoke to their comrades about serving the Union cause, and white abolitionist and woman's rights advocate Francis D. Gage "spoke very sensibly to the women." General Saxton joined the parade of speeches, which ended appropriately with the entire crowd of soldiers singing "John Brown's Body."[31]

At the time Tubman must have felt gratified to know that her predictions, first envisioned in a dream years before, had come to fruition, although it is apparent that she was also aware that the Emancipation Proclamation alone could not kill slavery. The document relied upon the Union army's invasion and occupation of Rebel territory, and it did not free the slaves still held by "loyal" slaveholders in the border states that remained in the Union. Tubman knew that a Union victory could actuate the promise of Lincoln's proclamation, and she did all she could to support the troops. Initially that meant helping to feed, clothe, and nurse the Union soldiers and contraband who occupied the region, but soon Tubman moved into more active service, first as an army scout and spy and then as a soldier herself.

* * *

Tubman and her fellow war workers confronted an unhealthy environment that featured disease-ridden swamps and marshes, where mosquitoes swarmed and infected the visitors with malaria and yellow fever. Furthermore, the army and contraband camps functioned as ideal breeding grounds for contagious diseases like typhoid fever, the measles, and dysentery, as thousands of men from disparate disease environments congregated in crowded and unsanitary conditions. Army policies, which naturally privileged military strategy, exacerbated these environmental hazards, by digging ditches that collected standing water and systematically exposing soldiers to the elements as they lived and worked in extreme heat and marched through rain and mud. As the war dragged on and conditions worsened, historian Jim Downs notes, "Emancipated slaves and soldiers also came in contact with diseased animals, from the horses and hogs that they were ultimately forced to eat to the rats that lived among them."[32]

Tubman immediately set to combat the negative consequences of these living conditions, providing medicine and nursing care to the sick and wounded. Tubman likely used common remedies such as quinine and plants like sassafras and dandelion to make teas and tinctures to soothe soldiers' ills. An army manual suggested mixing water or milk with ground slippery elm bark to treat nausea and vomiting, while one nurse made a cordial from blackberries and lemon extract to treat diarrhea.[33] Tubman recalled to interviewer Emma Telford that she cured a whole unit of soldiers who suffered from dysentery by digging up the roots of plants that grew near the water that had infected the troops and making a medicinal tea that she administered to the doctor on staff. "The disease stopped on him," Tubman remembered, "And then he said, 'give it to de soldiers.' So I boiled up a great boiler of roots and herbs, and the General told a man to take two cans and go round and give it to all in the camp that needed it, and it cured them."[34]

In addition to using roots and herbs, Tubman and other nurses relied on alcohol to treat wounded soldiers. Records indicate that in August of 1862 an army surgeon requested that "Moses" be issued "a little Bourbon whiskey for medicinal purposes," a common way of easing soldiers' pain when more powerful drugs like chloroform or opium were in short supply.[35] As with other drugs, however, alcohol had to be carefully rationed, and many nurses bemoaned the chronic shortage of "tonics" that many hospitals experienced. Judith McGuire, a nurse in Richmond, observed that her wounded patients were "suffering excessively for tonics, and I believe that many valuable lives are lost for the want of a few bottles of porter." She told the story of one soldier whom the surgeon believed was near death for lack of nourishment, after not being able to keep anything in his system for days. As a last-ditch effort, McGuire fed her patient spoonfuls of "India ale . . . cautiously at first, and when I found that [he] retained it, and feebly asked for more, tears of joy and thankfulness ran down my cheeks." She observed that "life seemed to return to his system . . . he began then to take milk, and I never witnessed anything like the reanimation of the whole man, physical and mental." As McGuire and Tubman could attest, alcohol was so important that items like sherry wine, whiskey, brandy, and port were commonly stocked next to castor oil, quinine, and morphine on hospital shelves.[36]

Medical supplies like these were particularly hard to come by in the contraband camps and freedmen's hospitals, however, where Tubman did much of her work; even when the necessary tonics were available, surgeons administered them differently to white and black soldiers and civilians, believing that whites and blacks were biologically distinct. For example, Doctor J.W. Compton submitted a report to the U.S. surgeon general in 1865 that claimed that a black man varied "as widely from the white man physiologically, as does his skin or hair; hence the importance of understanding his peculiarities." Because of these beliefs, surgeons often treated black illnesses differently from whites', or simply did not know how to treat them at all because some doctors had never before seen black patients. One Union doctor had never treated "black folks with small-pox," thinking that he had to approach the remedy differently than he would a white patient with the same disease. The fact that black soldiers received inferior medical care and were given unhealthy jobs like digging latrines, especially before they were allowed to fight, helps explain why their mortality rate was over twice as high as whites.[37]

Once Lincoln began to requisition black troops, however, many blacks happily laid down their latrine shovels to pick up a gun. The 1st South Carolina Volunteer Infantry (Colored), commanded by Colonel Higginson, had been organized in the fall and winter of 1862, and in the spring of 1863 the 2nd South Carolina formed, which would soon be known as the 34th United States Colored Infantry after the creation of the Bureau of Colored Troops in May.[38] Colonel James Montgomery organized the 2nd Infantry Regiment, South Carolina Colored Volunteers, and immediately began preparing his troops for his Jayhawker style of military justice. According to historian Keith Wilson, "Montgomery believed he was on a mission to inflict divine retribution on the slaveholding South," and he transferred these devout beliefs and his "western" style of guerilla warfare, first practiced in Kansas with John Brown, to his unit in South Carolina. Telling Adjutant General Lorenzo Thomas that the "religious element is the only foundation on which we can build, in making soldiers of these freedmen," Montgomery imposed rigid camp rules and instructed his chaplain, the Reverend Homer H. Moore, to conduct daily prayers and instill a "strict Christian regime" among his troops.[39]

Like her introduction to Colonel Higginson, Harriet Tubman knew about Colonel Montgomery from their mutual association with John Brown, and certainly Montgomery's pious commitment to waging a "holy war" on slavery resonated with Tubman's own faith. Similarly, Montgomery found in Tubman a kindred spirit and a qualified scout and spy, ready to serve the troops in whatever capacity was needed. The confidence the army leadership invested in Tubman is indicated by a military pass she carried in February 1863, just when Montgomery arrived in the region: "Pass the bearer, Harriet Tubman, to Beaufort and back to this place, and wherever she wishes to go; and give her free passage at all times, on all Government transports. Harriet was sent to me from Boston by Governor Andrew, of Massachusetts, and is a valuable woman. She has permission, as a servant of the Government, to purchase such provisions from the Commissary as she may need."[40] Clearly Tubman had already established herself as a valuable asset to the Union army when she joined Montgomery to lead the 2nd South Carolina in a series of controversial raids that would earn both of them headlines.

Since most of the plantation owners on the coast had fled to the interior and taken many of their slaves with them, one way to further weaken the heart of the Confederacy was to pursue these refugees and destroy their ability to wage war. The Combahee River formed an artery into the interior from Morgan Island, northeast of Beaufort, to plantations that dotted the riverbank for miles. As biographer Kate Larson notes, "Tubman was quite comfortable navigating on both land and by water. Although the fields sprouted rice and cotton rather than the grains of the Eastern Shore, the sameness of the physical landscape worked to Tubman's advantage." Tubman had already explored the region during her scouting missions the previous winter, moving into the interior and talking secretly with local slaves, determining Confederate troop positions and strengths, and recruiting other scouts to help further the Union's spying missions. As early as January of 1863, the government issued Tubman $100 in "secret service money," which she and her team of spies used to pay skeptical slaves for information, so that by June Tubman's team had sufficiently prepared the enslaved population for the Union gunboats' arrival and gathered enough information to plan a successful raid.[41]

But even with these extensive preparations, no one could have predicted how effective the Combahee River raid would be, nor how many accolades both Tubman and Montgomery would receive because of their leadership. Boarding three gunboats, the *John Adams*, *Harriet A. Weed*, and *Sentinel*, Tubman, Montgomery, and roughly 300 soldiers from the 2nd South Carolina moved up the Combahee from Port Royal on June 1st, carefully sailing around the many dangerous mines that Tubman's scouts had identified. Tubman also provided crucial information about the locations of Confederate warehouses and barns full of rice and cotton, and she apparently had no reservations about Montgomery's style of "western" guerilla warfare, which entailed the wholesale destruction of civilian property. On the morning of June 2nd, Montgomery sent a detachment of his troops up to the riverbanks, where they rooted out any remaining Confederate gunners, set fire to local houses and barns, and told any slaves they saw to find the Union gunboats and join the army. They also opened the sluices and flooded the rice crop, which according to one witness, were "growing beautifully" and would now be "a total loss." Finally, Union troops confiscated rice, corn, and cotton stores, along with horses, pigs, and cows, resulting in hundreds of thousands of dollars of captured and destroyed property that had belonged to Confederate masters.[42]

The most important source of Confederate wealth taken in the raid, however, were the 700 plus slaves that fled the once-wealthy plantations and took refuge on "Lincoln's gunboats." Tubman described the scene with a mixture of incredulity and joy, first noting that the slave drivers used their whips to try and stem the tide of slaves who flooded the riverbanks, but the force of freedom was too great. She told the exodus story to her biographer, Sarah Bradford:

> "I nebber see such a sight," said Harriet; we laughed, an' laughed, an' laughed. Here you'd see a woman wid a pail on her head, rice a smokin' in it jus as she'd taken it from de fire, young one hangin' on behind. . . . Sometimes de women would come wid twins hangin' roun' der necks . . . bags on der shoulders, baskets on der heads, and young ones taggin' behin,' all loaded; pigs squalin', chickens screamin', young ones squalin'.[43]

The desperate passengers overloaded the rowboats docked at the river's edge, making it impossible to row back to the gunboat, so Montgomery asked Tubman to sing and reassure the soon-to-be freedmen that these "arks of refuge" would return to collect them. Filled with her indomitable faith and spirit, Tubman sang, "Of all the whole creation in the east or the west, the glorious Yankee nation is the greatest and the best. Come along! Come along! Don't be alarmed, Uncle Sam is rich enough to give you all a farm."[44]

Ultimately the raid netted roughly 750 slaves, and the 2nd South Carolina left a trail of destruction in its wake: crumbling pontoon bridges, smoldering mansions, and abandoned plantations. One Confederate officer who later investigated what he referred to as an "abolition raid," said that the Union's "success was complete" and claimed that Montgomery had thwarted "all the rules of civilized warfare."[45] Major General Hunter likewise proclaimed the mission a resounding success and wrote to Massachusetts Governor Andrew that Montgomery (and Tubman) "had taken 'but the initial step of a system of operations' that would 'rapidly compel the Rebels,' to withdraw all their slaves into the interior," leaving the most fertile and lucrative land open for Union occupation. Indeed, even before the raid, the Confederate leadership stationed in the region issued a circular to planters in South Carolina that advised them to "remove their negroes as far as practicable into the interior of the State, as otherwise they are liable to be lost at any moment."[46] By mid-June, a correspondent for the *New York Post*, then stationed on Folly Island just outside of Charleston, reported that "great numbers of negroes are now coming into our lines, both here and in Georgia and Florida. They say there is a great movement among the negroes for an insurrection, and there are some who believe them."[47] The Combahee River raid represented the planters' worst nightmare and the beginning of a process that would eventually bring the Confederacy to its knees.

While some critics questioned the total war tactics employed during the Combahee raid, many abolitionists lauded Montgomery and Tubman's success, and the press reported widely on the victory and subsequent celebrations. One Philadelphia paper described the raid as "most gratifying to the Union men and most damaging to the Rebels," and recorded with some exaggeration that "about one thousand negroes carried off, and property to the amount of $1,000,000 destroyed."[48] The New York *Herald* noted that "the negroes at work in the fields ran towards the boats in spite of pistols in the hands of the drivers," and estimated that "seven hundred and over" returned to the camp, where "all the able bodied men" were drafted into Montgomery's unit.[49] Finally, the Washington, D.C., *Intelligencer* highlighted the raid's primary outcomes: "Col. Montgomery has brought off with him six hundred thousand dollars' worth of chattel property, has destroyed fifty dwelling houses, has demonstrated beyond all question that negro soldiers will follow wherever a brave man dare lead, and that the slaves on the rice plantations of South Carolina are eager to reach our lines." Papers from Atchison, Kansas, to Bangor, Maine, reprinted accounts of the increasingly famous Montgomery and his exploits.[50]

Not surprisingly, the vast majority of stories about the raid cited Montgomery's bravery and leadership and neglected to mention anything about Tubman's involvement in the mission. A few papers, however, noted Tubman's participation, and one Wisconsin reporter dubbed her a "Black She 'Moses'" and claimed that under Tubman's "supervision [the raid] was originated and conducted." Furthermore, this reporter lifted her up as an icon of black feminist accomplishment, arguing that Tubman was "head and shoulders above the many who vaunt their patriotism and boast their philanthropy, swaggering of their superiority because of the cuticle in which their Creator condescended to envelop them."[51] Similarly, the Boston *Commonwealth* reprinted parts of the story first published by the Wisconsin paper and made sure its readers knew that the "She 'Moses'" referenced in the story was, in fact, Harriet Tubman, since the reporter never mentioned her by name. Perhaps this oversight, and certainly the lack of reference to Tubman's involvement in the press at large, is an indication of how women's contributions to the war effort were often overlooked. It is also likely that she could have asked not to be named in deference to military or gender norms, or because she did not want to leave concrete evidence of her role in the raid for fear of enemy capture. But given that she shared details of the experience with Franklin Sanborn, who that July published a short biography of her in the *Commonwealth* that included information about the Combahee raid, it is doubtful that Tubman is to blame for her excision from the public record.

In contrast to these public silences, Generals Hunter and Saxton and Colonel Higginson all named Tubman as a key player in their private and official correspondence, and soon after the raid, she inferred that she would be involved in future missions in the region. First, however, she needed proper clothing, "a *bloomer* dress, made of some coarse, strong material, to wear on *expeditions*." Bloomers, named after woman's rights advocate Amelia Bloomer, offered women greater mobility with ballooned pants and skirts that only went down to the upper calf or knee rather than below the ankles. She recalled to Sanborn that during the raid, "I was carrying two pigs for a poor sick woman, who had a child to carry, and the order 'double quick' was given, and I started to run, stepped on my dress, it being rather long, and fell and tore it almost off.... I made up my mind then I would never wear a long dress on another expedition of the kind, but would have a *bloomer* as soon as I could get it."[52] It seems that the confines of traditionally feminine roles and fashion would not prevent Tubman from fulfilling her responsibilities to the Union and to her people.

For the time being Tubman temporarily retired her scouting garb to reassume her duties as a nurse and relief agent, helping the men and women who escaped the plantations dotted along the Combahee with their acclimation to freedom. In a dictated letter to Sanborn, she reported that the freedmen were "very destitute, almost naked," and others, like Colonel Higginson, also noted the freedmen's dire straits: "Never had I seen human beings so clad, or rather so unclad, in such amazing squalidness and destitution of garments." Finding proper clothing and feeding hundreds of new camp residents formed the first order of business, and then Tubman hoped to impart vital skills and knowledge that would assist the freedmen in their transition to wage labor and financial independence. She noted, "I am trying to find places for those able to work, and provide for them as best I can, so as to lighten the burden on the Government as much as possible, while at the same time they learn to respect themselves by earning their own living."[53] Tubman's philosophy reflected the official army policy of "self-reliance," articulated by Brigadier General Lorenzo Thomas in the Mississippi Valley, who emphasized the important links between black recruitment and free labor. Thomas wrote, "The families of colored soldiers were on the same footing as other Blacks," and were expected to work for their rations. They were now "free—free as I am," Thomas instructed," and "Now [that] you are free, you can learn—learn to work. Learn to read."[54]

Tubman continued to support the freedmen and the local troops as they prepared for an assault on Fort Wagner in July of 1863. The 54th Massachusetts, made famous by the Hollywood film "Glory," led the charge on the fort, and their commander, Colonel Robert Gould Shaw, received his last meal from Tubman and had likely come to know her during his unit's six-week stay in Beaufort before the battle.[55] On the evening of July 18th Shaw and roughly 600 soldiers and officers marched bravely toward the heavily defended fort and suffered significant casualties. According to historian

Edwin Redkey, the 54th "paid a price for the honor of proving that African American troops could and would fight well." Experiencing a casualty rate of over 40 percent, roughly 175 soldiers were wounded at Fort Wagner, and another seventy-five were killed, including Colonel Shaw, who was buried in a mass grave with his men.[56]

The dying and wounded men were farmed out to hospitals in Beaufort and Charleston, where nurses like Tubman greeted them and tried to minimize the mortality rate. Crude conditions and meager supplies made that difficult, however, and Tubman remembered how she did the best she could to care for the soldiers:

> I'd go to de hospital, I would, early eb'ry mornin'. I'd get a big chunk of ice, I would, and put it in a basin, and fill it with water; den I'd take a sponge and begin. Fust man I'd come to, I'd thrash away de flies, an' dey'd rise, dey would, like bees roun' a hive. Den I'd begin to bathe der wounds, an' b de time I'd bathed off three or four, de fire and heat would have melted de ice and made de water warm, an' it would be as red as clar blood. Den I'd go an' git more ice, I would an' by de time I got to de nex' ones, de flies would be roun' de fust ones black an' thick as eber.

It appears that Tubman never received payment for her nursing services, and according to her biographer Sarah Bradford, she "never drew for herself but twenty days' rations during the four years of her labors" in the war. Instead, as she had instructed her charges months earlier at Port Royal, she supported herself by baking pies and brewing root beer to sell in the camps.[57]

Like other freedpeople, Tubman struggled financially, and during a short leave in the fall of 1863, she tried to place her family in Auburn and Canada on stronger financial footing and traveled to St. Catharines in November. She might have participated in a "fact-finding trip" with Samuel Gridley Howe, an agent for the American Freedmen's Inquiry Commission (AFIC). The AFIC was founded in March of 1863 by Secretary of War Edwin Stanton, who charged the agency's commissioners to explore "the measures which may best contribute to the protection and improvement of the recently emancipated freedmen of the United States, and to their self-defense and self-support." The AFIC reported that contrary to popular belief, the commissioners found a "free colored population supporting themselves under grievous and depressing disabilities, without any aid whatever even from those legal sources appointed for the relief of indigent whites." Members of Tubman's family worked as coachmen and servants for white families in Auburn and as day laborers and farmers in St. Catharines, but steady, well-paying jobs remained out of reach for Tubman's family and for freedmen in general. Although they enjoyed legal freedom in Canada and wartime emancipation in the United States, blacks still confronted racist vitriol and discriminatory employment practices on a regular basis. Commissioners reported that even in St. Catharines, a "colored" woman named Mrs. Susan Boggs claimed, "If it was not for the Queen's law we would be mobbed here, and could not stay in this house. The prejudice is a great deal worse here than it is in the States."[58]

The commission also recognized, however, that prejudice against blacks was rapidly decreasing in certain sectors, especially where black soldiers were stationed and as news of their heroism spread throughout the country. "The whites have changed, and are still rapidly changing, their opinion of the negro. And the negro, in his new condition as freedman, is himself, to some extent, a changed being. No one circumstance has tended so much to these results as the display of manhood in negro soldiers. Though there are higher qualities than strength and physical courage, yet, in our present stage of civilization, there are no qualities which command from the masses more respect."[59] Like the commissioners, perhaps Tubman understood that her work with the army in South Carolina would eventually benefit her family in New York and in Canada, and she resolved to return to the front lines in November of 1863.

When Tubman arrived back in South Carolina, she received orders from General Quincy Adams Gillmore, who had replaced General Hunter, to take up residence on Folly Island, near Charleston. According to correspondence written by George Garrison, son of famed abolitionist William Lloyd Garrison, she served Brigadier General Alfred H. Terry, commander of Morris and Folly Islands, perhaps as his personal laundress and cook, but she also continued her spying and scouting ventures. When Tubman saw the younger Garrison, who was then stationed at Folly Island, George remembered that she "instantly threw her arms around me, and gave me quite an affectionate embrace, much to the amusement of those with me." Certainly seeing a familiar face must have warmed Tubman's heart, and she told Garrison how she intended to send money back to her family and wished to return to them soon. Garrison claimed that General Gillmore would not release her, however, because "she has made it a business to see all contrabands escaping from the rebels, and is [able] to get more intelligence from them than anybody else."[60] Tubman continued to work for the Department of the South throughout the winter and spring of 1864, when acting assistant surgeon Henry K. Durrant wrote that he was impressed with the "esteem" Tubman held among the soldiers, especially applauding "her kindness and attention to the sick and suffering of her own race."[61]

Apparently General Gillmore finally granted Tubman a leave in the summer of 1864 when she made the rounds to visit friends and family in New

York City, Auburn, and Boston. Wendell Garrison, George Garrison's brother, reported from Boston that "Moses Garrison, alias Harriet alias General Tubman has just arrived. . . . What times." Dr. John Rock, one of the country's first black doctors and also a noted abolitionist, hosted her in Boston, and Franklin Sanborn published a short article in the *Commonwealth* alerting the public to Tubman's stay in the city and reminding her supporters of her perpetual need for funds to help feed and clothe her own family and the freedmen she worked with in South Carolina.[62]

While in Boston Tubman had the opportunity to meet Sojourner Truth, a woman who in many ways shared a similar biography: an ex-slave, an activist for freedmen, and an increasingly vocal supporter for woman's rights. The two women initially held very different opinions of President Lincoln, however. Tubman questioned Lincoln's motivation for issuing the Emancipation Proclamation and critiqued what she perceived as his slow and reluctant embrace of black freedom. She also blamed Lincoln for the policies that perpetuated unequal pay and treatment for black soldiers. Sojourner Truth, in contrast, readily accepted Lincoln's reputation as the "Great Emancipator" and remarked after meeting him in the fall of 1864 that she had "never [been] treated with more kindness and cordiality than I was by the great and good man Abraham Lincoln, by the grace of God President of the United States for four more years."[63] Truth's more favorable opinion is not surprising given that during the war she was more enmeshed in northern antislavery circles than Tubman and was also a friend of Elizabeth Keckley's, Mary Todd Lincoln's confidante and personal dressmaker. Years later Tubman regretted not making the effort to try and meet the President, saying that she was "sorry [she] didn't see Master Lincoln and thank him." But at the time, she said, "we colored people didn't understand then that he was our friend. All we knew was that the first colored troops sent south from Massachusetts only got seven dollars a month, while the white regiments got fifteen. We didn't like that."[64]

Tubman was outraged about unequal pay for black soldiers, an injustice she personally experienced as a woman who was paid little to nothing, but during her leave she secured funding from the New England Freedmen's Aid Society, who agreed to pay her ten dollars a month to work as a "practical teacher" in South Carolina. The Aid Society's journal, the *Freedmen's Record*, published a biography of Tubman in its March 1865 issue and claimed that the society's members "considered her labors too valuable to the freedmen to be turned elsewhere," and thus funded her return to the Deep South. Tubman never made it back to the front, however, because while en route to South Carolina, a group of nurses who worked for the United States Sanitary Commission (USSC) persuaded her to stay in Virginia, where black soldiers at Fortress Monroe desperately needed her services.

By the end of the war, the USSC had grown from a skeleton organization to a national network of roughly 7,000 local soldier's aid societies administered by twelve regional branch offices with central locations in Chicago, New York, and Boston. The organization functioned much like the Red Cross does today, in that it was privately funded but authorized "to work in tandem with military authorities." Funneling much-needed food, clothing, and medical supplies to the front lines and field hospitals, the USSC provided over a million dollars' worth of aid to the Union war effort.[65] The Women's Central Association of Relief (WCAR), a core component of the USSC founded by Dr. Elizabeth Blackwell, solicited supplies and funds from thousands of local soldier's aid societies, organized and repackaged it, and forwarded it to Washington, D.C., where the USSC apparatus distributed it to the troops. Historian Judith Giesberg argues that the women of the USSC branches "combined grassroots women's activism with centralized access to political authority to offer a model of women's political culture that best served the needs of a new generation of women."[66] These women's wartime responsibilities gradually transitioned to post-war relief efforts and suffrage activism as the war drew to a close in the spring of 1865, and Tubman's work followed this same trajectory.

Stationed at Fortress Monroe in Virginia when the Confederate army surrendered at Appomatox, Tubman must have celebrated the Union victory with the very soldiers who helped ensure it. Together with the passage of the Thirteenth Amendment in January of that year, Confederate defeat spelled out a future for African Americans as a free people with renewed hopes of citizenship and suffrage. The scene at Ft. Sumter on April 14, 1865, captures that optimism when white abolitionists like William Lloyd Garrison and black abolitionists Martin Delaney and Robert Vesey, the son of a man who had been hanged for plotting a slave revolt forty years earlier, stood side by side to witness the raising of the stars and stripes. Delaney told the thousands of black troops and freedpeople gathered on the island that they should "do anything; die first! But don't submit again to them—never again be slaves."[67] The crowd cheered and praised the dawn of a lasting freedom. A similar scene played out in Richmond when President Lincoln entered the city on April 4th and was showered with praise and thronged by admirers. One reporter wrote that as Lincoln maneuvered his way through the crowds, "The colored population was wild with enthusiasm. Old men thanked God in a very boisterous manner, and old women shouted upon the pavement as high as they had ever done at a religious revival."[68]

Celebrations like these ended abruptly, however, after news of Lincoln's assassination spread throughout the country. The nation quickly turned from jubilation to depression, as it mourned the President's death and tried to heal the countless wounds inflicted by four years of loss and bloodshed.

The New Orleans *Black Republican* blamed "the fell spirit of slavery" that broke "from the knife of the assassin," and deified the President, saying, "He has sealed with his blood his Divine commission to be the liberator of a people." Other editorials voiced less reverence for Lincoln, and especially his policies, noting that "reconstruction on the principles which seemed uppermost in the mind of our late deeply lamented President" was "drifting" into dangerous territory, an "easy reconstruction" that valued peace over justice. Instead, the *Weekly Anglo-African* argued emphatically that all Confederates should be punished and disfranchised, while all black men should be given full citizenship rights, including the right to vote. Only then would "this terrible awakening" elicit real change, "real peace, and sounder, if slower prosperity" would inevitably result.[69] Like the variance in opinion between Sojourner Truth and Harriet Tubman, these editorials debated Lincoln's commitment to black equality and foreshadowed the challenges the nation would face as it mapped out a path toward Reconstruction.

Tubman's path led her from Hampton Hospital at Fortress Monroe back to Washington, D.C., because her promised commission as "Matron" of the hospital was never fulfilled, and she grew increasingly discouraged by the abuses she witnessed at the facility. Tubman reported in June to the Surgeon General, Dr. Joseph K. Barnes, and told him that over twice as many black soldiers were dying as white soldiers and reiterated the now common refrain that "colored hospitals" were understaffed and poorly funded.[70] Her frustration erupted in a dictated letter that was published by a New York paper, *The Independent*:

> I should be glad to write better news to you than this if I could, but how can I when there are dying around me, in the course of every day and night, twenty or twenty-five men? I truly believe the principal part of them suffer with hunger. . . . Neither the sick nor the well have enough to eat; brave men die with tears in their eyes, crying for something to eat. We found great fault with the rebels for their treatment of our prisoners, but it is worse among our friends by whose aide we have fought to put down this rebellion. We could not expect much from our enemies, but from our friends we looked for justice.

Although Barnes sent her to Hampton with the charge to remedy the dire situation there, Tubman found her task overwhelming and begged all "loyal and Union people" to consider "while they are at home enjoying comforts, their friends are suffering here."[71]

After enduring the deplorable conditions at Hampton for five weeks, she returned to Washington and worked briefly at a home for orphans funded by the National Association for the Relief of Destitute Colored Women and Children and administrated by Kansas abolitionist, Clarina Nichols.

Tubman might not have been able to influence policies at Hampton Hospital, but during her stay at the orphanage, she and Nichols restored order, cleanliness, and confidence in an organization that had recently suffered from extreme neglect and political scandal. Again, however, while her success at the home must have been gratifying, it is unlikely that Tubman was paid much, and her concerns about her family's financial and physical health forced a realization that she needed to find steady, paid work and attend to her family's well-being.[72]

Departing Washington for Auburn must have been bittersweet. The pull to remain near the center of activity and help reconstruct the nation and assist the freedpeople was strong, but the call to aid her family had always been the guiding light in Tubman's activism. As she boarded the train to leave D.C., Tubman undoubtedly reflected upon her service in the army and the many ways that she contributed to the war effort. She could take pride in the fact that she and other African American freedom seekers and "contraband" helped pressure Union generals and force Lincoln's hand to issue the Emancipation Proclamation. Furthermore, Tubman and the black and white soldiers she marched beside illustrated the utility of enlisting black men and using hard war tactics to crush the Confederacy. But Tubman and her fellow freedmen and women would not allow the sacrifices they made in wartime to go unnoticed by the American people. The war's true impact could not be fully realized until African Americans, in the North and the South, enjoyed freedom not just in name but in their daily lives. And while she might have gained a sense of accomplishment from her wartime achievements as "General Tubman," what would become a fateful train ride back to Auburn reminded her of the stubborn injustices that remained in post–Civil War America.

Notes

1. Qtd. in Kate Clifford Larson, *Bound for the Promised Land: Harriet Tubman, Portrait of an American Hero* (New York: Ballantine, 2004), 206, from a letter written by Lydia Maria Child to John Greenleaf Whittier, 21 January 1862 (Larson 364n16).
2. Larson, *Bound for the Promised Land*, 216–217.
3. Joseph T. Glatthaar, "Black Glory: The African-American Role in Union History," in Gabor S. Borritt, ed., *Why the Confederacy Lost* (New York: Oxford University Press, 1992), 138. Lincoln qtd. in Glatthaar, "Black Glory," 138.
4. Larson, *Bound for the Promised Land*, 203.
5. Larson, *Bound for the Promised Land*, 185–189; William Still, *The Underground Railroad: Authentic Narratives and First-Hand Accounts* (New York: Dover Publications, 2007; first published by Porter & Coates, 1872),261–262. Still records the family name as Ennets, but Larson notes that this was likely a mistake and/or typographical error.
6. Jean H. Baker, *James Buchanan* (New York: Times Books, 2004), 151.
7. John A. Lupton, "Abraham Lincoln and the Corwin Amendment," *Illinois Periodicals Online*, http://www.lib.niu.edu/2006/ih060934.html. See also Daniel Crofts, "The Other 13th Amendment,"

Disunion Blog, *The New York Times*, 3 March 2011; Harold Holzer, *Lincoln President-Elect: Abraham Lincoln and the Great Secession Winter* (New York: Simon & Schuster, 2008), 429; and Christopher A. Bryant, "Stopping Time: The Pro-Slavery and 'Irrevocable' Thirteenth Amendment," *Harvard Journal of Law and Public Policy* 26, No. 2 (March 2003): 501.

8. Alice Lucas Brickler, qtd. in Larson, *Bound for the Promised Land*, 196–198.

9. Larson, *Bound for the Promised Land*, 198–202. Alice Lucas Brickler wrote, "Strange to say mother looked very much like Aunt Harriet, and there was a hardness about her character in the face of adversity that must have been hereditary," (Larson, 199).

10. Paul Finkelman, "Lincoln, Emancipation and the Limits of Constitutional Change," *Supreme Court Review* (2008): 349–387.

11. Ira Berlin, "Who Freed the Slaves?: Emancipation and Its Meaning," in David Blight and Brooks Simpson, eds., *Union and Emancipation: Essays on Politics and Race in the Civil War Era* (Kent, OH: Kent State University Press, 1997), 111, 110.

12. Butler qtd. in Ira Berlin, Joseph P. Reidy, and Leslie Rowland, eds., *Freedom's Soldiers: The Black Military Experience in the Civil War* (Cambridge: Cambridge University Press, 1998), 4. See also Joseph Glatthaar, *Forged in Battle: The Civil War Alliance of Black Soldiers and White Officers* (New York: The Free Press, 1990), 4.

13. But since Missouri was still in the Union, this order was flagrantly illegal and unconstitutional, and when Frémont refused to revoke it, President Lincoln countermanded it. See Finkelman, "Lincoln, Emancipation and the Limits of Constitutional Change," 368–370.

14. Diane Mutti Burke, *On Slavery's Border: Missouri's Small-Slaveholding Households* (Athens: University of Georgia Press), 271, 282–285; John David Smith, "Let Us All Be Grateful That We Have Colored Troops That Will Fight," in John David Smith, ed., *Black Soldiers in Blue: African American Troops in the Civil War Era* (Chapel Hill: The University of North Carolina Press, 2002), 20.

15. John David Smith, "Let Us All Be Grateful," 21.

16. Finkelman, "Lincoln, Emancipation and the Limits of Constitutional Change," 375–380.

17. Smith, "Let Us All Be Grateful," 13–14.

18. Larson, *Bound for the Promised Land*, 196, 204.

19. Howard Westwood, *Black Troops, White Commanders, and Freedmen during the American Civil War* (Carbondale: Southern Illinois University Press, 2008), 56–57.

20. Edward S. Philbrick to Mrs. E.S. Philbrick, 19 February 1862, cited in Elizabeth Ware Pearson, ed., *Letters from Port Royal: Written at the Time of the Civil War* (Boston: W.B. Clarke Co., 1906), 1–2.

21. Larson, *Bound for the Promised Land*, 205.

22. Keith P. Wilson, *Campfires of Freedom: The Camp Life of Black Soldiers during the Civil War* (Kent, OH: Kent State University Press, 2002), 204.

23. Richard M. Reid, ed., *Practicing Medicine in a Black Regiment: The Civil War Diary of Burt G. Wilder, 55th Massachusetts* (Amherst: University of Massachusetts Press, 2010), 130–131; 217.

24. Ella Forbes, *African American Women during the Civil War* (New York: Routledge, 1998), 55–57.

25. Larson, *Bound for the Promised Land*, 203, 208.

26. Letters from Charles P. Ware, 14 March 1863, and Harriet Ware, 10 March 1862, cited in Pearson, *Letters from Port Royal*, 173, 172. See also Glatthaar, *Forged in Battle*, 6–7.

27. Sarah H. Bradford, *Scenes in the Life of Harriet Tubman* (Auburn, NY: W.J. Moses, 1869), 38–39.

28. Keith Wilson, "In the Shadow of John Brown: The Military Service of Colonels Thomas Higginson, James Montgomery, and Robert Shaw in the Department of the South," in Smith, ed. *Black Soldiers in Blue*, 308, 313.

29. Thomas Wentworth Higginson, *Army Life in a Black Regiment* (Boston: Fields, Osgood, and Co., 1870), 59. Note—I have modernized the dialect recorded by Higginson.

30. Higginson, *Army Life in a Black Regiment*, 40–41.

31. Higginson, *Army Life in a Black Regiment*, 41–42.

32. Jim Downs, *Sick from Freedom: African-American Illness and Suffering during the Civil War and Reconstruction* (New York: Oxford University Press, 2012), 28. See also Gretchen Long, *Doctoring Freedom: The Politics of African American Medical Care in Slavery and Emancipation* (Chapel Hill: The University of North Carolina Press, 2012) for more evidence of blacks' inferior medical care during the war years.

33. Woman's Central Association of Relief to the Army, "Manual of Directions, Prepared for the Use of the Nurses in Army Hospitals, by a Committee of Hospital Physicians of the City of New York" (New York: Baker and Godwin, 1861), qtd. in Patricia B. Mitchell, *Civil War Plants & Herbs* (Chatham, VA: privately printed, 2010), 22–23.

34. Qtd. in Larson, *Bound for the Promised Land*, 224. See also Mitchell, *Civil War Plants & Herbs*, 26.

35. Larson, *Bound for the Promised Land*, 208.

36. Judith White Brockenbrough McGuire, *Diary of a Southern Refugee, During the War, By a Lady of Virginia*, 3rd ed. (Richmond, VA: J.W. Randolph & English Publishers, 1889), 187–188; Charles F. Johnson, *The Long Roll; Being a Journal of the Civil War, as set down during the years 1861–1863* (East Aurora, NY: The Roycrofters, 1911), 90–96.

37. J.W. Compton cited in Downs, *Sick from Freedom*, 34–35; Smith, "Let Us All Be Grateful," 41–42.

38. Transcript of War Department General Order 143, Creation of the U.S. Colored Troops, http://www.ourdocuments.gov/doc.php?flash=true&doc=35&page=transcript.

39. Lorenzo Thomas qtd. in Wilson, "In the Shadow of John Brown," 318.

40. Larson, *Bound for the Promised Land*, 209–210.

41. Larson, *Bound for the Promised Land*, 210.

42. Larson, *Bound for the Promised Land*, 212–213; Wilson, "In the Shadow of John Brown," 319–320.

43. Bradford, *Scenes*, 40–41.

44. Bradford, *Scenes*, 41–42.

45. Captain John F. Lay, qtd. in Wilson, "In the Shadow of John Brown," 319–320.

46. James Lowndes, "By order of Brigadier-General Walker," 23 March 1863, qtd. in Robert N. Scott, ed., *War of the Rebellion: A Compilation of the Official Records of the Union and Confederate Armies*, Series 1-Volume XIV (Washington, D.C.: Government Printing Office, 1885), 293.

47. *New York Post*, qtd. in "The Combahee Expedition," *Philadelphia North American and United States Gazette*, 10 June 1863, 19th Century U.S. Newspapers Index (USNI).

48. "State of the Campaign," *Philadelphia North American and United States Gazette*, 9 June 1863, USNI.

49. "Our Hilton Head Correspondence," *New York Herald*, 9 June 1863, USNI.

50. "A Foray in South Carolina," *Daily National Intelligencer*, 11 June 1863; see for example, the *Banghor Daily Whig and Courier*, 10 June 1863, and the (Atchison, KS) *Freedom's Champion*, 13 June 1863.

51. "Colonel Montgomery's Raid—the Rescued Black Chattels—A Black 'She Moses' ...," *The Wisconsin State Journal*, 20 June 1863, cited in Larson, *Bound for the Promised Land*, 214–216.

52. Larson, *Bound for the Promised Land*, 219–220, 225; Franklin Sanborn, "Harriet Tubman," *Boston Commonwealth*, 17 July 1863.

53. Larson, *Bound for the Promised Land*, 218; Higginson, *Army Life in a Black Regiment*, 172.

54. Wilson, *Campfires of Freedom*, 185; Michael T. Meier, "Lorenzo Thomas and the Recruitment of Blacks," in Smith, *Black Soldiers in Blue*, 257.

55. Larson, *Bound for the Promised Land*, 220.

56. Edwin S. Redkey, "Brave, Black Volunteers: Profile of the Fifty-fourth Massachusetts Regiment," in Donald Yacavone, ed., *Hope and Glory: Essays on the Legacy of the Fifty-Fourth Massachusetts Regiment* (Amherst: University of Massachusetts Press, 2001), 29–30; Joseph

Glatthaar, *Forged in Battle: The Civil War Alliance of Black Soldiers and White Officers* (New York: The Free Press, 1990), 138–140.

57. Bradford, *Scenes,* 37–38.

58. Robert Dale Owen, James McKaye, and Samuel G. Howe, "Final Report of the American Freedmen's Inquiry Commission to the Secretary of War," 15 May 1864, http://www.civilwar-home.com/commissionreport.htm.

59. Owen, McKaye, and Howe, "Final Report," http://www.civilwarhome.com/commissionreport.htm.

60. George Garrison to William Lloyd Garrison II, 10 February 1864, qtd. in Larson, *Bound for the Promised Land,* 222.

61. Larson, *Bound for the Promised Land,* 225.

62. Jean Humez, *Harriet Tubman: The Life and the Life Stories* (Madison, WI: The University of Wisconsin Press, 2003), 54–55.

63. Nell Irvin Painter, *Sojourner Truth: A Life, A Symbol* (New York: Norton, 1996), 203–206.

64. Larson, *Bound for the Promised Land,* 226–227. Tubman perhaps unfairly pinned all the blame for blacks' mistreatment in the army on Lincoln; she likely was unaware that blacks could not by law be paid as soldiers because they were initially enrolled as laborers. Once Congress changed their designation, black soldiers received back pay from their enlistment date, but that law did not take effect until March 1865. See John F. Marszalek, *Lincoln and the Military* (Carbondale: Southern Illinois University Press, 2014), 81–82.

65. Judith Ann Giesberg, *Civil War Sisterhood: The U.S. Sanitary Commission and Women's Politics in Transition* (Boston: Northeastern University Press, 2000), 5; Margaret Humphreys, *Marrow of Tragedy: The Health Crisis of the American Civil War* (Baltimore: Johns Hopkins University Press, 2013), 103.

66. Giesberg, *Civil War Sisterhood,* 54–56.

67. Wilbert L. Jenkins, *Seizing the New Day: African Americans in Post-Civil War Charleston* (Bloomington: Indiana University Press, 1998), 38–39; Delaney qtd. in Robert J. Zalimas, Jr., "A Disturbance in the City: Black and White Soldiers in Postwar Charleston," in Smith, ed., *Black Soldiers in Blue,* 367.

68. Rollin [R. Morris Chester] to the *Philadelphia Press,* 6 April 1865, in Donald Yacavone, ed., *Freedom's Journey: African American Voices of the Civil War* (Chicago: Lawrence Hill Books, 2004), 284.

69. New Orleans *Black Republican,* 22 April 1865, and New York *Weekly Anglo-African,* 22 April 1865, in Yacavone, *Freedom's Journey,* 302–304.

70. Larson, *Bound for the Promised Land,* 229–230.

71. Harriet Tubman, "Soldiers Dying from Hunger and Neglect: A Woman's Appeal," *The Independent . . . Devoted to the Consideration of Politics, Social and Economic Tendencies, History, Literature, and the Arts* (New York), 27 July 1863. Thanks to Kate Larson for forwarding me this important reference.

72. Marilyn S. Blackwell and Kristen T. Oertel, *Frontier Feminist: Clarina Howard Nichols and the Politics of Motherhood* (Lawrence: University Press of Kansas, 2010), 217–218.

CHAPTER 4

AUNT HARRIET

"Harriet's door was always open to those in need."
—Faith Ringgold, *Aunt Harriet's Underground Railroad in the Sky*[1]

In October 1865, Harriet Tubman boarded a train bound for New York from Philadelphia and climbed into the passenger car, carrying the half-fare ticket she earned because of her wartime service. When a conductor arrived to collect the ticket, he ordered her to the smoking car, the car often reserved for blacks, drunken men, and otherwise "rowdy characters" and positioned directly behind the engine where smoke belched out of the coal-fired furnace. Tubman protested, grabbed on to the interior of the car, and refused to leave, citing her government privilege (and perhaps her gender) to ride in the non-smoking or "ladies' car," as it was often called. The conductor yelled, "Come, hustle out of here! We don't carry niggers for half fare," and wrenched Tubman from her seat, injuring her arm and shoulder and possibly breaking a rib in the process of tossing her into the smoking car. Several bystanders joined the conductor and verbally harassed Tubman, but Tubman stood strong, dubbing the conductor a "Copperhead scoundrel," and claiming that she was, "as proud of being a black woman as he was being white." When she got off the train in New York City, Tubman's satisfaction with the Union's victory and emancipation, accomplishments she helped secure, was tarnished by the reality of racism.[2]

Although her resistance and proud words indicated otherwise, Tubman had been physically and emotionally beaten on this northern-bound train, an unfortunate harbinger of blacks' future challenges in post–Civil War America. Like most African Americans, Tubman struggled to secure fair wages, adequate housing for her and her family, basic civil rights like sharing public space with whites, and political rights like voting and running for office. But for a relatively brief moment immediately following the war, it appeared that America might make good on its promise of emancipation. Radical Republican policies and the ratification of the 14th and 15th Amendments to the Constitution offered a window of opportunity for black men to run and hold political office and for women to sue in court to maintain their right to ride on integrated streetcars and trains. Roughly 2,000 black men held a wide variety of political offices during Reconstruction, and black women from California to Pennsylvania successfully sued train and streetcar companies for discrimination. These triumphs did not last long, however, as Reconstruction turned to Redemption in 1877, and state after state began tossing black men out of office and denying white and black Republicans political power through violent repression.[3]

Tubman and her fellow black Americans met these and other obstacles to exercising their new freedoms head on, extending a legacy of resistance to white oppression rooted in slavery times and stretching from the Civil War and Reconstruction into the Jim Crow era. The slaves who broke tools, slowed down production, or ran away from abusive masters became freedmen and women who demanded fair wages, exited the fields if planters violated labor agreements, or moved to a neighboring county if promises of better wages beckoned them. Similarly, the free blacks who had organized antislavery societies and established black churches before the war continued their work for racial and social justice by advocating for black and woman's suffrage, desegregation in public spaces and schools, and equal wages and working conditions for African Americans. Formerly free and enslaved, hailing from the North and the South, black Americans throughout the country agitated in small and large ways to actuate the changes initiated by emancipation and Reconstruction.

Tubman might have been beaten on that train back to New York, but she was not defeated, nor was she alone in her fight to maintain her dignity and ride in a "ladies'" train car. Other well-known black women like Sojourner Truth and Ida B. Wells resisted removal from segregated streetcars and trains in the nineteenth century, almost a century before Rosa Parks most famously refused to give up her seat on a city bus in Montgomery, Alabama.[4] Black women "criticized laissez-faire Reconstruction policy, and advocated radical measures like land reform," and "challenged white perceptions of race, equal rights, free labor, and dependency." Tubman and her peers maintained a tradition of what historians have variously called "oppositional politics," "infrapolitics," and "visionary pragmatism," actions that challenged the racial and political status quo and pushed the boundaries of freedom to include property, voting, economic, and civil rights in the post-war era.[5]

But black women's politics, like Tubman's own activism during the late nineteenth century, cannot be defined by liberal political concepts such as individual rights and personal freedom; what many black women worked toward was a collective freedom, a political process that "operated out of a notion of community, wherein all—men, women, and children; freeborn and formerly slave; native and migrant—had inherent rights and responsibilities requiring no higher authority than their commitment to each other."[6] The motto of the most famous black women's organization of the late nineteenth and early twentieth centuries, the National Association of Colored Women (NACW), connotes this very philosophy; the NACW adopted "Lifting as We Climb" as their mantra and "pledged to help others as they helped themselves." The NACW, an organization that Tubman supported and whose motto she embodied, worked especially to relieve poverty in black communities and helped establish nurseries, schools, and homes for the elderly.[7]

Tubman's activism in Auburn typified these larger trends in black women's politics, as she worked first to house and feed her own family and then turned immediately to help others in her community, as well as reaching out to the freedmen in the South. Noted by many for her benevolence, Tubman established herself as a consummate Good Samaritan, and her nineteenth-century biographer, Sarah Bradford, claimed that "Harriet's charity for all the human race is unbounded." When raising money for a Freedman's Fair in 1867, she asked her old friend, former Secretary of State William Seward to support her cause. He quipped, "Harriet, you have worked for others long enough. It is time you should think of yourself. If you ask for a donation for *yourself*, I will give it to you; but I will not help you to rob yourself for others." But "Aunt Harriet," as so many called her in her final decades, practiced what others often only preached, that the Golden Rule reigned supreme and freedom could only be enjoyed if everyone was free.[8]

* * *

When Tubman returned to Auburn in the fall of 1865, she found a house full of mouths to feed, including her elderly parents, Rit and Ben, who were feeble from the strain of the war years. Seven other extended family members also lived with her parents: Katherine Kane Stewart, the widow of Tubman's brother James Stewart (née Ben Ross, Jr.), and her three children; Ann Marie Stewart (James Stewart's daughter from a previous marriage) and her husband, Thomas Elliott; Tubman's adopted daughter, Margaret Stewart; and a boarder, Thornton Newton. Tubman continued to suffer from the injuries caused by her ejection from the train car, which made it impossible for her to work and support her extended family during that first winter after the war. The family was forced to burn their own fence posts for firewood, and Tubman once visited the market with an empty basket and empty pockets, trusting that God would provide in her time of need. As with so many times before, when Tubman was at her most anxious, God answered her prayers; she left the market with a full basket, complete with a soup bone offered by a "kind-hearted butcher," and an assemblage of produce from other benevolent vendors. Certainly Tubman's esteem in the local community helped sustain her and her family at desperate times like these, but Tubman knew that she needed more than charity to survive in freedom.[9]

Her experiences during the war informed her understanding of the importance of financial independence. When Tubman helped ex-slaves set up a washing house in wartime South Carolina, she was actuating one of the main objectives of the ever-evolving freedmen's aid movement: inculcating the ideals and practices of free labor in black communities. The Freedmen's Bureau, founded in 1865, helped administer the South's transition from slavery to free labor, with the goal of laying "the foundation for a free labor society—one in which blacks labored voluntarily, having internalized the values of the marketplace, while planters and civil authorities accorded them the rights and treatment enjoyed by Northern workers."[10] General Oliver Otis Howard was appointed to head the Bureau in Washington, D.C., and dozens of assistant commissioners worked at the state and local levels. One assistant commissioner articulated the "Herculean task" facing the Bureau: "I had often felt depressed at the extent of work before us, but never doubtful of final success in restoring not only the Union in its integrity but of infusing correct notions of government and liberty into the minds of the old slave holders . . . and also of the freedmen."[11]

The most radical commissioners advocated land redistribution and located the key to African American economic success in blacks' ownership and cultivation of land. For example, General Rufus Saxton, whom Tubman served under in the Department of the South, expressed confidence in the freedmen's ability to adopt free labor farming. Saxton was appointed Assistant Bureau Commissioner for the states of South Carolina, Georgia, and Florida, and after experiencing success with the Port Royal experiment during the war, he believed that "to lay a short basis for the substantial freedom and permanent improvement of the Negroes . . . they should be owners of the land they cultivate." Furthermore, Saxton claimed, when an ex-slave became a landowner, "he becomes practically an independent citizen, and a great step towards his future elevation has been made."[12] Saxton began distributing abandoned and conquered lands to contraband and emancipated slaves during the war, and he continued these policies during early Reconstruction, sometimes straining relations with federal officials who were more reluctant to redistribute Confederate property.

The issue of land redistribution divided Reconstruction politicians and policymakers in the immediate aftermath of the war. Radical Republicans in Congress, like Thaddeus Stevens and Charles Sumner, argued that African Americans deserved the fruits of their labor that had been denied to them by whites for centuries. Stevens asked rhetorically, "How can republican institutions, free schools, free churches, free social intercourse exist in a mingled community of nabobs and serfs? If the South is ever to be made a safe republic let her lands be cultivated by the toil of the owners or the free labor of intelligent citizens." Accordingly, Stevens suggested that the federal government seize 400 million acres of conquered Confederate land and provide 40 acres to each adult freedman.[13] On the other hand, more moderate Republicans and all Democrats believed that the South had suffered enough during the war, and that private property should remain in the hands of its original owners. President Johnson aligned himself with the moderates and then with his former party stalwarts, the Democrats, and began to thwart Freedmen's Bureau policies at every turn. He issued Circular 15 in the fall of 1865, a directive that ordered the restoration of land to all pardoned Confederates and countered the confiscated land policies first administered by Howard and Saxton.[14]

In contrast to Johnson's policies, Tubman embraced the radical vision of Reconstruction and perhaps even directly supported Saxton's policies in South Carolina and Georgia. Through her nephew James A. Bowley, who worked with the Freedmen's Bureau in South Carolina, and likely others who were still stationed in the region, Tubman maintained a connection with Reconstruction efforts on the ground. Tubman organized at least two Freedmen's Fairs at the Central Presbyterian Church in Auburn to raise money for the freedmen communities in South Carolina. Patterned after the successful antislavery and Sanitary Commission fairs that raised thousands of dollars before and during the war, these Freedmen's Fairs encouraged local citizens to donate clothing, bedding, and cash to facilitate the Bureau's programs in the Deep South. Tubman's old abolitionist friends like Martha Wright, Lucretia Mott, and Eliza Wright Osborne all collected goods for the fair that Tubman organized in December 1868, which raised over $500 for the freedmen's cause.[15]

Tubman's Auburn friendships continued to bear fruit for her family and the freedmen, and her wartime alliances also brought a former U.S. soldier to her doorstep sometime in 1866. Nelson Davis, a former slave who fought with the 8th United States Colored Troops (USCT) during the war, began boarding at the Tubman residence, and even though Davis was twenty-one years younger than Tubman, they fell in love and married in 1869. Observers alternately described Davis as a "black, true African" who was "a magnificent specimen in appearance," but also as someone who was "tubercular" and "colorless" because he suffered from the debilitating lung disease throughout his adult life.[16] Whatever Tubman's attraction to Davis, it is possible the two first met in South Carolina or Florida in 1864 because both were stationed in the region at that time; Davis's unit, the 8th USCT, fought at the Battle of Olustee, along with Colonel Montgomery's brigade, and evidence suggests that Tubman probably nursed and attended to these soldiers in Jacksonville. Regardless of how they met or whether they maintained contact after their service in Florida, Davis and Tubman obviously shared much in common during the war, which might have strengthened their bond.[17]

Their marriage epitomized the joy many African Americans experienced during Reconstruction when their loving partnerships could be officially recognized by the church and state. Reports from the Tubman-Davis wedding popped up in Auburn newspapers, and it appears that the town's elite attended the wedding and wished the couple well. Whether any gossip circulated regarding their age difference is unknown, but certainly a few tongues must have been wagging as the small, elderly-looking Tubman walked down the aisle with the much younger, strapping ex-soldier.[18] Unlike her first marriage to John Tubman, which was not recognized by the state and ended in heartbreak, Tubman and Davis enjoyed almost twenty years together, just one of the benefits of freedom that blacks could exercise in the wake of emancipation.

Harriet Tubman's marriage to Nelson Davis followed close on the heels of the tragic news that her ex-husband, John Tubman, had been murdered in Maryland. According to newspaper accounts of the incident, Tubman and a white man named Robert Vincent quarreled on the morning of September 30, 1867, exchanged threats, but eventually parted ways; however, later that afternoon the two confronted each other again, whereupon Vincent shot Tubman in the head and killed him. Tubman's 13-year-old son, Thomas, was the only witness, so it was no surprise that an all-white, male jury took only ten minutes to acquit Vincent of the crime. Vincent claimed that Tubman had come after him with a club, arguing self-defense and certainly banking on the fact that his word would trump a young black boy's.[19] John Tubman left behind his son Thomas; his wife, Caroline (whom he had taken up with after Harriet's escape from Maryland in 1849); and three other children, and regardless of the pain his and Caroline's union had caused her almost twenty years earlier, Harriet undoubtedly lamented the injustice of his murder.

Unfortunately, John Tubman's death was emblematic of the epidemic of white-on-black violence in the South during Reconstruction. One journalist who traveled throughout the Deep South in the late 1860s and early 1870s observed "a condition of lawlessness toward blacks," noting that southern whites had a "disposition ... to trample [blacks] underfoot, to deny them equal rights, and to injure or kill them on slight or no provocations." The famous Civil War nurse, Clara Barton, recorded a horrific example of this type of violence in Georgia, when a former master bucked and gagged his female employee and then whipped her for not performing her spinning tasks correctly. Barton noted that "she must have been whipped with a lash half as large [wide] as my little finger . . . [because] the flesh had been cut completely out most of the way."[20] General Rufus Saxton, whom Tubman served under during the war, reported from Edgefield County, South Carolina, that a freedman and three children "were stripped naked, tied up, and whipped severely" by recalcitrant whites. One Freedmen's Bureau official in New Orleans believed that as soon as the Union army left, southern whites would wantonly murder the freedmen, while another official went even further, claiming that he "expected in ten years to see the whole colored race exterminated." Legal historian Paul Finkelman argues that the "openly homicidal intentions of whites . . . underscored the refusal of many southern whites to accept black freedom or the outcome of the War that they had started."[21]

Reports of southern intransigence, along with pleas from Freedmen's Bureau agents, helped provide the political capital necessary to pass both the Fourteenth and Fifteenth Amendments to the Constitution. Republicans in Congress argued that African Americans needed a federal guarantor of citizenship and voting rights to ensure that southern whites could not quash their newly gained freedoms. The Fourteenth Amendment, ratified in 1868, deemed any person born in the United States a citizen with "equal protection of the laws" and prohibited individual states from depriving "any person of life, liberty, or property without due process of law." The Fifteenth Amendment, ratified in 1870, guaranteed the right to vote without reference to "race, color, or previous condition of servitude."[22] President Grant summed up the significance of the Fifteenth Amendment in a special message to Congress on March 30, 1870: "A measure which makes at once four millions of people voters, who were heretofore declared by the highest tribunal in the land *not citizens* of the United States, nor eligible to become so . . . is indeed a measure of grander importance than any other one act of the kind from the foundation of our free Government to the present day."[23]

Armed with the legal protections provided by these Reconstruction amendments, black men began voting in droves and electing their own candidates to local, state, and even federal offices. Between 1867 and 1877, fourteen black men were elected to Congress, along with two black Senators, Hiram Rhodes Revels and Blanche Kelso Bruce. These politicians were among the twenty-two blacks who served in Congress during the nineteenth century, but approximately 2,000 black men held some kind of political office at the local and state levels during Reconstruction. From Alabama and Georgia to Virginia and North Carolina, Republican voters sent black representatives to Congress, and black majority states like Mississippi and South Carolina produced black electorates that eventually numbered in the hundreds of thousands.[24]

Black women were still denied the right to vote and hold office, but they used Reconstruction-era laws to pursue the rights they did have. Caroline LeCount, a black school teacher and principal in Philadelphia, cited a Pennsylvania law passed in 1867 that "allowed judges to either fine or imprison (or both) conductors who denied service to black riders" to have a conductor arrested who refused her service on a streetcar. LeCount and other black women formed the Ladies' Union Association during the war to support black soldiers and their families in Philadelphia. They used this organization as a platform from which to launch an attack on the city's segregated transportation system, arguing that their wartime commitments to black soldiers and the Union required full and equal mobility. The organization noted, "We hope that our friends will make some efforts to gain us admission to the city cars, as we find great difficulty in reaching the Hospitals." Another Philadelphia woman, "Mrs. Derry," argued that "she and others of her race were engaged in providing comforts for the wounded soldiers," and thus needed access to all forms of city transportation. Derry won a lawsuit against a Philadelphia streetcar conductor who was forced by the court to pay Derry $50 in damages "for the injuries she incurred when she was wrongfully ejected from the train."[25]

After Tubman continued to suffer from the arm and shoulder injuries that she endured on the train from Philadelphia to New York, her friends encouraged her to sue the railroad company responsible. They placed ads in local newspapers seeking out a witness who had given Tubman his card and seemed sympathetic after the incident. But the witness never materialized, and Tubman decided not to pursue the case any further, even though she remained handicapped by the injury throughout the winter of 1865–1866. Sojourner Truth, on the other hand, successfully prosecuted one conductor who threw her out of a streetcar and wrenched her shoulder in the process. Truth and her white colleague, Laura Haviland, attempted to board a car together when another passenger yelled, "[H]ave you got room for niggers here?" The conductor tried to remove Truth, but she resisted and suffered injuries in the ensuing tussle. Haviland and Truth recorded the conductor's I.D. number and used a recent federal law that desegregated streetcars in Washington, D.C., to bolster their prosecution of the conductor, who was later convicted of assault and battery for causing Truth's injuries.[26]

Black leaders like Truth and Tubman endured individual acts of violence as they worked and lived in the North, but their counterparts in the South faced large-scale violence and intimidation designed to curb rising black political and economic power. While the Ku Klux Klan is the most infamous white vigilante organization, in places like Colfax, Louisiana, and Hamburg, South Carolina, various groups of armed white men gunned down hundreds of black men with the goal of preventing them from voting and holding office. The Colfax Massacre, which took place on Easter Sunday in 1873, resulted in 150 slain blacks and 3 whites. Hundreds of white paramilitary fighters from the Knights of the White Camelia and the Ku Klux Klan attempted to occupy the county courthouse in Colfax, which at the time was guarded by black militiamen. What shocked many observers was the bold-faced shooting of dozens of unarmed black men who sought refuge from the melee at the courthouse. One militia colonel reported finding six black bodies under a warehouse, victims who had apparently tried to hide from their pursuers, but who were "shot like dogs . . . one man still lay with his hands clasped in supplication; the face of another was completely flattened by blows from a gun. . . . Many of them had their brains literally blown out."[27]

Although not as large in scale as Colfax, whites in Hamburg used a similar playbook in July of 1876, claiming that several members of a local black militia had threatened whites during a marching drill. In response, a group of armed ex-Confederates attacked the black militia and killed seven black men, causing the militia to disband and ultimately forcing the resignation of the town's black trial judge, Prince Rivers.[28] The Atlanta *Daily Constitution* predicted that violence would erupt in places like Hamburg and Colfax in their derogatory portrait of Justice Rivers a year before the massacre:

> He is a man of unbounded ambition and much influence and it is thought that it will be found that the spirit of insurrection pervades other states. The idea among the Negroes that the land is theirs, and that their fathers earned it by their labor, has been preached to them for years, until they have become imbued with that feeling to such an extent that a *war of races would not be the most surprising occurrence* of the day.[29]

The Atlanta paper blamed radical blacks like Rivers for the impending "race war," but more often than not, it was unruly whites who initiated the violence during Reconstruction. In fact, historian Eric Foner argues that "the Klan during Reconstruction offers the most extensive example of homegrown terrorism in American history."[30]

While Tubman did not suffer or witness large-scale violence in upstate New York, she too was the victim of conniving men who took advantage of blacks trying to gain a financial foothold after the war. In 1873 Tubman and her family continued to live hand to mouth, so when two men approached Tubman's brother John Stewart and claimed to have access to $5,000 worth of gold bars, Stewart and Tubman were easily drawn in to what became a notorious swindle. The men, named Stevenson and Thomas, had a "contraband" friend named Harris from South Carolina who had allegedly hidden a trunk filled with gold since the close of the war, and remarkably, Stevenson only wanted $2,000 in cash for the $5,000 worth of gold. Tubman had heard of similar stories while stationed in the Department of the South, plus Harris claimed to know Tubman's nephew in the Freedmen's Bureau, Alfred Bowley, so while the story seemed far-fetched to some, Tubman believed it. Tubman agreed to secure the funds from her local benefactors, but her go-to sources, like the Osbornes, were skeptical and refused to help. So Tubman turned to a fellow Central Presbyterian church member and well-known local real estate investor Anthony Shimer, who agreed to float her the $2,000 cash.

Stevenson told Shimer and Tubman that Harris was too frightened to deal directly with white men, so he convinced Tubman to go alone with Harris to the rendezvous point with the cash in hand. Tubman testified that Harris seemed "scared and troubled" as he walked with her to the trunk, which was partially submerged in the ground. Harris demanded the money, but Tubman balked, asking to see the gold first. Harris then claimed that he needed a key to the trunk and scurried off into the woods to retrieve it. But when he didn't return and Tubman noticed that the trunk didn't even have a keyhole, she became anxious that she had been swindled; her worst fears were realized when she woke up sometime later bound and gagged, sporting a bump on her head, and missing the $2,000 cash.[31]

Thankfully Tubman's upstanding reputation in the community and Shimer's well-known propensity for risk taking garnered sympathy for her and deflected any suspicions that she had tried to trick Shimer. Her friend Emily Howland offered her care and shelter so that Tubman could recover from her injuries, which must have been emotional as well as physical. For so long Tubman had trusted her instincts and her faith, a formula that had kept her safe from harm for decades, but this time her personal compass steered her toward disaster and humiliation and was driven by a sense of desperation borne out of financial need. Freedom had come, but the fruits of her labor were not yet sufficient to feed and clothe her family and sustain her community.

Tubman recuperated at Howland's home in nearby Sherwood, New York, where undoubtedly they discussed Howland's work with the freedmen, which included purchasing land in the town of Heathsville, Virginia, and selling it to ex-slaves. Howland also set up a freedmen's school in the community that boasted an average daily attendance of thirty students, including a few poor whites who overcame local prejudice by sitting next to black children in the classroom. Howland's efforts were funded by family wealth, which gave her the independence to distribute the land parcels and run the school as she desired. Although she ceased orchestrating the Reconstruction plans directly and returned to upstate New York in the 1870s, she remained committed to the Heathsville community and supported it financially. Reflecting on the importance of black land ownership in the South, Howland wrote, "Since coming here and learning the frauds and extortions practiced on the people I see it has been a great benefit to them for land to be owned in their midst held for them to buy at fair price and sure title." She hoped that her formula would be replicated in other communities and believed it would "be a great check of the wicked wills of the old slaveocracy, who let no whit of a chance escape to oppress [the freedmen]."[32]

Tubman and Howland continued to sustain the freedmen's aid movement even as they engaged in other social reform movements like temperance and woman's suffrage. While not much is known about Tubman's commitment to the temperance movement, Eliza E. Peterson, who headed the "colored division" of the Women's Christian Temperance Union (WCTU) in Texas, was at her bedside when she died, which indicates she maintained friendships with temperance reformers late in life.[33] Furthermore, many of Tubman's colleagues in upstate New York, like Howland, openly and actively supported temperance in their local communities. In May of 1873, Howland issued a petition to the Board of Excise signed by "222 voters and 465 non-voters, asking you to grant no licenses for the sale of intoxicating liquors in this town." The petition cited the deleterious effects that alcohol waged on women and families, claiming that one woman "returned to her home from a day's work and found her husband in a raving state. He thrust her outdoors, knocked her down and kicked her, so that she was not able to work for a fortnight. He is a peaceable man when he is sober, she remarked."[34]

Petitioning and lobbying male politicians was by now familiar political terrain for female reformers, and the WCTU used these tools to great effect. Frances Willard, president of the WCTU from 1879 until her death nineteen years later, dubbed the WCTU's approach as the "New Politics," which merged petitioning with door-to-door canvassing and mailing campaigns to influence temperance-minded voters. Willard asked her fellow WCTU members to "thoroughly canvass the community and secure the largest possible number of pledges to support these [prohibitionist] candidates. Accompany the work by the circulation of temperance literature and holding prayer meetings." Willard couched her activism in service to God, home, and family, cognizant of the potential for admonition from male critics. She argued that "no person of intelligence will deny that it is womanly work to strive thus for the protection of the home."[35]

Early suffragists often embraced a similar political ideology, claiming that women needed the vote to protect home and family, but Tubman may have relied on a more practical philosophy when she argued in favor of woman's suffrage. She cited her fellow Civil War nurses and their heroism as justification for the vote, telling one group of suffragists that these women "were on the scene to administer to the injured, to bind up their wounds and tend them through weary months of suffering in the army hospitals. If those deeds do not place woman as man's equal, what do?" Undoubtedly speaking from experience, she noted that the "brave and fearless" nurses who "moved in battle when bullets mowed down men" and who "sacrificed all for their country" deserved the right to vote. When a friend asked her late in life if she thought women should have voting rights, she famously replied, "I suffered enough to believe it."[36]

Perhaps Tubman recognized how black men, particularly black soldiers, used their service in the Civil War as a bridge to gaining formal political rights. President Lincoln himself planted the seed of this argument in April of 1865 when he said that he "would myself prefer that it [the ballot] were conferred on the very intelligent, and on those who serve our cause as soldiers."[37] Two years later, when future President Rutherford B. Hayes was campaigning for governor of Ohio, he openly supported black male suffrage, saying at one campaign rally, "Our government . . . is not the government of any class, or sect, or nationality, or race, it is the government of the freeman; and when colored men were made citizens, soldiers, and freemen by our consent and votes, we were stopped from denying them the right of suffrage." Black soldiers themselves joined the chorus of voices advocating for their suffrage rights, and one group of ex-soldiers lobbied as early as 1865 that since they "had the privilege of fighting for our country," they also wanted "the privilege of voting." One black soldier from Tubman's native state of Maryland argued that when the "three or four thousand brave colored soldiers, who have endured privation and suffering to crush the wicked rebellion, return to their homes in Maryland," they should be "entitled to equal rights and privileges."[38] The connection between "ballots and bullets" resonated with Congress and provided justification for the passage of the Fifteenth Amendment in 1869 and its ratification in 1870.[39]

Ten days after the Fifteenth Amendment was ratified, Wendell Phillips and the other leaders of the American Anti-Slavery Society agreed to dissolve the organization, satisfied that their primary goals had been achieved. Frederick Douglass assured the society's members that the "spirit" of the organization would live on "through new instrumentalities" and would pursue justice for "suffering humanity everywhere." Douglass cited women and Indians as part of that "suffering humanity," and the "new instrumentalities" that he mentioned likely referred to the many woman's suffrage organizations that emerged in the wake of the passage of the Fifteenth Amendment. The historic and causal connection between antislavery and woman's rights activism remained in spirit and was embodied by many of the movements' major players, like Susan B. Anthony and Henry Blackwell, but the structure of these alliances within the suffrage movement changed dramatically.[40]

The battle over the Fifteenth Amendment split the suffrage movement into two main factions, the National Woman's Suffrage Association (NWSA), led by Susan B. Anthony and Elizabeth Cady Stanton, and the American Woman's Suffrage Association (AWSA), whose founders included Lucy Stone and Henry Blackwell. The NWSA withdrew its support from the Fifteenth Amendment because it only enfranchised black men, and Anthony and Stanton regrettably joined forces with vitriolic racists such as Democrat George Francis Train to campaign against black suffrage in places like Kansas. Stanton even argued, "All wise women should oppose the Fifteenth Amendment," in part because she believed that "black men on the stump and in their conventions repudiate women." Stanton's blanket assessment did not incorporate several outspoken black men who supported woman's suffrage, like Louis Willis Menard, a black Congressman from Louisiana, who claimed, "They [blacks] had but one voice in the South, and that was to know *no distinctions of color or sex*. Unless they concentrated their power, they would never attain to any political power."[41] Instead Stanton focused on men like Frederick Douglass, who believed that it was "the Negro's hour." Douglass, while never questioning the efficacy of universal suffrage, cited intransigent racist violence as the primary motivating factor to give black men the right to vote before women: "When women, because they are women, are hunted down through the cities of New York and New Orleans; when they are dragged from their houses and hung upon lampposts; when their children are torn from their arms and their brains dashed out upon the pavement . . . then they will have an urgency to obtain the ballot equal to our own."[42]

Tubman, like many black women, maintained friendships in both suffrage camps, but she openly supported the NWSA, once referring to it as "Miss Anthony's organization." And while many African Americans preferred the AWSA, Tubman stuck with the NWSA, even in the face of Stanton and Anthony's racism, likely because she cherished her relationships with women like Emily Howland and Eliza Wright Osborne, who hosted Anthony in their homes and whose commitments to each other had already survived decades of political turmoil. Biographer Kate Larson also posits that for Tubman, who "counseled John Brown, and commanded raids and advised generals during the Civil War, the thought that men should vote 'for' her may have been too much."[43] Thus perhaps Tubman questioned the logic of the AWSA, an organization spawned from its support for black male suffrage, and instead chose to affiliate with women whom she had trusted since her days on the Underground Railroad.

Tubman's suffrage activism peaked in the late 1880s, 1890s, and early 1900s, even as her age and physical health posed more challenges to traveling long distances to meetings and events. In addition, her tenuous financial situation continued to impinge upon her mobility, but several efforts to secure a government pension finally met success in the 1880s and 1890s, which likely freed up time and money for her to participate in suffrage activities. Beginning in 1868, when William Seward initiated the process, and not ending until 1899, when she received recognition and payment as a Union nurse, Tubman and several friends and political allies made multiple attempts to seek financial justice for her wartime service. Early in the process General Rufus Saxton wrote a letter that chronicled the many roles she filled in the Department of the South: "She was employed in the hospitals and as a spy. She made many a raid inside the enemy's lines, displaying remarkable courage, zeal, and fidelity. She was employed by General Hunter, and I think by Generals Stevens and Sherman, and is as deserving of a pension from the Government for her services as any other of its faithful servants."[44]

But despite Seward's support and Saxton's testimony, along with a bill introduced by New York Congressman McDougall that advocated for her relief, Tubman would not receive any pay from the government until after her husband, Nelson Davis, died in 1888. Following the Dependent Pension Act of 1890, Tubman was now eligible, as the "dependent" of Davis, to seek a widow's pension, which she eventually received five years after first requesting it. The $8 per month payment did not match the value she or her husband had rendered the government, but it did help ensure some financial stability and would later be augmented by monies she earned outright for her wartime service as a nurse.[45]

New York Congressman Sereno E. Payne felt that Tubman deserved more than a widow's pension and introduced a bill in 1897 requesting that Congress grant "a pension to Harriet Tubman Davis, late a nurse in the United States Army, at the rate of $25 a month." He also advocated that Tubman receive official recognition of her wartime service as a scout and a spy, and his claims were supported by a petition from Auburn residents. After two years of negotiation, Payne's bill met partial success, and Tubman was awarded a new pension of $20 a month, which included the $8 a month she received as Davis's widow and $12 a month for her service as a nurse. Members of Congress balked at offering a woman such a large pension and rejected any recognition of her service as a scout and spy, so Payne lobbied her claim as a nurse, a more gender-appropriate and ultimately successful argument. Thus Tubman's significant work for General Saxton and Colonel Montgomery as a scout and spy was never recognized by the U.S. government, but she undoubtedly welcomed the larger and more predictable income that came with the new pension.[46]

Tubman received her first pension payments in 1895, which might help explain her re-entry on to the public stage a year later at two important women's conventions. The National Association of Colored Women (NACW) asked Tubman to speak at its first meeting in July 1896, and Tubman accepted the invitation and travelled to Washington, D.C., for the event. According to historian Bettye Collier-Thomas, the NACW was a "manifestation of Christian women's belief that it was their responsibility to speak for and uplift less fortunate women," and one woman noted that to be a "true 'race' woman was one who was 'deeply interested in every good work designed to benefit her race.'" The NACW's motto, "Lifting as We Climb," reflected the group's belief in racial progress facilitated by Christian benevolence, ideals that Tubman had embraced her entire life, so it was particularly fitting that she helped open their inaugural meeting.[47] The convention's program featured a tribute to Tubman along with a picture of her holding a shotgun. The tribute had been originally published in a black women's newspaper, *The Woman's Era*, and it called upon all black women to band together "in the benign presence of this great leader." The convention lauded Tubman's "actions that caused strong men to quail," and asked its members to "uncover from partial oblivion and unconscious indifference the great characters within our ranks," calling Tubman a "Black Joan of Arc." They rallied around "this noble mother of Israel!" and used Tubman as an icon of liberation.[48]

The NACW merged two national black women's organizations that had formed in part because of the racism embedded in the white woman's suffrage movement. The feuding between the NWSA and the AWSA persisted for decades, but in 1891 the two groups finally bridged their differences, in part because they both agreed to assuage southern white women's concerns about black female suffrage. The newly formed National American Woman Suffrage Association (NAWSA) adopted the AWSA's state-by-state strategy, which focused on passing state suffrage laws rather than advocating for a federal amendment that enfranchised all women. Laden with "negrophobia" proffered by women like Louisiana suffragist Kate Gordon, "The racist sentiments that underlay this 'states' rights' approach were never difficult to discern as over and over again white southern suffragists made the case that white women's votes should be viewed as a 'means to the end of securing white supremacy.'" The NACW, in contrast, continued to support a federal woman's suffrage amendment, making it one of the only women's groups to reject the state-by-state strategy at the turn of the twentieth century.[49]

The same year that Tubman attended the inaugural NACW meeting, she also enjoyed top billing with Susan B. Anthony at the New York State's Woman's Suffrage Association convention in Rochester, New York. The two women clasped hands as they walked through the crowd, and Tubman took the stage after being introduced as the "great Black liberator." Tubman made a speech on behalf of woman's suffrage, but she reminded the audience of her feats on the Underground Railroad, voicing the now oft-quoted words that would secure her mythical reputation as a hero of that organization: "I was the conductor on the Underground Railroad for eight years, and I can say what most conductors can't say—I never ran my train off the track and I never lost a passenger."[50] Even if some of the leaders of the white suffrage organizations had lost sight of the movement's origins in the antislavery movement, Tubman's presence and speech served as a powerful reminder of that crucial connection, one that Tubman would always embrace.

Perhaps these white suffragists invited Tubman to their meetings and honored her in public forums in part to deflect charges of racism within their organizations. Undoubtedly Tubman witnessed the racism embedded in these groups, so that when she remarked that "she saw nothing venomous" in a group of white women whom she met in the late 1890s, one can imagine that maybe other women had not been so kind. But it is just as likely that Tubman maintained genuine friendships with former abolitionists like Ednah Dow Cheney and William Lloyd Garrison, Jr., and she trusted and relied upon their persistent support of her causes. The affection was mutual, as expressed by Anthony, who wrote after her final meeting with Tubman that she, Eliza Wright Osborne, Emily Howland, and other members of the "old guard" of the movement enjoyed "a real love feast of the few that are left," remarking that "this most wonderful woman—*Harriet Tubman*—is still alive."[51]

Even with the added pension income and continued support from women like Eliza Osborne, Tubman remained financially unstable, as indicated by her need to sell a cow in order to pay for a train ticket to Boston in 1897 for a series of receptions held in her honor. The white suffrage newspaper, the *Woman's Journal*, announced the Boston-area receptions, which included stops at Garrison's offices and a speech at the Old South Meetinghouse.[52] She met with her longtime friend Franklin Sanborn, who had published a biography of their comrade John Brown after the war, and she also visited Wilbur H. Siebert, a history professor who was then writing his master narrative, *The Underground Railroad from Slavery to Freedom*, which was first published in 1898. Siebert interviewed Tubman and, like many of her biographers, identified her spirituality as a motivating force in her abolitionism: "she saw in the oppression of her race the sufferings of the enslaved Israelites, and was not slow to demand that the pharaoh of the South should let her people go." Furthermore, he reiterated how often she used God as her compass on the Underground Railroad, and noted that Quaker Thomas Garrett remembered Tubman as someone "who had more confidence in God, as spoken to her soul," than "any person, of any color."[53]

Tubman's faith continued to inspire her activism as the nineteenth century drew to a close, and she invested a great deal of time and money in Auburn's AME Zion Church. Although she had initially attended the antislavery (predominantly white) Central Presbyterian Church, where she and Nelson Davis were married, Tubman began attending the AME Zion Church at some point in the 1870s, after Davis was elected to serve as a trustee. The Reverend James E. Mason recalled that when he first met Tubman in the late 1870s, she asked him if he had been saved. When he replied, "Yes," she responded, "Glory to God," and gave "testimony to God's goodness and long-suffering." Mason noted that she "possessed such endurance, vitality and magnetism," that others joined her as she shouted out in praise and thanksgiving. But Tubman did more than evangelize; she collected clothes and supplies for black Auburn's old and infirm residents, and in 1891, when the church moved locations, Tubman pledged $500 to support the new building's construction (though she likely did not have $500 and intended to raise the money).[54]

In addition to fulfilling her own religious commitments, Tubman might have pledged funds for the church with the hope that the church would, in turn, support her efforts to build a nursing home in Auburn. Tubman already maintained an informal home for the elderly and indigent at her own house on South Street, offering shelter and food to a revolving door of residents who sought comfort from "Aunt Harriet," knowing that she rarely, if ever, turned anyone away. One observer who visited Tubman's home in 1886 remarked that it was "an asylum for the poor people of her own color. Sometimes she has three or four invalids at a time for whom she is caring." Another visitor made similar observations a decade later, noting that Tubman "devotes herself to the succor of colored men and women more aged and wretched than herself, and she cares for helpless children who are allied to her race. Her house is a hospital for the infirm and sick." Tubman and her brother William H. Stewart and her husband, Nelson, raised livestock and grew fruits and vegetables on the surrounding property to feed their flock; they even created a garbage disposal service, collecting the refuse thrown out by Auburn's residents and feeding it to their hogs and chickens.[55]

As Tubman herself increased in age and feebleness, she recognized the need for more space and an institutional presence to sustain her mission: to create a low or no-cost nursing and housing facility she wanted to call the "John Brown Hall." She first purchased an adjacent lot and the attendant buildings to expand the operation, seeking help from the AME Zion Bishop in Syracuse to raise $350 from local contributors, while mortgaging the remaining $1,000 to pay for the property.[56] While Tubman must have been pleased to secure the twenty-five-acre property, the debt it carried only increased her financial burden, which forced her to rent out the buildings and land until she could raise enough money to establish the nursing facility. In the mean time she continued to house and feed Auburn's needy, both young and old. By the turn of the century, when Tubman was in her early 80s, Emma Telford wrote that Harriet cared for "the aged ... the babe deserted, the demented, the epileptic, the blind, the paralyzed, [and] the consumptive." Similarly, her biographer Sarah Bradford remembered that at one point Tubman was "providing for five sick and injured ones," along with a blind woman who soon gave birth to a child who also lived in the house.[57]

Tubman believed that she could sell another edition of Bradford's biography to raise the money she needed to open John Brown Hall. Bradford had already reissued the original 1869 version of *Scenes in the Life of Harriet Tubman* in 1886 with a new title, *Harriet, The Moses of Her People*. In the preface of the 1886 edition Bradford wrote, "She needs help again not for herself, but for certain helpless ones of her people. Her own sands are nearly run, but she hopes, 'ere she goes home, to see this work, a hospital, well under way. Her last breath and her last efforts will be spent in the cause of those for whom she has already risked so much."[58] Undoubtedly the same motivations and sentiments drove the publication of the 1901 edition, which Tubman's friends like Edna Dow Cheney and Franklin Sanborn supported. Tubman dictated a letter to one of her benefactors, remembering fondly that "Miss Cheney has done very well by me and I do not wish to ask for money [but] if through her influence I can get the friends to help me I shall be ever thankful. My home is incorporated [sic] for an asylum for aged colored people that will hold the mortgage and I won't be trouble[d] now." The new edition added twenty-five pages of additional material, which perhaps explains its greater (and some said substantial) cost of $1; Bradford kept all of the profits, though took no royalties herself, and paid Tubman's bills as necessary because she said Harriet "was surrounded by a set of beggars who I fear *fleece* her of everything sent her."[59]

Unfortunately the sales of the new edition were not sufficient to sustain the mortgage, let alone remodel and open the buildings for residents, and Tubman finally accepted the reality that she could not retain financial responsibility for the facility. She first turned to the NACW and offered to donate the property to the group if they could then assume its debt, but the NACW declined ownership because of the size of the mortgage. She then began a long process of negotiation with the AME Zion Church and its male leadership, which eventually resulted in her signing over the deed to the property in 1903. The church began raising funds for what was now called the "Harriet Tubman Home for Aged and Infirm Negroes" and for an industrial training school for girls, the latter of which was never part of Tubman's original vision. Although no evidence exists to suggest that she openly opposed such a school, she did support "higher education" for African Americans and never mentioned industrial education as part of that philosophy, perhaps implying that she questioned the church's efforts to raise money in the white community for "domestic science" education.[60]

We do know she butted heads with the church's leadership over their administration of the Harriet Tubman Home, which finally opened in 1908 after years of financial and bureaucratic delays. She initially "broke off participation in its management" because she wanted the home to be free of charge for all residents. She complained, "When I give the home over to Zion Church what suppose they done? Why, they make a rule that nobody should come in without they have a hundred dollars. Now I wanted to make a rule that nobody would come in unless they didn't have no money at all." The church won that argument and charged a $150 entrance fee against Tubman's wishes. No one knows how or why, but by the time the home opened, Tubman had reconciled with the church board and retained a seat on the home's board of directors, serving as its only female member. A "board of lady managers" began orchestrating the home's day-to-day operations, however, and these women were credited with ensuring the facility's financial viability. The local Auburn paper reported, "The friends of Aunt Harriet had lost all hope of ever seeing the home open. . . . Owing to the stringency of money matters, the work was delayed until a few weeks ago, when the board of lady managers took hold of the work with the result that the home was so auspiciously opened yesterday."[61]

Church, state, and local officials, along with members of the Empire State Federation of Women's Clubs celebrated the Harriet Tubman Home's grand opening with a parade and a day full of festivities. Local black dignitaries marched at the head of the parade, including black veterans like "Comrade Perry Williams in white coat and blue trousers," who was "proudly bearing the national flag," and "the Ithaca colored band," which "hit off some lively quicksteps." The Auburn paper noted that "'Aunt Harriet' and her brother, William Henry Stewart," rode at the head of a "long string of carriages containing prominent colored people of the city," and Tubman had "the stars and stripes wound about her shoulders." The audience enjoyed a short speech from the home's namesake, then nearing 90 years old. Tubman told the crowd that she "did not take up this work for my own benefit . . . but for those of my race who need help. The work is now well started and I know God will raise up others to take care of the future." Expressing her everlasting faith in God and trusting in the community's benevolence, she asked the white and black audience members for a "united effort, for 'united we stand: divided we fall.'"[62]

Tubman herself could not stand much longer and was soon confined to a wheelchair around 1910. Quite simply, it is remarkable that she wasn't wheelchair bound earlier given the physical challenges she faced throughout her life, beginning with the persistent headaches and seizures caused by the blow to her head as a child, punctuated by bouts of disease during the Civil War, and sustained by further physical abuse at the hands of train conductors and swindlers. She did find some relief from her chronic and painful headaches after undergoing brain surgery sometime in the late 1890s at Massachusetts General Hospital. During an unrelated trip to Boston, she made an impromptu visit to the hospital and asked a doctor, "Sir, do you think you could cut my head open?" She told the doctor that her head was causing her "a powerful sight of trouble lately, with achin' and buzzin'," so bad that she "couldn't get no sleep at night." The doctor agreed to perform the surgery and tried to give her anesthetic to ease the pain, but Harriet refused, choosing instead to clench a bullet in her teeth, like her fellow soldiers had done during the war. She recalled later that she "just lay down like a lamb before the slaughter, and he sawed open my skull, and raised it up." The procedure worked, and Tubman claimed that after the surgery her head felt "more comfortable" and even tried to walk herself home from the hospital. Her legs "kind of g[a]ve out under me," however, and an ambulance carried her to a friend's residence where she recuperated.[63]

Tubman suffered fewer headaches as a result of the surgery, but her physical mobility declined significantly in these final years, so much so that she had lost the use of her legs in 1910 and was forced to move into the Harriet Tubman Home in 1911. Newspapers from New York to Minnesota reported Tubman's move, and these stories highlighted her extreme poverty and advanced age, one claiming that she was between 95 and 100 years old. One headline read, "Negro 'Moses' a Pauper," while another announced, "Noted Negress Broke," furthering the painful irony of such a famous woman being defined as an "inmate" of a home for aged and "penniless negroes." Most of the stories clarified that Tubman's poverty was rooted in her benevolence, however. The New York *Sun* reported that she "gave her all to establish the home for aged colored men and women of which she is now an inmate," while *The Forest Republican* (Tionesta, Pennsylvania) noted that she "devoted all of her savings to the establishment of this institution."[64] Word of her financial need spread throughout the country, and colored women's clubs, like the Empire State Federation of Women's clubs, answered the call for help. Women at the Fleet Street AME Zion Church in Brooklyn donated $5 toward Tubman's care at the home, and the church claimed that "the women's clubs have decided to assist Mrs. Tubman, who is in need in her declining years."[65]

Black women's club members like Mary Talbert, founding member and second President of the Empire State Federation of Women's clubs, and AME Zion Church members provided much needed funds and nursing care for Tubman until she died from pneumonia on March 10, 1913. Tubman's last words to Talbert articulated these lasting alliances with the church and women's organizations, as she instructed Talbert to "tell the women to stand together, for God will never forsaken [sic] us." Tubman's longtime friends like Eliza Wright Osborne and Janet Seward (William H. Seward's daughter-in-law) also stuck by her side until the very end, another example of the ways Tubman bridged racial differences and maintained her friendships with the descendants of the old abolitionist community that had first welcomed her in Auburn six decades earlier.[66]

It was that very community that encircled her casket before it was lowered into the ground at Auburn's Fort Hill cemetery on March 13th. Hundreds of mourners gathered to commemorate "Aunt Harriet's" passing, and services were conducted at both the Harriet Tubman Home and the Thompson Memorial AME Zion Church. A conductor till the very end, the local paper noted that the "arrangements for the funeral were practically made by 'Aunt Harriet' some time ago, and her wishes will be carried out."[67] If, indeed, her mourners followed her instructions, then the three significant objects buried with her were not an accident; her hands grasped a crucifix, a medal given to her by Queen Victoria lay on her body, and her casket was wrapped in an American flag. Perhaps Tubman wanted to be remembered in death with symbols that identified the cause she fought for in life: freedom, both for her race and her sex. The crucifix signified her everlasting faith and the spirit that motivated her activism; the royal medal, sporting an image of the Queen, had been given to her in recognition of her accomplishments on the Underground Railroad by the only female world leader at the time; and the flag, for which she fought as a Union scout and spy during the Civil War, represented freedom, not only for Tubman but for the millions of slaves emancipated by the Union victory. The pall bearers closed the casket with these symbolic reminders inside and laid her in the ground, placing her next to her brother's grave, another indication of Tubman's lasting inspiration, her family.[68]

Newspapers across the country published eulogies of Tubman in the coming months and captured these lifelong commitments in their columns. The *Washington Herald* announced, "Colored Moses of Her People Dies in Home She Founded," and claimed that "she was regarded by many as one of the most remarkable women of this continent." The *New York Tribune* enhanced her celebrity by noting that famous men like Ralph Waldo Emerson and John Brown "esteemed her highly for her unusual attainments and personality." The paper reported that "one of her most picturesque assets" was her "tremendous physical strength," which "served her well on several occasions when she personally rescued slaves from their masters and whisked them away North to safety." News of her death travelled west as well, with eulogies appearing in Iowa, Utah, Texas, California, and Washington. The *Seattle Republican* included her in a list of "notable persons," writing that Tubman was "born a slave, but escaped and worked in harmony with the great anti-slave leaders in the freedom of her people." Similarly, her hometown paper proudly chronicled a "Sketch of Her Career," noting that although she was "born lowly, she lived a life of exalted self-sacrifice . . . [her death] closes a career that has taken its place in American history."[69]

Certainly Tubman's life has "taken its place" in our history, but that place has shifted dramatically over the last century. Tubman's story has been rescued from relative obscurity—when in the 1940s famous suffragist Carrie Chapman Catt denied knowing that Tubman (or any black women for that matter) was ever involved in woman's suffrage activism—to fantastic celebrity, when President Barack Obama deemed her "an American hero" and signed a proclamation that created the "Harriet Tubman Underground Railroad National Monument" in Maryland in 2013.[70] These vast differences in Tubman's notoriety illustrate the power of historical memory in shaping the public's perceptions of the American past. The public memory of Tubman stretches from the eulogies of the early twentieth century that dubbed her the "Colored Moses" to the internet blogs of the twenty-first century that call her "the baddest sistah ever on the planet," and these variegated memories can teach us as much about our own history as hers.

NOTES

1. Faith Ringgold, *Aunt Harriet's Underground Railroad in the Sky* (New York: Dragonfly Books, 1995), back cover.
2. Kate Clifford Larson, *Bound for the Promised Land: Harriet Tubman, Portrait of an American Hero* (New York: Ballantine, 2004), 232.
3. For example, the black electorate in Louisiana declined from 130,000 men to 1,000 by the end of the nineteenth century. See Eric Foner, *Forever Free: The Story of Emancipation and Reconstruction* (New York: Vintage, 2005), 129, 207; Judith Giesberg, *Army at Home: Women and the Civil War on the Northern Home Front* (Chapel Hill: The University of North Carolina Press, 2009), 92–118.
4. For example, Truth had at least two conflicts with streetcar conductors in the 1860s. See Nell Irvin Painter, *Sojourner Truth: A Life, A Symbol* (New York: Norton, 1996), 210–211; for Wells-Barnett see Patricia A. Schechter, *Ida B. Wells-Barnett and American Reform, 1880–1930* (Chapel Hill: The University of North Carolina Press, 2001), 43, 71.
5. Carol Faulkner, *Women's Radical Reconstruction: The Freedmen's Aid Movement* (Philadelphia: University of Pennsylvania Press, 2004), 67. For more on the concepts of oppositional politics or infrapolitics see Giesberg, *Army at Home*, 96, and James Scott, *Domination and the Arts of Resistance: Hidden Transcripts* (New Haven: Yale University Press, 1990), 183. For "visionary pragmatism" see Schechter, *Ida B. Wells-Barnett*, 3, 9.
6. Elsa Barkley-Brown, "To Catch the Vision of Freedom: Reconstructing Southern Black Women's Political History, 1865–1880," in Ann Gordon and Bettye Collier-Thomas, eds., *African American Women and the Vote, 1837–1965* (Amherst: University of Massachusetts Press, 1997), 86.

7. Deborah Gray White, *Too Heavy a Load: Black Women in Defense of Themselves, 1894–1944* (New York: Norton, 1999), 54.

8. Seward qtd. in Sarah Bradford, *Scenes in the Life of Harriet Tubman* (Auburn, NY: W.J. Moses, 1869), 112.

9. Larson, *Bound for the Promised Land*, 233–234.

10. Eric Foner, *Reconstruction: America's Unfinished Revolution, 1863–1877* (New York: Harper and Row, 1988), 143–144.

11. Mary Farmer Kaiser, *Freedwomen and the Freedmen's Bureau: Race, Gender, and Public Policy in the Age of Emancipation* (New York: Fordham University Press, 2010), 1, 20.

12. Paul Cimbala, *Under the Guardianship of the Bureau: The Freedmen's Bureau and the Reconstruction of Georgia, 1865–1870* (Athens: University of Georgia Press, 1997), 3.

13. Thaddeus Stevens qtd. in Foner, *Reconstruction*, 235–236.

14. Foner, *Reconstruction*, 158–160.

15. Larson, *Bound for the Promised Land*, 240–241, 249–250.

16. For evidence of Nelson Davis, a.k.a. Nelson Charles's Civil War service, see "An Act Granting an Increase of Pension to Harriet Tubman Davis," Records of the House of Representatives, H.R. 4982, 5 December 1898, http://www.archives.gov/legislative/resources/education/tubman/. Physical descriptions of Davis are quoted from Larson, *Bound for the Promised Land*, 253.

17. The 8th U.S. Colored Infantry's battle history can be found at http://www.nps.gov/rich/learn/historyculture/8th-usct.htm

18. Larson, *Bound for the Promised Land*, 252. See also the *Auburn Morning News*, 19 March 1869.

19. Larson, *Bound for the Promised Land*, 239–241.

20. Charles Nordhoff, *The Cotton States in the Spring and Summer of 1875,* and Clara Barton, *Reconstruction Report*, both qtd. in W.E.B. Du Bois, *Black Reconstruction in America* (New York: Atheneum, 1992, 1935), 672–673.

21. Saxton and Freedmen's Bureau quotes from *Report of the Joint Committee on Reconstruction*, H.R. Rep. No. 30–39 (1866), cited in Paul Finkelman, "The Long Road to Dignity: The Wrong of Segregation and What the Civil Rights Act of 1964 Had to Change," *Louisiana Law Review* 74 (2014): 1045–1046, 1048, 1050.

22. For full text of the amendments see http://www.senate.gov/civics/constitution_item/constitution.htm#amdt_14_(1868).

23. Ulysses S. Grant qtd. in Du Bois, *Black Reconstruction*, 594. For full text of Grant's message see http://www.nps.gov/ulsg/historyculture/grant-and-the-15th-amendment.htm.

24. Eric Foner, "Rooted in Reconstruction," *The Nation* 287, No. 18 (November 2008): 30; Stephen Middleton, ed., *Black Congressmen during Reconstruction: A Documentary Sourcebook* (Westport, CT: Greenwood Press, 2002), xv, xvii; and Xi Wang, *The Trial of Democracy: Black Suffrage and Northern Republicans, 1860–1910* (Athens: University of Georgia Press, 1997), 40.

25. Giesberg, *Army at Home*, 113, 108–109, 93.

26. Larson, *Bound for the Promised Land*, 232–233; Painter, *Sojourner Truth*, 210–211.

27. LeAnna Keith, *The Colfax Massacre: The Untold Story of Black Power, White Terror, and the Death of Reconstruction* (New York: Oxford University Press, 2008), 112.

28. For the Hamburg Massacre, see Carole Emberton, *Beyond Redemption: Race, Violence, and the American South after the Civil War* (Chicago: University of Chicago Press, 2013), 195–198, and Stephen Budiansky, *The Bloody Shirt: Terror after Appomattox* (New York: Penguin, 2008), 219–254.

29. "The Would-be Massoniello of Georgia," *The Atlanta Daily Constitution*, 29 August 1875, ProQuest Historical Newspapers (author's emphasis).

30. Foner, *Forever Free*, 171.

31. Larson, *Bound for the Promised Land*, 255–259.

32. Faulkner, *Women's Radical Reconstruction*, 106–108.

33. Larson, *Bound for the Promised Land*, 288–289. For information on Eliza E. Peterson see Bruce A. Glasrud and Merline Pitre, eds., *Black Women in Texas History* (College Station: Texas A & M University Press, 2008), 111.

34. Mildred D. Myers, *Miss Emily: Emily Howland, Teacher of Freed Slaves, Suffragist, and Friend of Susan B. Anthony and Harriet Tubman* (Charlotte Harbor, FL: Tabby House, 1998), 135.

35. Willard qtd. in Rebecca Edwards, *Angels in the Machinery: Gender in American Party Politics from the Civil War to the Progressive Era* (New York: Oxford University Press, 1997), 45.

36. Larson, *Bound for the Promised Land*, 273; Jean Humez, *Harriet Tubman: The Life and the Life Stories* (Madison, WI: The University of Wisconsin Press, 2003), 256.

37. Lincoln qtd. in Faye E. Dudden, *Fighting Chance: The Struggle over Woman Suffrage and Black Suffrage during the Civil War and Reconstruction* (New York: Oxford University Press, 2012), 61.

38. Hayes qtd. in Wang, *The Trial of Democracy*, 143; Richard Reid, "USCT Veterans in Post-Civil War North Carolina," in John David Smith, ed., *Black Soldiers in Blue: African American Troops in the Civil War Era* (Chapel Hill: University of North Carolina Press, 2002), 404; and Sergeant Norman B. Sterrett, reprinted in the (Philadelphia) *Christian Recorder*, 26 August 1865, cited in Edwin S. Redkey, *A Grand Army of Black Men: Letters from African-American Soldiers in the Union Army, 1861-1865* (New York: Cambridge University Press, 1992), 227–228.

39. Richard M. Re and Christopher M. Re, "Voting and Vice: Criminal Disenfranchisement and the Reconstruction Amendments," *The Yale Law Journal* 121, No. 7 (May 2012): f.n. 455.

40. Philip S. Foner, *The Life and Writings of Frederick Douglass: Reconstruction and After* (New York: International Publishers, 1950), 45.

41. Dudden, *Fighting Chance,* 182–183.

42. Douglass qtd. in Philip S. Foner, ed., *Frederick Douglass on Women's Rights* (New York: Da Capo Press, 1992), 87.

43. Larson, *Bound for the Promised Land*, 272. For example, Anthony spoke with the Auburn Women's Political Equality Club in 1897 and stayed at Eliza Osborne's home. See Ann Gordon, ed., *The Selected Letters of Elizabeth Cady Stanton and Susan B. Anthony* (New Brunswick: Rutgers University Press, 2013), 132–133, f.n. 2.

44. Saxton qtd. in Sarah Bradford, *Harriet Tubman: The Moses of Her People* (New York: G.R. Lockwood & Son, 1886), 76.

45. Larson, *Bound for the Promised Land*, 276–277.

46. Larson, *Bound for the Promised Land*, 278–279.

47. Bettye Collier-Thomas, *Jesus, Jobs, and Justice: African American Women and Religion* (New York: Knopf, 2010), 121.

48. Larson, *Bound for the Promised Land*, 275; Humez, *Harriet Tubman*, 88–89.

49. Allison L. Sneider, *Suffragists in an Imperial Age: U.S. Expansion and the Woman Question, 1870-1929* (New York: Oxford University Press, 2008), 96–97, 125.

50. Tubman qtd. in Humez, *Harriet Tubman*, 101.

51. Earl Conrad, *Harriet Tubman* (Washington, D.C.: Associated Publishers, 1943), 215–216.

52. Larson, *Bound for the Promised Land*, 281; Humez, *Harriet Tubman*, 101.

53. Wilbur H. Siebert, *The Underground Railroad in Slavery and Freedom* (New York: The MacMillan Company, 1898), 185, 188. Siebert cited both Bradford's biography of Tubman and his own interview with her.

54. Humez, *Harriet Tubman*, 82; Larson, *Bound for the Promised Land*, 263, 279.

55. Humez, *Harriet Tubman*, 83–84.

56. Humez, *Harriet Tubman*, 83–85; Larson, *Bound for the Promised Land*, 279–280.

57. Larson, *Bound for the Promised Land*, 282, 276–277.

58. Bradford, *Harriet Tubman*, 5.

59. Larson, *Bound for the Promised Land*, 280, 283.

60. Larson, *Bound for the Promised Land*, 284–285; Humez disagrees somewhat from my and Larson's interpretation of the evidence and thinks Tubman might have supported the "professionalization" of domestic work to give it more social value. See Humez, *Harriet Tubman*, 94–95.

61. Larson, *Bound for the Promised Land*, 285; Humez, *Harriet Tubman*, 95.

62. Larson, *Bound for the Promised Land*, 285, 286–287; Humez, *Harriet Tubman*, 95–96. See also the *Auburn Daily Advertiser*, 24 June 1908, reprinted at http://harriettubman.com/dedication.html.

63. Larson, *Bound for the Promised Land*, 281–282.

64. *The (New York, NY) Sun*, 3 June 1911 and *The Forest Republican* (Tionesta, PA), 7 June 1911. See also *The Appeal* (St. Paul, MN), 10 June 1911 and the *Marion (Ohio) Daily Mirror*, 3 June 1911. All cited from "Historic American Newspapers," http://chroniclingamerica.loc.gov

65. *The Brooklyn Daily Eagle*, 16 February 1912, cited from http://newspapers.com/image/54536905; Larson, *Bound for the Promised Land*, 288.

66. Larson, *Bound for the Promised Land*, 288–289.

67. *Auburn Daily Advertiser*, 11 March 1913, reprinted at http://harriettubman.com/memoriam2.html

68. Larson, *Bound for the Promised Land*, 289.

69. *New-York Tribune*, 13 March 1913 and *The Seattle (WA) Republican*, 28 March 1913, both reprinted at http://chroniclingamerica.loc.gov; *Auburn Citizen*, 11 March 1913, reprinted at http://harriettubman.com/memoriam2.html

70. When Tubman's biographer Earl Conrad wrote to Catt in 1940 for information about Tubman, Catt replied, "To tell the truth, I had never heard of Harriet Tubman when you first wrote me." Catt qtd. in Larson, *Bound for the Promised Land*, 293; Barack Obama, "Presidential Proclamation— Harriet Tubman Underground Railroad National Monument," 25 March 2013, reprinted at https://www.whitehouse.gov/the-press-office/2013/03/25/presidential-proclamation-harriet-tubman-underground-railroad-national-m

CHAPTER **5**

MYTH, MEMORY, AND HISTORY

On February 1, 2014, the Google "doodle" debuting black history month featured an image of Harriet Tubman. (See image at: http://www.google.com/doodles/celebrating-harriet-tubman). The doodle included a sketch of Tubman holding a lantern and wearing her characteristic head scarf. Some criticized the image, and it generated a lively discussion on the web, particularly after celebrity Nick Cannon tweeted, "#Really Google? . . . #racist much," because he took offense at Tubman sporting a "do-rag." One supporter of the doodle posted, "Nick, would we have been happier if Google just ignored the baddest Sistah ever on the planet?"[1] The doodle and the controversy that emerged in its wake both illustrate the mythical status attained by Tubman and the battle over historical memory that rages in the present day. The American public has embraced Tubman as a hero, as the "baddest Sistah ever," and yet, which vision of Tubman do they see? Does the mythical Tubman trump the historical one in American memory?

Historian Milton Sernett correctly observes that Tubman's "larger-than-life image has until very recently overpowered the historical evidence available about the real person."[2] Americans have embraced grandiose, simplified visions of Tubman and other famous historical actors, erasing the complexity, human frailty, and paradox that characterizes actual lived experience. Several scholars identify this process of historical amnesia when exploring the contrast between Thomas Jefferson's public image as a benevolent, "ideal master" and the more critical accounts journalists and historians have recently constructed. The mythical memory of Jefferson originated in the nineteenth century and even influenced his former slaves, leading one of them, Peter Fossett, to remember Jefferson as a "kind and indulgent" master "who we all loved." Similarly, the Jefferson that

America lauds today is a "Statesman and Visionary for the founding of the Nation" who believed that "commerce between master and slave is despotism," according to the words etched on the Thomas Jefferson Memorial in Washington, D.C. No matter that young boys at age 10 or 11 were whipped at Monticello's nail factory, a tactic explicitly endorsed by Jefferson to increase productivity at the operation. Thus it is not the slave master, the "Henry Ford of slavery," who is first remembered by the American public, but rather the "Visionary." Better to lift up Jefferson's words and ideals, than to reveal his flaws or lived reality.[3]

On the surface, Tubman's biography is easier to digest in part because her story is less paradoxical than Jefferson's; she repeatedly triumphed over tragedy and against incredible odds, but no one, as of yet, has found the Tubman equivalent of a Sally Hemings in the historical closet. Perhaps this apparent simplicity and untarnished image is why the Tubman myth carries so much weight in the American memory. Sernett recently argued that Tubman's story "taps into a quintessentially American myth: the notion that, with hard work and persistence, anyone can rise above the circumstances of their birth." But like Jefferson's life story, Tubman's history is more complex and varied then her myth has portrayed.[4]

Tubman is not a singular heroic figure standing above the crowd on the Underground Railroad. She did not, as many published figures suggest, return to the South dozens of times before the Civil War and rescue over 300 slaves single-handedly. Rather, she was an integral part of a network of activists, both black and white and male and female, and she succeeded not only because of her courage and individual determination but also because she resided on the border between slavery and freedom, a border that had been tested repeatedly and that contained black and white residents who were willing to challenge the institution of slavery. Furthermore, her work did not stop when the guns fired on Ft. Sumter; she continued the hard, slow work of emancipation during the Civil War, first serving as a nurse, helping members of her race to rebound physically and emotionally after years of enslavement, and then as a scout and spy, planning military strategy and opening the floodgates of freedom for hundreds of South Carolina slaves. Finally, her efforts to achieve justice and equality did not cease after the war, and she worked tirelessly for economic justice and woman's rights in the final decades before her death. Throughout her life she persistently challenged the physical and ideological boundaries that constrained her race and her sex, and her courage and activism serve as examples of righteous humanity in the present day. And yet, she died in 1913 as she also lived: in poverty, without the right to vote because of her sex, and unable to bridge the chasm between her mythical status and the reality of living in Jim Crow America as an African American woman.

While the Tubman myth and the academic history of her "flesh-and-blood person" both continue to inspire, one must not neglect the lessons that they both convey. Myths often reveal as much about the society in which they were created as they do about the persons they valorize.[5] This final chapter will examine how the Tubman myth was created, by whom, and in which time periods, and will then consider the recent uptick in attention by academics to her "flesh-and-blood" history, along with the simultaneous, meteoric rise of Tubman's status in pop culture. By following the twentieth- and twenty-first-century chronology of the Tubman myth, we open a window into the struggle over black civil rights, feminism, and the emerging histories of these movements and peoples, in addition to revealing the ongoing contest over Tubman's historical memory. Finally, we will explore the opportunities and dangers related to how technology, like Google and its cousin YouTube, has nurtured the explosion of knowledge about Tubman and her world.

***

As many scholars have noted, Tubman herself participated in the original construction of her myth. Providing interviews with journalists and writers like Franklin Sanborn and Sarah Bradford, Tubman overcame the pitfalls of illiteracy by sharing her story with sympathetic ears who published it for posterity. Sanborn also chronicled John Brown's life and, perhaps not coincidentally, published the first biographical sketch of Tubman in the Boston *Commonwealth* in July 1863 after learning about the Combahee River raid.[6] As a member of Brown's "Secret Six," Sanborn undoubtedly earned Tubman's trust, and his article cast Tubman as a heroine that should be remembered for all time: "The whole world now sit(s) as spectators, and the desperation or the magnanimity of a poor black woman has power to shape the nation that so long was deaf to her cries. We write of one of these heroines, of whom our slave annals are full,—a woman whose career is as extraordinary as the most famous of her sex can show."[7] Sanborn recounted Tubman's accomplishments on the Underground Railroad and referred to her as a "good angel" who shepherded the "frost—bitten, hungry, and naked" runaways from slavery to freedom in Canada. Sanborn, a radical abolitionist and a former ally of Brown's, clearly used Tubman's story to champion the strength and resilience of African Americans and to endorse the righteousness of emancipation.

Tubman's second biographer, Sarah Bradford, also possessed antislavery credentials, but her motivation to record Tubman's story was rooted less in radical politics and more in practical economics. As the introduction to *Scenes in the Life of Harriet Tubman* states, Bradford wrote the book in collaboration with Tubman "with the single object of furnishing some help to the subject of the memoir."[8] Bradford arranged for all the proceeds from the sale of her book to be donated to Tubman because Tubman had not been able to secure any back pay or financial compensation from the U.S. government in the four years since the war ended. Bradford recognized that this motivation and the remarkable nature of Tubman's story would invite critics who might question the narrative's authenticity. In anticipation of the book's detractors, Bradford wrote:

> There are those who will sneer . . . at this quixotic attempt to make a heroine of a black woman, and a slave; but it may possibly be that there are some natures, though concealed under fairer skins, who have not the capacity to comprehend such general and self-sacrificing devotion to the cause of others as that here delineated, and therefore they resort to scorn and ridicule, in order to throw discredit upon the whole story.[9]

To further bolster the claims Tubman made in her book, Bradford solicited letters and testimonials from abolitionists and army personnel involved with Tubman's exploits. She reprinted letters from the likes of Gerrit Smith, Henry K. Durrant (acting assistant surgeon for the U.S. army), and Brigadier General Rufus Saxton in the appendix of the book to substantiate its contents. So while Bradford's intended audience appears to have been a small abolitionist circle in the Northeast, made up of people who had already supported Tubman, her efforts to authenticate Tubman's story indicate that she recognized the book would have a wider appeal and might be read by the general public, people who were less inclined to trust an illiterate black woman's biography.

Bradford's book, and the reprint of it in 1886, did reach a larger audience, but not necessarily in the nineteenth century. It appears that the vast majority of children's and youth biographies written about Tubman in the mid- to late twentieth century often used Bradford's text as the single authority on Tubman's life, which reinforced the mythical status created by Tubman's retelling of her autobiography and her abolitionist publishers who desired its dissemination. The problem with accepting Bradford's text at face value is that the facts she reportedly conveys were rarely checked by subsequent biographers. For example, while Bradford's claim (via Thomas Garrett's testimony) that Tubman rescued between sixty and eighty people from the Eastern Shore of Maryland has stood the test of time and careful research, the assertion that she "never drew for herself but twenty days rations during the four years of her labors" during the Civil War does not hold up to historical scrutiny, as documents exist that reveal the army supplied Tubman with funds for her operations and likely paid her rations sporadically throughout her service. And although many children's biographers write with the stated goal of casting their subjects in a laudatory light, few of them questioned Bradford's historical position within antislavery circles or her inevitable bias in presenting Tubman as a "sagacious heroine."[10]

Subsequent biographers, particularly those writing for children, also did not challenge the inherent racism expressed in Bradford's book, especially the second edition, when Bradford changed key aspects of Tubman's biography and described Harriet and her peers in ways that fulfilled white stereotypes about African Americans. For example, Bradford described the young Harriet in starkly racialized terms, claiming that Tubman was

> darker than any of the others, and with a more decided *woolliness* in the hair; a pure unmitigated African. She was not so entirely in a state of nature as the rollers in the dust beneath her; but her only garment was a short woolen skirt, which was tied around her waist, and reached about to her knees. . . . Behold here, in the stupid little Negro girl, the future deliverer of hundreds of her people.[11]

Scantily dressed and "stupid," Bradford made the Harriet of 1886 less threatening than the Harriet of 1869. Sernett notes that "Bradford took literary license with Tubman's oral accounts and repackaged them to make them palatable for readers in post-Reconstruction America, a time when racism thrived and African-Americans suffered from stereotypical characterizations that offend readers of Bradford's *Moses* today." Thus, a change in political atmosphere and perhaps a desire to sell the text to a broader audience, elicited an interpretive shift between the two visions of Tubman. And yet both visions maintained Tubman's heroic status; in the second edition, by picturing Tubman as a stereotypical dumb, "merry, little dark[y]," Bradford made her accomplishments seem all the more remarkable given that the 1886 readers were repeatedly reminded of her membership in an "inferior race." As Bradford remarks, "certainly all should not be judged by the idle, miserable darkies who have swarmed about Washington and other cities since the War."[12]

The racial stereotypes that seeped into Bradford's second edition of *Moses* help explain why it would take another sixty years before a new biography of Tubman would be published. In fact, racism almost prevented the publication of the next complete biography of her in 1943, as Earl Conrad, a white journalist from Auburn, New York, sought out dozens of publishers for his piece and was rejected by "nearly all of the New York City publishers." In 1940 an editor at Simon and Schuster said, "It is an original biography all right, almost in fact, *a freak subject*," while Alfred A. Knopf wrote that they were "unable to see how we can obtain a sufficient sale to warrant making you a publication offer. The market for books on topics of this kind is limited to begin with, and furthermore, your book suffers somewhat from the inflation of the factual material beyond reasonable bounds." Conrad's interpretation of Tubman was clearly influenced by his own desire to paint Tubman in the most favorable light, and he unabashedly dubbed her the "greatest heroine of the age."[13] But potential publishers questioned his "factual material," not only because of his bias but also because they could not or did not want to believe that a black woman had accomplished so much against incredible odds.

Conrad searched for years in vain to find a place for his Tubman biography, and he finally met success with an African American publisher, Carter G. Woodson, founder of the *Journal of Negro History*, who at the time also owned Associated Publishers in Washington, D.C. The book debuted in the fall of 1943, and not surprisingly, black and Leftist newspapers reviewed it favorably, while it went unnoticed by most mainstream newspapers. Celebrated writer Langston Hughes recommended Conrad's biography to the readers of the *Chicago Defender*, saying that it would inspire young black Americans to resist oppression. "To read about Harriet Tubman, who broke her own shackles of slavery and risked her life many times to liberate others," wrote Hughes, "is to put to shame those who say they can do nothing because of color and Jim Crow." In the *People's Voice*, a black paper in New York, future Congressman Adam Clayton Powell said: "It is to be hoped that every one of us will have this volume in our home. It is further hoped that such a volume will be included in the school systems of our country as a required reading."[14]

Powell's dream that Tubman's biography would become "required reading" for school children would eventually come true, although it appears that most youth biographers gleaned their knowledge of Tubman from Bradford's books, not Conrad's. Perhaps authors turned to Bradford because unlike the hagiographic depiction of Tubman presented by Conrad, Bradford claimed she simply recorded the personal interviews she conducted with Tubman while she was alive. The eyewitness promise connoted more authority to Bradford, and perhaps her experience writing children's books supplied a tone that appealed to children's authors. Or maybe 1960s and 1970s authors chafed at Conrad's explicit Leftist and anti-racist politics, illustrated by a dedication that boldly indicted white racism in the publishing industry; on the frontispiece he referred to the book as, "The one that the white publishers would not issue."[15] Regardless, both Bradford and Conrad cast Tubman in a heroic mold, a model that would inform every children's biography of her published in the twentieth century.

The most popular and widely printed youth biography in the mid-twentieth century was Ann Petry's *Harriet Tubman: Conductor on the Underground Railroad*, first published in 1955. Petry, an African American originally from Massachusetts, said she wrote the book to address the paucity of accurate information about the history of slavery and African Americans in school textbooks.[16] For example, in the 1953 textbook *The United States: From Wilderness to World Power*, editor Ralph Volny Harlow claimed that "on the average plantation the slaves were not harshly treated. Many of the owners were kindly, humane men." If some textbook depictions of slavery were not as sugarcoated as Harlow's, they were almost always brief. In another text from the 1950s, *Story of American Democracy*, authors Mabel B. Casner and Ralph H Gabriel summed up their discussion of slavery in one short paragraph: "These laborers worked on the plantation fields in gangs. The planter fed, clothed, and cared for his slaves. He took care of the old people when they could no longer work. Slavery made life in the South very different from life in the North."[17] Fearing southern white protests and thus decreased sales, textbook publishers continued to placate their white customers by depicting slavery as a benign institution and slaves as objects that were controlled by white masters.

Petry's biography of Tubman certainly remedied some of the problems endemic to textbook interpretations of slavery, but it wasn't until the post–Civil Rights era that children's biographies and textbooks more accurately reflected the brutality of slavery and the injustice of sexism that Tubman and her peers experienced. More than half a dozen youth biographies of Tubman were published in the 1960s, and perhaps more importantly, she took her place among other female "greats" of American history, as a number of books that hailed the accomplishments of women like Harriet Beecher Stowe, Susan B. Anthony, and Eleanor Roosevelt also included Tubman. One book argued that Tubman was "the epitome of physical courage as well as moral dedication," and an illustrated history magazine featured Tubman in their 1966 issue.[18] The Tubman myth endured in all of these texts, and as the Black Power and feminist movements progressed, her strength and resilience fit nicely with politicized notions of racial and gendered pride.

These trends continued in the 1970s and 1980s, and juvenile literature was joined by TV miniseries and feature-length films that highlighted the black experience. In 1977 ABC aired the now iconic miniseries *Roots*, based on Alex Haley's novel that chronicled protagonist Kunta Kinte's capture in Africa and his life on a southern plantation. Running for eight consecutive nights, the miniseries was "a virtually unprecedented gamble for ABC." The gamble cashed in, however, and over half of all Americans who watched television that week watched *Roots*, and the series was viewed in almost 32 million homes.[19] Haley's depiction of slavery and its reception by so many Americans clearly reflected the post–Civil Rights era shift in Americans' thinking about race and slavery. With its explicit whipping scenes and sympathetic and empowering portrait of Kunta Kinte, *Roots* challenged the dominant narrative available in textbooks and called its audience into a national conversation about the peculiar institution.

Adding to the popular discussions stimulated by television's wide reach, NBC offered a two-night miniseries on Harriet Tubman called "A Woman Called Moses," which debuted in December 1978. Starring Cicely Tyson, an Emmy-award winning actress who had played the role of Kunta Kinte's mother in *Roots*, the show garnered critical praise, but also elicited controversy because the script was based on a novel written by Marcy Heidish. Why the producers of the television show chose to use a fictional portrait of Tubman as their roadmap rather than Conrad's or Bradford's biographies remains unknown, but Heidish's portrayal of Tubman, which included naked sex scenes with John Tubman and drinking binges, was clearly not based on any surviving evidence. While these particular scenes were not included in the television series, factual errors persisted, like the assertion by narrator Orson Welles that Tubman freed more than 3,000 slaves or that she was the sole "founder of the Underground Railroad."[20]

In addition to showing up on the silver screen, the Tubman myth that she was a superhero conductor on the UGRR also wove its way into theatrical interpretations of her life in the late twentieth and early twenty-first centuries. Scottish composer Thea Musgrave wrote and directed an opera based on Tubman's life story called *Harriet, the Woman Called Moses*, which was first produced in Norfolk, Virginia, in 1985. Twenty-five years later, Nkeiru Okoye composed words and music for the opera, *Harriet Tubman: When I Crossed That Line to Freedom*, which has been performed in New York, Baltimore, and Philadelphia. Musgrave explicitly embraced the Tubman myth, writing that Tubman was "gifted with those rare qualities of courage and imagination which enabled her to overcome seemingly insuperable odds," and compared her with famous women in history like Joan of Arc and Mother Teresa.[21] Okoye also highlighted Tubman's heroic qualities, writing an aria called "I am Moses the Liberator," where the Tubman character sings, "dead Negroes tell no tales" as she walks through the audience waving a revolver.[22] One might cite creative license in both of these cases and certainly operas (and other creative ventures, for that matter) should not be held to strict historical standards, but neither opera presents a nuanced portrait of Tubman's life. Furthermore, both productions focus only on Tubman's life as a slave and her subsequent work on the Underground Railroad, and they end before the Civil War even begins, thus truncating Tubman's long career of activism.

To her credit, however, Okoye does include several important supporting characters in her opera, like Thomas Garrett and William Still, thus complicating the idea that Tubman was a singular historical force on the UGRR, and she consulted the recent scholarly biographies of Tubman that informed her more complex narrative. After a dry spell of nearly sixty years, four academic biographies of Tubman were published between 2003 and 2007; in fact, given that neither Bradford nor Conrad were trained historians, one could argue that the first full-length scholarly biography of Tubman was not published until 2004, when historian Kate Clifford Larson issued *Bound for the Promised Land: Harriet Tubman, Portrait of an American Hero*. Larson's detailed and impeccably researched biography followed close on the heels of women's studies professor Jean Humez's "spiritual biography," an exploration of Tubman's religious identity and a literary analysis of the published writings about her life. Renowned historian Catherine Clinton also published a Tubman biography in 2004, and African American studies professor Milton Sernett offered an insightful and provocative exploration of Tubman's place in American memory in 2007. As Sernett notes, the Baltimore *Sun* expressed what many had been thinking, that "182 years after her birth, 139 years after the end of the Civil War, 91 years after her death—the world has known Tubman only through the grandly mythologized accounts of two amateur historians and the scores of children's books they inspired. Suddenly, three new books written by academic historians have appeared."[23]

That four academics, three of whom were trained in universities in the post–Civil Rights era, simultaneously identified Tubman and their disciplines' inattention to her as an area ripe for exploration is not an accident of fate. Women's and African American history came of age in the 1970s and 1980s, and M.A. and Ph.D. programs offering mentors and courses in these fields ballooned in the 1990s and early 2000s. For example, established in 1970, the Afro-American Studies Department at the University of Wisconsin-Madison "is an outgrowth of the student concern for relevance in higher education which was so dramatically evidenced on many college campuses during the late 1960s." What began as a small program at a white-dominated university now offers over seventy-five undergraduate and graduate courses in African American studies. Furthermore, women's history courses continue to be added in colleges and universities across the country, and now over fifty colleges and universities offer graduate degrees in women's history and women's studies.[24]

These recent biographies of Tubman are testaments to the widespread attention to women's and African American history in the academy over the past generation; they all provide, to varying degrees, comprehensive portraits of Tubman's life and place her biography within the context of the history of slavery, the Civil War, and social activism in the nineteenth century. Larson's is the most ambitious and successful in its attempt to uncover the many unknown details of Tubman's life; it is because of Larson's discovery of a receipt for payment of a midwife, for example, that we know Tubman was most likely born in March of 1822, not 1820 or 1821 as previously believed. But the public's reception of her biography has been mixed, with academics, on the one hand, praising its careful detective work, and some of Tubman's descendants and an "inner circle" of devoted fans, on the other, questioning her debunking of long-held beliefs about Tubman's heroics. For example, Larson documents each of Tubman's trips back to Maryland between 1849 and 1860 and significantly lowers the number of fugitives Tubman rescued from the commonly cited figure of 300 to somewhere between 70 and 75. Tubman devotees chafe at the modesty of the new numbers, perhaps worried that it somehow diminishes the importance of her story. But Larson insists the opposite; that the truth of Tubman's story is "far more compelling" than the myth.[25]

Perhaps what's more important than these biographies is not their individual or collective worth, but rather, the wider impact of the scholarship from which they emerged. Unlike the history textbooks and biographies of Tubman from the 1950s and 1960s, slavery now takes center stage in the American narrative, as historians acknowledge the profound influence the institution had on the development of American society. For example, take the widely used college textbook, *Nation of Nations*, now in its sixth edition and issued by publishing giant McGraw-Hill. It gives primacy to the centrality of slavery in American history, along with dedicated attention to the history of Indian nations and women:

> . . . everywhere in the American South and Southwest, white people's lingering dreams were realized only through the labor of the least free members of colonial America. In the Southwest the Spanish made servants of the Indians. Along the southern Atlantic coast and in the Caribbean, English plantation owners turned for labor to the African slave trade. Only after slavery became firmly established as a social and legal institution did England's southern colonies begin to settle down and grow. . . . That stubborn reality would haunt Americans of all colors who continued to dream of freedom and independence.[26]

Like the narrative found in *Nation of Nations*, most high school and college level textbooks now provide social and cultural history in addition to more traditional political chronologies, and thus students explore life in the slave cabins along with life in the White House. The most recent text published by Oxford University Press, *Of the People: A History of the United States*, offers a detailed and graphic account of a slave auction:

> The slave market was a ghastly collision of worlds: for potential buyers, sellers, and onlookers, it was a lively gathering place (like a club or tavern) for white men, whose easy camaraderie stood in stark contrast to the terror of the black people about to be offered for sale. Indeed the amiability of the market helped potential buyers more easily to see themselves as rational, well-motivated businessmen, rather than purveyors of misery. And yet the truth of the transaction permeated the place—in the audible sobs of mothers and children, in the harsh calculations and coarse comments of attendees, and in the absence of white females, a powerful silent admission that what was occurring at the slave market was so nakedly brutal as to taint the purity of white women.[27]

Whitewashing the sins of the past is no longer standard operating procedure in textbook publishing, even though recent headlines indicate that resistance to teaching what critics call "revisionist history" persists, as states like Texas excise discomfiting passages from its common textbooks and reject publishers who emphasize this more complex narrative.[28]

But rather than engendering guilt in its readership, which for so long has been a concern of social conservatives who advocate censorship of the unseemly in American history, many textbook authors and educators recognize the benefits of teaching the valleys as well as the mountain tops in American history. In his study of United States history textbooks, scholar Joseph Moreau praises the merits of conveying a fuller, more complicated historical narrative to America's students: "[Jefferson], the champion of local democracy, political and economic egalitarianism, and the (White) yeoman farmer is the same Jefferson who owned slaves and wrestled with his own racism. His personal dilemma, handled with honesty in the classroom, can shed light on what has been a great national dilemma."[29] America's tragic flaws must be paired with its triumphs because much of American identity is embedded in that central tension between the ideals of democracy and the practice of oppression; furthermore, American students need to see the human in history. A litany of heroic acts and larger-than-life historical figures places the past on a pedestal, making it more difficult for students to connect with history and learn from it.

Thus Harriet Tubman's courageous feats on the Underground Railroad and her accomplishments while serving in the Union army must be discussed alongside the unfortunate truths of black and female inequality in order to absorb the full breadth of her life and its challenges. Tubman, like many African Americans living in the nineteenth century, struggled with poverty, racism, and sexism throughout her lifetime and died nearly penniless. The fact that one of the most well-known black women in the United States repeatedly found herself in dire living conditions attests to the larger structural inequalities that wove their way into American society. If we only focus on the hero, on the Tubman who stands above the crowd and "beats" the slave catchers, we forget a much larger part of the story, the injustices that persistently weighed Tubman down before and after her storied career on the UGRR.

And yet, the Tubman myth prevails in American culture, even as more complicated portraits of her show up on library shelves and in college classrooms. The proliferation of children's books that focus on Tubman continues, but the more recent texts take into account the centrality of slavery in American history and offer a surprisingly honest account of its brutality. For example, *Harriet Tubman, Secret Agent*, published by National Geographic in 2006, opens with a bold and unadulterated vision of the institution: "Long before the Civil War began, Harriet Tubman started her own war against slavery. Born a slave, she worked day after day and year after year on Maryland farms. The daughter of one master whipped her, scarring her for life. Another master fractured her skull. She saw her sisters taken away by slave traders." Author Thomas B. Allen expanded the typical chronology presented in many children's books and highlights Tubman's service in the Union army. In fact, the subtitle of the book, *How Daring Slaves and Free Blacks Spied for the Union During the Civil War*, reveals this focus, and Allen provides a cast of characters that includes lesser-known abolitionists like Alexander Milton Ross and other female spies like Elizabeth Van Lew. He acknowledges that Tubman worked inside a network of free blacks and slaves, claiming, "She was not alone. She was one of countless—and usually unknown—African-Americans who served the Union as spies."[30]

Allen must be credited with shifting his audience's focus from one decade of Tubman's life to two or three decades and for placing Tubman within a larger narrative of black resistance and activism, but his story perpetuates Tubman's heroic status, extending her superhuman courage from her prewar feats on the Underground Railroad to her spying and scouting during the Civil War. Allen claims that although Colonel James Montgomery "was in charge as the commanding officer, Harriet was the *real* leader of the black soldiers," during the Combahee River raid. The information Tubman helped gather from her scouts, and her mere presence certainly helped ensure the raid's success, but the likelihood that a white male commissioned officer would defer to a black woman's authority is extremely far-fetched. Furthermore, Allen ends his story with Tubman serving as a nurse at Fortress Monroe, Virginia, placing her in a more traditional feminine environment and perhaps reminding the reader that the gendered disruption of war would return to normal upon its closure. But as we know, when Tubman left Virginia to return home, neither her gender nor her status as a trusted army spy protected her from the racialized assault she suffered on that fated train ride back to New York.[31]

Perhaps it is Tubman's position within this double bind of race and gender oppression that makes her myth so impervious to destruction; in addition, her very longevity, dying at the age of 91, defied the odds of a poor black woman living in the nineteenth century. It is often this enduring, non-threatening image of an elderly woman of small stature that pops up everywhere in the twenty-first century, from the History Channel to the pages of web blogs and the stages of elementary theater productions. For example, politician Al Sharpton helps narrate a documentary in which he describes Tubman "in physical terms, not a mighty woman," but asserts, "No one struck more fear in the hearts of slave owners than Harriet Tubman because tens of thousands of slave owners had to deal with for the first time the fact that these people are going to rebel."[32] Shown in the video wearing her lace neck scarf and a simple black wool dress, Tubman appears as a demure, unassuming figure that suddenly struck the fear of God into southerners. Never mind that Tubman joined a long line of well-known slave rebels, like Denmark Vesey and Nat Turner, who had elicited anxiety and fear throughout the South for decades. For Sharpton and the History Channel, she almost single-handedly "developed the Underground Railroad" and caused slaveholders to "look at their servants differently" for the first time in American history. Similarly, in a play produced by the New Jersey Performing Arts Council Arts Education Department, Tubman's life is presented as a "thrilling play about danger, friendship, spies, fugitives, soldiers, and the pursuit of the American dream," where she forges new pathways on the Underground Railroad and rescues over 300 slaves before the Civil War.[33] Furthermore, accomplished playwright and actor Leslie McCurdy repeats the oft-quoted (and inaccurate) number of 300 slaves rescued in her one-woman show, "The Spirit of Harriet Tubman," which she presents between 100 and 150 times a year to schoolchildren across the country.[34]

The larger-than-life Tubman portrait emerges in video games as well, and although the game has not yet debuted, the National Endowment for the Humanities recently funded the development of a video game that features Tubman and other activists on the Underground Railroad.[35] Likewise, the American Girl Doll company offers an online game that pits the runaway slave girl, Addy, against other characters in this fictionalized replay of a mother and daughter escaping to freedom during the Civil War. The game is based on the popular doll and accompanying book that shows "a courageous girl determined to be free," who works to reunite her family in the midst of war and segregation.[36] Fast forward in age but travel back in time, and instead of the innocent, lovable Addy, you can find, Aveline, a lead character in the popular video game series Assassin (M+ rating). Aveline is the daughter of a French merchant and formerly enslaved black woman, and she inhabits Revolutionary-era New Orleans, inciting slave revolts and murdering Spanish soldiers. According to the game developer's website, "Whether silently eliminating her enemies with slow-motion chain kills or luring them into deadly traps, Aveline strikes mortal fear into the hearts of those who stand in her way," and she is deemed a "triple threat assassin."[37]

Perhaps historians should welcome the advent of a strong black female slave rebel on XBoxes and PlayStations worldwide, but dangers lurk in pop culture portrayals of historical figures and can engender painful and harmful misrepresentations of the past. The most egregious online interpretation of Tubman elicited outrage and disbelief from Americans across the political spectrum when hip-hop mogul Russell Simmons produced the now infamous "Harriet Tubman Sex Tape" in 2013. Released in early August, the three-minute video depicts Tubman having sex with her white master while a fellow slave videotapes them from a closet near the bed, purportedly to use as incriminating evidence against their master. Simmons debuted the video on his Def Jam Digital YouTube channel and immediately received a hailstorm of criticism. From *The New York Times* to numerous websites and discussion blogs, black women, in particular, railed against Simmons and the video. Online petition site Change.org circulated a statement that read, "Rape is not a joke, nor is the sexual violation of African American women a punchline," and director Spike Lee tweeted, "Why do we desecrate our ancestors? Why do we hate ourselves?"[38] One woman who posted a comment on the YouTube channel said, "I do not find anything about this funny. . . . Slavery, was no DAM joke, and women being forced to have sex against their will because they were sold and bought as community property was no joke either."[39]

Simmons soon apologized for the video and took it down from his Def Jam Digital channel. His self-censorship was unprecedented, which perhaps indicates the amount of vitriol that got thrown his way and the "teachable moment" that emerged from the controversy:

> . . . once someone explained to me what it was [why it was so offensive], for the first time in 30 years I took down some content. I never took down a piece of content in my life. They shot up my office over Public Enemy. They had people under the desk hiding. Snipers were outside of my office. . . . So I've been through it. But in this case I understood how hurt people were, especially black women. And it just made me feel like, "I don't want to do that. I don't want to be

that kind of source of pain for that many people." So I pulled it down instantly when I understood it. So it is what it is. It's behind me, I hope. It's a different world.[40]

A different world indeed, but one that would still benefit from a thorough understanding of slavery and its wounds, rather than gleaning historical knowledge from pop culture shorts by Simmons or Comedy Central skits like "The Auction Block," in which actors Key and Peele pretend to be slaves being sold at auction.[41]

Humor can be a handmaiden to history, but historical literacy requires more than pop culture interpretations of serious topics like racism and slavery. Take for example another Key and Peele sketch, one that features Tubman played by a cross-dressing Jordan Peele. The caption to the video clip reads, "Harriet Tubman was the defender of liberty, the protector of liberty, and the inventor of parkour," and shows Tubman leading a reluctant group of slaves on an obstacle course. Tubman sprints and flips over hay bales and crashes through windows, demonstrating the skills necessary to follow her "to freedom," and after several attempts, her followers give up saying, "Forget this, man, I'm goin' back!" On the one hand, the hilarious skit gives credence to Tubman's physical strength and testifies to the difficulty of successfully travelling hundreds of miles in secret. But it also diminishes her accomplishments by simplifying them, implying that acrobatics alone helped Tubman accomplish her goals, thus neglecting her intelligence and her alliances with other abolitionists.[42] Finally, and perhaps most importantly, it freezes Tubman's memory in an 1850s time capsule that emphasizes her role as a conductor on the Underground Railroad and lauds her in only that capacity.

By unpacking the humor, myth, and memories that swirl around Tubman's story, we can begin to appreciate the historical Tubman and all the complexity and tragedy that accompanies her biography. The mythical Tubman lives on the shelves of elementary school libraries, and children all over the world learn about her as they read the latest edition of *Minty: A Story of Young Harriet Tubman*.[43] And yet, the historical Tubman never learned to read and spent her childhood enslaved, working on a Maryland plantation and suffering the indignities and physical abuse that characterized slavery in the antebellum United States. The mythical Tubman rescued over 300 slaves and founded the Underground Railroad single-handedly, but in reality, Tubman rescued approximately seventy slaves before the Civil War and moved among hundreds, perhaps thousands, of like-minded black and white abolitionists who populated the network to freedom from Maryland to Canada. And the Tubman who lives in American memory does not exist outside her feats on the Underground Railroad. Only recently have children's authors, playwrights, and artists begun to incorporate Tubman's accomplishments during the Civil War, and virtually no one attends to her work in poverty relief and woman's suffrage. Thanks to recent work by academic biographers, however, we can find Tubman scouting on the battlefield and caring for soldiers during the war, and we can watch her walk through the halls of suffrage conventions at the turn of the century. None of these historical pictures diminishes the accomplishments Tubman made throughout her ninety-one years, and even those studies that explore and often debunk the myths that reign supreme in pop culture offer historical narratives that sustain her heroic status in American history.[44]

The disconnect that exists between the Tubman myth and history and the controversy that often surrounds processes of historical revision parallels the dialectic dance that has characterized the larger American narrative for decades. When the College Board released a new version of the AP United States History (APUSH) guidelines in 2014, conservatives cried foul, arguing that the liberal college professors who designed the AP curriculum teach "I hate America 101" and are only covering "the bad things in history and leaving the good things out."[45] James Grossman, president of the American Historical Association in 2014, defended the new curriculum and urged teachers and parents to resist the desire to "use history to unite a people" by teaching a "comfortable national history." Grossman points out that "we do it in our families" as well: "You have a set of family stories that makes your children feel comfortable and proud, and you have stories about the not-so-great things. Is it better to tell children just the comfortable things or should they learn the rest?"[46] "The rest" defies mythologizing but it embodies the human experience, a story that is both positive and negative, triumphant and tragic.

Tubman's optimism can guide us as we wade through "the rest," just as it motivated her when she crossed the swollen rivers of Maryland or knocked on doors to raise money to house and feed Auburn's elderly and disabled. She died when women were still denied the right to vote and when African Americans continued to suffer the daily injustices of Jim Crow. But Tubman died as she lived, a visionary whose steadfast faith in a benevolent and just God sustained her faith in humanity. In the final hours before she passed, her friends recorded her last words, paraphrased from a biblical passage: "I go away to prepare a place for you, and where I am ye may be also."[47] History can prepare a place for us and our ancestors to reside, but only if that history reflects the complexity and fullness of human existence, a narrative that features Minty, Moses, "General Tubman," and "Aunt Harriet" in joy and in pain, suffering and celebrating, living and dying—a story that deconstructs the myth but reminds us that heroes emerge only when they have villains to fight. That story is Harriet's, and it is also America's story.

Notes

1. Comment by SecondSaturdayblog Sacramento, "Nick Cannon Blows a Gasket over Google's Tribute to Harriet Tubman," http://www.kulturekritic.com/2014/02/news/nick-cannon-blows-gasket-googles-tribute-harriet-tubman/.

2. Milton C. Sernett, *Harriet Tubman: Myth, Memory, and History* (Durham: Duke University Press, 2007), 9.

3. Peter Fossett, qtd. in Lucia C. Stanton, *"Those Who Labor for My Happiness": Slavery at Thomas Jefferson's Monticello* (Charlottesville: University of Virginia Press, 2012); Annette Gordon-Reed, *The Hemingses of Monticello: An American Family* (New York: Norton, 2008), 581; National Park Service, "Thomas Jefferson Memorial," quotation from Panel 3, http://www.nps.gov/thje/index.htm; and Henry Wiencek, *Master of the Mountain: Thomas Jefferson and His Slaves* (New York: Farrar, Straus, and Giroux, 2012), 4, 9–11.

4. Sernett, *Harriet Tubman*, 319. For a fascinating and comprehensive discussion of Tubman's complexity see Janell Hobson, "Harriet Tubman: A Legacy of Resistance," and the special issue dedicated to Tubman in *Meridians: Feminism, Race, Transnationalism* 12, No. 22 (2014).

5. Sernett, *Harriet Tubman*, 296–297. The literature on memory studies is too expansive to summarize here, but for some representative texts related to Civil War memory in particular see David Blight, *Race and Reunion: The Civil War in American Memory* (Cambridge, MA: Belknap/Harvard University Press, 2001) and *American Oracle: The Civil War in the Civil Rights Era* (Cambridge, MA: Belknap/Harvard, 2011); Alice Fahs and Joan Waugh, eds., *The Memory of the Civil War in American Culture* (Chapel Hill: The University of North Carolina Press, 2004); and Carolyn Janney, *Remembering the Civil War: Reunion and the Limits of Reconciliation* (Chapel Hill: The University of North Carolina Press, 2013).

6. Franklin B. Sanborn, "Harriet Tubman," *The (Boston) Commonwealth*, 17 July 1863; Sanborn, *The Life and Letters of John Brown: Liberator of Kansas, and Martyr of Virginia* (Boston: Roberts Brothers, 1891).

7. Sanborn, "Harriet Tubman," 17 July 1863, reprinted in Bradford, *Scenes in the Life of Harriet Tubman* (Auburn, NY: W.J. Moses, 1869), 72.

8. Samuel M. Hopkins, "Introduction," 1 December 1859, in Bradford, *Scenes*. For a more detailed description of Bradford and the publication process for both *Scenes* and *The Moses of Her People* see Sernett, *Harriet Tubman*, 105–130.

9. Bradford, *Scenes*, 3–4.

10. Kate Clifford Larson, *Bound for the Promised Land: Harriet Tubman, Portrait of an American Hero* (New York: Ballantine, 2004), 212, 225; Bradford, *Scenes*, 38, 48.

11. Sarah Bradford, *Harriet Tubman: The Moses of Her People* (New York: Dover, 2004; G.R. Lockwood & Son, 1886), 9.

12. Sernett, *Harriet Tubman*, 127; Bradford, *Harriet Tubman*, 9, 37.

13. Qtd. in Sernett, *Harriet Tubman*, 197, 216–217 [emphasis added]; Earl Conrad, *Harriet Tubman* (Washington, D.C.: Associated Publishers, 1943), 101.

14. Langston Hughes, "HERE TO YONDER," *The Chicago Defender*, 25 December 1943. ProQuest. Web, 31 July 2014; Powell qtd. in Sernett, *Harriet Tubman*, 222–223.

15. Sernett, *Harriet Tubman*, 222. Based on his detailed survey of dozens of children's biographies, Sernett claims that more authors relied upon Bradford than Conrad for their information about Tubman. See Sernett, *Harriet Tubman*, 22.

16. Sernett, *Harriet Tubman*, 27–28; Ann Petry, *Harriet Tubman: Conductor on the Underground Railroad* (New York: Harper Collins, 1955, reprint 1996).

17. Qtd. in Joseph Moreau, *Schoolbook Nation: Conflicts over American History Textbooks from the Civil War to the Present* (Ann Arbor: University of Michigan, 2003), 273–274.

18. Senator Margaret Chase Smith and H. Paul Jeffers, qtd. in Sernett, *Harriet Tubman*, 29–30.

19. Allison Landsberg, *Prosthetic Memory: The Transformation of American Remembrance in the Age of Mass Culture* (New York: Columbia University Press, 2004), 102–103.

20. Sernett, *Harriet Tubman*, 234–238, quote on p. 237.

21. Thea Musgrave, *Harriet, A Woman Called Moses*, Norfolk, VA, 1985; see plot synopsis, http://www.theamusgrave.com/html/harriet_woman_called_moses.html.

22. Nkeiru Okoye, *Harriet Tubman: When I Cross That Line to Freedom*, production website, http://www.harriettubmanopera.com. For video clip of the aria, "I Am Moses, the Liberator," see https://www.youtube.com/watch?v=U1JtSvtXc8Q.

23. Quoted in Sernett, *Harriet Tubman*, 296.

24. The first graduate degree in women's history was offered by Sarah Lawrence College in 1972, and now over fifty colleges and universities offer graduate degrees in women's history and/or women's studies See http://www.slc.edu/womens-history/character/ and http://www.smith.edu/swg/graduate.php. For Wisconsin's Afro-American Studies program see "Home-Mission Statement" and "Courses," at www.afroamericanstudies.wisc.edu.

25. Larson, *Bound for the Promised Land*, xv. For a summary of each of Tubman's trips back to Maryland and the "passengers" she ferried, see "Chronology," 300–303. For an example of the continued belief that Tubman "led at least 300 slaves to freedom," see the *Washington Post*, http://www.washingtonpost.com/local/sharing-the-harriet-tubman-story--through-wax-at-madame-tussauds/2012/02/07/gIQAxn7sxQ_story.html.

26. James West Davidson, et.al., *Nation of Nations: A Narrative History of the American Republic*, 5th ed. (New York: The McGraw-Hill Companies, 2005), 79–80.

27. James Oakes, et.al., *Of the People: A History of the United States*, 2nd ed. (New York: Oxford University press, 2014), 407.

28. James C. McKinley, "Texas Conservatives Win Curriculum Change," *The New York Times*, 12 March 2010, http://www.nytimes.com/2010/03/13/education/13texas.html?_r=0.

29. Moreau, *School Book Nation*, 336–337.

30. Thomas B. Allen, *Harriet Tubman, Secret Agent: How Daring Slaves and Free Blacks Spied for the Union During the Civil War* (New York: National Geographic Society, 2006), 9, 12.

31. Allen, *Harriet Tubman, Secret Agent*, 149.

32. Al Sharpton, "Harriet Tubman," The History Channel, 2009, http://www.history.com/topics/black-history/harriet-tubman/videos/harriet-tubman-and-the-underground-railroad?m=528e394da93ae&s=undefined&f=1&free=false.

33. New Jersey Performing Arts Council, "Harriet Tubman and the Underground Railroad," *Passport to Culture: Teachers Resource Guide*, 2008–2009, http://duponttheatre.com/downloads/studyguides/tubman_studyguide.pdf.

34. Leslie McCurdy, "The Spirit of Harriet Tubman," 2013; see information about McCurdy at http://lesliemccurdy.ca/harriet.html or video clip of one performance at http://vimeo.com/90332027.

35. Lia Russell, "Video game Teaches about Underground Railroad," *The Virginia Pilot*, 8 June 2010; the NEH grant was awarded to Professor Cassandra Newby-Alexander of Norfolk State University who is seeking additional funding for development of the game.

36. Connie Porter, *Meet Addy* (New York: American Girl Publications, 2012). For Addy's website see http://www.americangirl.com/play/historical-character/addy/ #page=home&popup=meet.

37. Ubisoft, "Assassins Creed III: Liberation," released October 2013, http://assassinscreed.ubi.com/en-us/games/assassins-creed-3-liberation.aspx.

38. Josh Voorhees, "Russell Simmons No Longer Thinks His 'Harriet Tubman Sex Tape' Parody Is Hilarious," *Slate.com*, 15 August 2013, http://www.slate.com/blogs/the_slatest/2013/08/15/harriet_tubman_sex_tape_video_russell_simmons_apologizes_for_yanks_controversial.html; and Jen Yamato, "Russell Simmons Pulls Controversial 'Harriet Tubman Sex Tape' after YouTube Channel Launch," *Deadline.com*, 15 August 2013, http://www.deadline.com/2013/08/russell-simmons-pulls-controversial-harriet-tubman-sex-tape-after-youtube-channel-launch/. For several insightful analyses of the sex tape controversy see Karsonya Wise Whitehead, "Harriet Tubman: From Maternal Mother to Jezebel," Janell Hobson, "The Rape of Harriet Tubman," and Treva B. Lindsey and Jessica Marie Johnson, "Searching for Climax: Black Erotic Lives in Slavery and Freedom," all found in *Meridians: Feminism, Race, Transnationalism* 12, No. 22 (2014): 156–195.

39. La Tonya White, comment posted in June 2014, https://www.youtube.com/watch?v=78Ovn OmZvTg&google_comment_id=z13esbxjhzjef5aaj04cezm5owfotlhw0zs0k.

40. Russell Simmons quoted in Brennan Williams, "Russell Simmons Talks 'Harriet Tubman Sex Tape' Backlash and All Def Digital Launch," *The Huffington Post*, 20 August 2013, http://www. deadline.com/2013/08/russell-simmons-pulls-controversial-harriet-tubman-sex-tape-after-youtube-channel-launch/.

41. Key and Peele, "The Auction Block," Comedy Central, video clip at https://www.youtube.com/ watch?v=zB7MichlL1k. As of January 2015, this video had been viewed over 13 million times.

42. Key and Peele, "Harriet Tubman: Freedom Runner," Comedy Central, video clip at http:// vimeo.com/channels/keypeele/54162827.

43. Alan Schroeder and Jerry Pinkney, *Minty: A Story of Young Harriet Tubman* (New York: Puffin Books, 1996, 2000).

44. A similar call for understanding and teaching a more complex historical Tubman rather than a mythical Tubman was made by Vivian M. May in "Under-Theorized and Under-Taught: Re-examining Harriet Tubman's Place in Women's Studies," *Meridians*, 28–49. May argues that Tubman "is more often remembered in ways that misrecognize, distort, or flatten," and asks for scholars to "remember her lifetime of differently courageous acts of working in solidarity with others on multiple fronts" (31, 36).

45. Jenny Deam, "New U.S. History Curriculum Sparks Education Battle of 2014," *Los Angeles Times*, 1 October 2014.

46. James Grossman quoted in Karen Tumulty and Lyndsey Layton, "Changes in AP History Trigger a Culture Clash in Colorado," *The Washington Post*, 5 October 2014.

47. Auburn *Citizen*, "Harriet Tubman Is Dead," 11 March 1913, reprinted at http://www.harriet tubman.com/memoriam2.html.

RUNAWAY ADVERTISEMENT FOR MINTY (HARRIET TUBMAN) AND HER TWO BROTHERS OCTOBER 3, 1849

Harriet Tubman's owner, Eliza Brodess, took out this ad in the *Cambridge Democrat*, a newspaper published on the Eastern Shore, roughly two weeks after "Minty" and her brothers ran away. Slave owners often waited to place ads until they were certain the slaves would not return of their own accord, a common practice across the South. Contrary to many ads that offered less money for female slaves, Brodess's ad indicates that she valued Tubman as much as her brothers, offering $100 each for their return.

Three Hundred Dollars Reward. Ranaway from the subscriber on Monday the 17th ult., three negroes, named as follows: HARRY, aged about 19 years, has on one side of his neck a wen, just under the ear, he is of a dark chestnut color, about 5 feet 8 or 9 inches hight; BEN, aged aged [sic] about 25 years, is very quick to speak when spoken to, he is of chestnut color, about six feet high; MINTY, aged about 27 years, is of a chestnut color, fine looking, and about 5 feet high. One hundred dollars reward will be given for each of the above-named negroes, if taken out of the State, and $50 each if taken in the State. They must be lodged in Baltimore, Easton or Cambridge Jail, in Maryland.

Eliza Ann Brodess, Near Bucktown, Dorchester county, Md. Oct. 3d, 1849.

The Delaware Gazette will please copy the above three weeks, and charge this office.

SOURCE

Cambridge Democrat, Cambridge, MD, 3 October 1849, reprinted in Kate Clifford Larson, *Bound for the Promised Land: Harriet Tubman, Portrait of an American Hero* (New York: Ballantine, 2004), 79.

"A LETTER TO AMERICAN SLAVES" FROM THE FUGITIVE SLAVE CONVENTION AT CAZENOVIA, NY AUGUST 22, 1850

White abolitionist Gerrit Smith and former fugitive slave Frederick Douglass likely co-authored this letter and circulated it at the Fugitive Slave Convention in Cazenovia, New York, in the summer of 1850. The convention gathered over 2,000 abolitionists to protest the impending passage of the Fugitive Slave Law of 1850. The attendees included famous fugitive slaves like Mary and Emily Edmonson (along with Douglass), and prominent abolitionist leaders like Smith and Theodore Weld. The convention was remarkable for its diversity; rarely did black and white, male and female gather in a public forum in the nineteenth century. The letter's bold message pledging support to fugitive slaves only added to the convention's radicalism.

––––––––

Afflicted and beloved Brothers:—The meeting which sends you this letter, is a meeting of runaway slaves. We thought it well that they who had once suffered as you still suffer, that they who had once drank of that bitterest of all bitter cups which you are still compelled to drink of, should come together for the purpose of making a communication to you.

The chief object of this meeting is to tell you what circumstances we find ourselves in—that so you may be able to judge for yourselves whether the prize we have obtained is worth the peril of the attempt to obtain it.

The heartless pirates who compelled us to call them "master" sought to persuade us, as such pirates seek to persuade you, that the condition of those who escape from their clutches is thereby made worse instead of better. We confess that we had our fears that this might be so. Indeed, so great was our ignorance that we could not be sure that the Abolitionists were not the fiends which our masters represented them to be. When they told us that the Abolitionists could they lay hands upon us, would buy and sell us, we could not certainly know that they spoke falsely; and when they told us that Abolitionists are in the habit of skinning the black man for leather and regaling their cannibalism on his flesh, even such enormities seem to us to be possible. But owing to the happy change in our circumstances, we are not as ignorant and credulous now as we once were; and if we did not know it before, we know it now, that slaveholders are as great liars as they are great tyrants. . . .

Including our children, we number in Canada, at least, twenty thousand. The total of our population in the free States far exceeds this. Nevertheless, we are poor, we can do little more to promote your deliverance than pray for it to the God of the oppressed. We will do what we can to supply you with pocket compasses. In dark nights, when his good guiding star is hidden from the flying slave, a pocket compass greatly facilitates his exodus. Besides, that we are too poor to furnish you with deadly weapons, candor requires the admission, that some of us would not furnish them, if we could; for some of us have become non-resistants and have discarded the use of these weapons: and would say to you: "love your enemies; do good to them, which hate you; bless them that curse you; and pray for them, which despitefully use you." Such of us would be glad to be able to say that all the colored men of the North are non-resistants. But, in point of fact, it is only a handful of them who are. When the insurrection of the Southern slaves shall take place, as take place it will unless speedily prevented by voluntary emancipation, the great mass of the colored men of the North, however, much to the grief of any of us, will be found by your side, with deep-stored and long-accumulated revenge in their hearts, and with death-dealing weapons in their hands. . . . This truth you are entitled to know, however the knowledge of it may affect you, and however you may act in view of it.

We have said, that some of us are non-resistants. But while such would dissuade you from all violence toward the slaveholder, let it not be supposed that they regard it as guiltier than those strifes which even good men are wont to justify. If the American revolutionists had excuse for shedding but one drop of blood, then have the American slaves excuse for making blood to flow "even unto the horsebridles." . . .

We do not forget the industrious efforts which are now making to get new facilities at the hands of Congress for re-enslaving those who have escaped from slavery. But we can assure you that, as to the State of New York and the New England States, such efforts must prove fruitless. Against all such devilism—against all kidnappers—the colored people of these States will "stand for their life"; and, what is more, the white people of these States will not stand against them. A regenerated public sentiment has forever removed these States beyond the limits of the slaveholders' hunting ground. Defeat—disgrace—and it may be death—will be their only reward for pursuing their prey into this *abolitionized* portion of the country. . . .

There are three points in your conduct when you shall have become inhabitants of the North on which we cannot refrain from admonishing you.

1st. If you will join a sectarian church, let it not be one which approves of the Negro-pew, and which refuses to treat slaveholding as a high crime against God and man. It were better that you sacrifice your lives than that by going into the Negro pew, you invade your self-respect—debase your souls—play the traitor to your race—and crucify afresh Him who died for the one brotherhood of man.

2d. Join no political party which refuses to commit itself fully, openly, and heartily, in its newspapers, meetings, and nominations, to the doctrine that slavery is the grossest of all absurdities, as well as the guiltiest of all abominations, and that there can no more be a law for the enslavement of man, made in the image of God than for the enslavement of God himself. Vote for no man for civil office who makes your complexion a bar to political, ecclesiastical, or social equality. Better die than insult yourself, and insult every person of African blood, and insult your Maker, by contributing to elevate to civil rule the man who refuses to eat with you, to sit by your side in the House of Worship, or to let his children sit in the school by the side of your children.

3d. Send not your children to the school which the malignant and murderous prejudice of white people has gotten up exclusively for colored people. Valuable as learning is, it is too costly, if it is acquired at the expense of such self-degradation. . . .

And now brethren, we close this letter with assuring you that we do not, cannot forget you. You are ever in our minds, our hearts, our prayers. Perhaps you are fearing that the free colored people of the United States will suffer themselves to be carried away from you by the American Colonization Society. Fear it not. In vain is it, that this greatest and most malignant enemy of the African race is now busy devising new plans and in seeking the aid of Government to perpetuate your enslavement. It wants us away from your side, that you may be kept in ignorance. But we will remain by your side to enlighten you. . . . The land of our enslaved brethren is our land, and death alone shall part us.

We cannot forget you, brethren, for we know your sufferings, and we know your sufferings because we know from experience what it is to be an

American slave. So galling was our bondage that to escape from it we suffered the loss of all things, and braved every peril and endured every hardship. Some of us left parents, some wives, some children. Some of us were wounded with guns and dogs, as we fled. Some of us, to make good our escape, suffered ourselves to be nailed up in boxes, and to pass for merchandise. Some of us secreted ourselves in the suffocating holds of ships. Nothing was so dreadful to us as slavery; and hence it is almost literally true that we dreaded nothing which could befall us in our attempt to get clear of it. Our condition could be made no worse, for we were already in the lowest depths of earthly woe. Even should we be overtaken, and subjected to slavery, this would be but to return to our old sufferings and sorrows; and should death itself prove to be the price of our endeavor after freedom, what would that be but a welcome release to men, who had all their lifetime been killed every day and "killed all the day long."

We have referred to our perils and hardships in escaping from slavery. We are happy to be able to say, that every year is multiplying the facilities for leaving the Southern prison house. The Liberty Party, the Vigilance Committee of New York, individuals, and companies of individuals in various parts of the country, are doing all they can, and it is much, to afford you a safe and a cheap passage from slavery to liberty. They do this, however, not only at great expense of property, but at great peril of liberty and life. Thousands of you have heard, ere this, that within the last fortnight, the precious name of William L. Chaplin has been added to the list of those who, in helping you gain your liberty, have lost their own. Here is a man, whose wisdom, cultivation, moral worth, bring him into the highest and best class of men:—and yet, he became a willing martyr for the poor, despised, forgotten slave's sake. Your remembrance of one such fact is enough to shed light and hope upon your darkest and most desponding moments.

Brethren, our last word to you is to bid you be of good cheer and not to despair of your deliverance. Do not abandon yourselves, as have many thousands of American slaves, to the crime of suicide. Live! Live to escape from slavery! Live to serve God! Live till He shall Himself call you into eternity! Be prayerful—be brave—be hopeful. "Lift up your heads, for your redemption draweth nigh."

SOURCE

Frederick Douglass and Gerrit Smith, "Letter to the American Slaves," reprinted at http://national humanitiescenter.org/pds/maai/community/text7/ltramerslaves1850.pdf.

THOMAS GARRETT DESCRIBES HARRIET TUBMAN DECEMBER 16, 1855

Thomas Garrett, white abolitionist and conductor for the Underground Railroad in Wilmington, Delaware, wrote to fellow Quaker and secretary of the Edinburgh (Scotland) Ladies Emancipation Society to chronicle Tubman's accomplishments. Wigham sent money to Garrett, which he used to facilitate Tubman's success on the UGRR. The Garrett-Wigham correspondence is but one example of the transatlantic network of abolitionists that provided ideological and financial support to the antislavery movement in the United States.

I feel as if I could not close this already too long letter, without giving some account of the doings of a noble woman, but a black one, in whose veins flows not one drop of Caucasian blood. She is strong & muscular, now about 55 years of age; born a Slave, and raised what is termed a field hand. She escaped from Slavery some 8 years since; her master lived nearly 100 miles below this. She has made 4 successful trips to the neighborhood she left; & brought away 17 of her brothers, sisters, & friends & has mostly made the journeys down on foot, alone, & with her companions mostly walked back, traveling the whole distance at night, and secreting themselves during the day. She has three times gone to Canada with those she brought, and spent every dollar she could earn, or get in the cause. She, in one instance, was in the immediate neighborhood of her Master for three months, before she could get off safely with her friends; & but one family, &

they colored, where she stopped, knew her. She twice in that time met her master in open day, in the fields, but he did not know her; having always worked in the open air fields, her color had changed so much, that her own brother & sister did not know her.

Last week, after a trip of two weeks, she brought up one man. She took tea with me, & has left again with a determination (during the Christmas holidays) to bring away her sister, now the last left in slavery, & her three children, a sister in law & her three children, (the husband of the latter has been a Year in Canada), & one male friend. She says if she gets them away safely, she will be content, & give up such hazardous journeys, but says she will either accomplish it or be arrested, & spend the remainder of her days in Slavery; for should she be arrested for assisting a slave, even if she had been free-born, she would be sold a slave for life; were a white person, man or woman, to peril life & health, & spend everything he or she had earned in such a noble & disinterested cause, the name would be trumpeted over the land; but be sure you do not trumpet her noble deeds in the Newspapers. I can assure you I am proud of her acquaintance.

SOURCE

Thomas Garrett to Eliza Wigham, 16 December 1855, reprinted in Jean Humez, *Harriet Tubman: The Life and the Life Stories* (Madison: University of Wisconsin Press, 2003), 281.

CHARLES NALLE RESCUE
APRIL 27, 1860

On her way to a meeting in Boston, Tubman was staying in Troy, New York, when fugitive slave Charles Nalle was arrested and held at the U.S. Commissioner's office in downtown Troy. Local free blacks and sympathetic whites gathered outside the commissioner's office when news spread of Nalle's capture. Tubman and the expanding crowd battled with the local sheriff and police officials and eventually rescued Nalle. The antislavery community in Troy then raised enough money to purchase Nalle's freedom from his Virginia master. The following newspaper report details the dramatic rescue and illustrates how local citizens challenged the Fugitive Slave Act.

––––––––

Yesterday afternoon, the streets of this city and West Troy were made the scenes of unexampled excitement. For the first time since the passage of the Fugitive Slave Law, an attempt was made here to carry its provisions into execution, and the result was a terrific encounter between the officers and the prisoner's friends, the triumph of mob law, and the final rescue of the fugitive. Our city was thrown into a grand state of turmoil, and for a time every other topic was forgotten, to give place to this new excitement. People did not think last evening to ask who was nominated at Charleston, or whether the news of the Heenan and Sayers battle had arrived—everything was merged into the fugitive slave case, of which it seems the end is not yet.

Charles Nalle, the fugitive, who was the cause of all this excitement, was a slave on the plantation of B. W. Hansborough, in Culpepper County, Virginia, till the 19th of October, 1858, when he made his escape, and went to live in Columbia, Pennsylvania. A wife and five children are residing there now. Not long since he came to Sandlake, in this county, and resided in the family of Mr. Crosby until about three weeks ago. Since that time, he has been employed as coachman by Uri Gilbert, Esq., of this city. He is about thirty years of age, tall, quite light-complexioned, and good-looking. He is said to have been an excellent and faithful servant.

At Sandlake, we understand that Nalle was often seen by one H. F. Averill, formerly connected with one of the papers of this city, who communicated with his reputed owner in Virginia, and gave the information that led to a knowledge of the whereabouts of the fugitive. Averill wrote letters for him, and thus obtained an acquaintance with his history. Mr. Hansborough sent on an agent, Henry J. Wall, by whom the necessary papers were got out to arrest the fugitive.

Yesterday morning about 11 o'clock, Charles Nalle was sent to procure some bread for the family by whom he was employed. He failed to return. At the baker's, he was arrested by Deputy United States Marshal J. W. Holmes, and immediately taken before United States Commissioner Miles Beach. The son of Mr. Gilbert, thinking it strange that he did not come back, sent to the house of William Henry, on Division Street, where he boarded, and his whereabouts was discovered.

The examination before Commissioner Beach was quite brief. The evidence of Averill and the agent was taken, and the Commissioner decided to remand Nalle to Virginia. The necessary papers were made out and given to the Marshal.

By this time it was two o'clock, and the fact began to be noised abroad that there was a fugitive slave in Mr. Beach's office, corner of State and First Streets. People in knots of ten or twelve collected near the entrance, looking at Nalle, who could be seen at an upper window. William Henry, a colored man, with whom Nalle boarded, commenced talking from the curb-stone in a loud voice to the crowd. He uttered such sentences as, "There is a fugitive slave in that office—pretty soon you will see him come forth. He is going to be taken down South, and you will have a chance to see him. He is to be taken to the depot, to go to Virginia in the first train. Keep watch of those stairs, and you will have a sight." A number of women kept shouting, crying, and by loud appeals excited the colored persons assembled.

Still the crowd grew in numbers. Wagons halted in front of the locality, and were soon piled with spectators. An alarm of fire was sounded, and hose carriages dashed through the ranks of men, women, and boys; but they closed again, and kept looking with expectant eyes at the window where the negro was visible. Meanwhile, angry discussions commenced. Some persons agitated a rescue, and others favored law and order. Mr. Brockway, a lawyer, had his coat torn for expressing his sentiments, and other melees kept the interest alive.

All at once there was a wild hulloa, and every eye was turned up to see the legs and part of the body of the prisoner protruding from the second-story window, at which he was endeavoring to escape. Then arose a shout! "Drop him!" "Catch him!" "Hurrah!" But the attempt was a fruitless one, for somebody in the office pulled Nalle back again, amid the shouts of a hundred pair of lungs. The crowd at this time numbered nearly a thousand persons. Many of them were black, and a good share were of the female sex. They blocked up State Street from First Street to the alley, and kept surging to and fro.

Martin I. Townsend, Esq., who acted as counsel for the fugitive, did not arrive in the Commissioner's office until a decision had been rendered. He immediately went before Judge Gould, of the Supreme Court, and procured a writ of habeas corpus in the usual form, returnable immediately. This was given Deputy Sheriff Nathaniel Upham, who at once proceeded to Commissioner Beach's office, and served it on Holmes. Very injudiciously the officers proceeded at once to Judge Gould's office, although it was evident they would have to pass through an excited, unreasonable crowd. As soon as the officers and their prisoner emerged from the door, an old negro, who had been standing at the bottom of the stairs, shouted, "Here they come," and the crowd made a terrific rush at the party.

From the office of Commissioner Beach, in the Mutual Building, to that of Judge Gould, in Congress Street, is less than two blocks, but it was made a regular battle-field. The moment the prisoner emerged from the doorway, in custody of Deputy-Sheriff Upham, Chief of Police Quin, Officers Cleveland and Holmes, the crowd made one grand charge, and those nearest the prisoner seized him violently, with the intention of pulling him away from the officers, but they were foiled; and down First to Congress Street, and up the latter in front of Judge Gould's chambers, went the surging mass. Exactly what did go on in the crowd, it is impossible to say, but the pulling, hauling, mauling, and shouting, gave evidences of frantic efforts on the part of the rescuers, and a stern resistance from the conservators of the law. In front of Judge Gould's office the combat was at its height. No stones or other missiles were used; the battle was fist to fist. We believe an order was given to take the prisoner the other way, and there was a grand rush towards the West, past First and River Streets, as far as Dock Street. All this time there was a continual melee. Many of the officers were hurt—among them Mr. Upham, whose object was solely to do his duty by taking Nalle before Judge Gould in accordance with the writ of habeas corpus. A number in the crowd were more or less hurt, and it is a wonder that these were not badly injured, as pistols were drawn and chisels used.

The battle had raged as far as the corner of Dock and Congress Streets, and the victory remained with the rescuers at last. The officers were completely worn out with their exertions, and it was impossible to continue their hold upon him any longer. Nalle was at liberty. His friends rushed him down Dock Street to the lower ferry, where there was a skiff lying ready to start. The fugitive was put in, the ferryman rowed off, and amid the shouts of hundreds who fined the banks of the river, Nalle was carried into Albany County.

As the skiff landed in West Troy, a negro sympathizer waded up to the waist, and pulled Nalle out of the boat. He went up the hill alone, however, and there who should he meet but Constable Becker? The latter official seeing a man with manacles on, considered it his duty to arrest him. He did so, and took him in a wagon to the office of Justice Stewart, on the second floor of the corner building near the ferry. The Justice was absent.

When the crowd on the Troy bank had seen Nalle safely landed, it was suggested that he might be recaptured. Then there was another rush made for the steam ferry-boat, which carried over about 400 persons, and left as many more—a few of the latter being soused in their efforts to get on the boat. On landing in West Troy, there, sure enough, was the prisoner, locked up in a strong office, protected by Officers Becker, Brown and Morrison, and the door barricaded.

Not a moment was lost. Up stairs went a score or more of resolute men—the rest "piling in" promiscuously, shouting and execrating the officers. Soon a stone flew against the door—then another—and bang, bang! went off a couple of pistols, but the officers who fired them took good care to aim pretty high. The assailants were forced to retreat for a moment. "They've got pistols," said one. "Who cares?" was the reply; "they can only kill a dozen of us—come on." More stones and more pistol-shots ensued. At last the door was pulled open by an immense negro, and in a moment he was felled by a hatchet in the hands of Deputy Sheriff Morrison; but the body of the fallen man blocked up the door so that it could not be shut, and a friend of the prisoner pulled him out. Poor fellow! he might well say, "Save me from my friends." Amid the pulling and hauling, the iron had cut his arms, which were bleeding profusely, and he could hardly walk, owing to fatigue.

He has since arrived safely in Canada.

SOURCE

Troy (NY) *Whig*, 28 April 1860, reprinted in Sarah Bradford, *Scenes in the Life of Harriet Tubman* (Auburn, NY: W.J. Moses, 1869), 92–100.

The Corwin Amendment (1861) and the Thirteenth Amendment (1863) to the Constitution

During the winter of 1860–1861, Congress scrambled to find ways to hold the country together in the wake of South Carolina's secession. Representative Thomas Corwin of Ohio, as chairman of the "Committee of 33," which offered several last-ditch attempts at compromise, sponsored the joint resolution to protect slavery in states where it already existed. The proposed amendment passed Congress in March of 1861, and President Lincoln transmitted the would-be Thirteenth Amendment to the state Governors for ratification per his executive duty. Ironically, the actual Thirteenth Amendment, which officially abolished slavery in the United States, stands in direct opposition to the Corwin Amendment.

Joint Resolution to Amend the Constitution of the United States

Resolved, By the Senate and House of Representatives of the United States, of America in Congress assembled, that the following article be proposed to the Legislatures of the several States as an amendment to the Constitution of the United States, which, when ratified by three-fourths of said Legislatures, shall be valid, to all intents and purposes, as part of the said Constitution, viz:

Article XIII

No amendment shall be made to the Constitution which will authorize or give to Congress the power to abolish or interfere, within any State, with the domestic institutions thereof, including that of persons held to labor or service by the laws of said State.

WILLIAM PENNINGTON

Speaker of the House of Representatives.

JOHN BRECKINRIDGE

Vice President of the United States, and
President of the Senate
Approved March 2, 1861.

JAMES BUCHANAN

SOURCE

"A Proposed Thirteenth Amendment to Prevent Secession," reprinted at http://www.gilderlehrman. org/history-by-era/failure-compromise/resources/proposed-thirteenth-amendment-prevent-secession-1861.

ARTICLE XIII

Section 1. Neither Slavery nor involuntary servitude, except as a punishment for crime; whereof the party shall have been duly convicted, shall exist within the United States, or any place subject to their jurisdiction.

Section 2. Congress shall have power to enforce this article by appropriate legislation.

SOURCE

http://memory.loc.gov/cgi-bin/query/r?ammem/mal:@field(DOCID+@lit(d4361100)).

COMBAHEE RIVER RAID
JUNE 1–2, 1863

On June 1st and 2nd, 1863, Colonel James Montgomery and Harriet Tubman led a raid up the Combahee River that resulted in the destruction of hundreds of thousands of dollars of Confederate property and the freedom of over 700 slaves. Tubman's scouting and spying ventures facilitated the raid, and she and Montgomery received a heroes' welcome back at Camp Saxton. A reporter from the *Wisconsin State Journal* was stationed in Beaufort and recorded the group's homecoming to the camp. This story was subsequently reprinted in other papers, like the Boston *Commonwealth*, and it illustrates how the press helped construct and circulate reports of Tubman's heroism but also how it perpetuated sexism and racism.

JUNE 6, 1863

At Beaufort a few days since, I had the satisfaction of witnessing the return of the gallant Col. Montgomery from a successful raid into the enemy's country, having with him the trophies of war in the shape of 780 black chattels, now recreated and made freemen, and thousands of dollars worth of rice and other property.

As I witnessed the moving mass of recreated black humanity on its way from the boat to the church in Beaufort, where they were quartered for the moment, with the filth and tatters of slavery still hanging to their degraded persons, my heart went up in gratitude to God for the change which had been wrought on South Carolina soil. The emblem of liberty and a nation's glory, as it floated over these poor, defenseless children of oppression, never looked to me so glorious, and never thrilled any heart with a more honest pride. . . .

I doubt whether this church was ever before filled with such a crowd of devout worshippers—whether it was ever before appropriated to so good a purpose—whether so true a gospel had ever before been preached within its walls. I certainly never felt such swelling emotions of gratitude to the Great Ruler as at this moment.

Col. Montgomery and his gallant band of 300 black soldiers, under the guidance of a black woman, dashed into the enemies' country, struck a bold and effective blow, destroying millions of dollars worth of commissary stores, cotton and lordly dwellings, and striking terror to the heart of rebellion, brought off near 800 slaves and thousands of dollars worth of property, without losing a man or receiving a scratch. It was a glorious consummation.

After they were all fairly disposed of in the church, they were addressed in strains of thrilling eloquence by their gallant deliverer; to which they responded in a song—"There is a white robe for thee." A song so appropriate and so heartfelt and cordial as to bring unbidden tears.

The Colonel was followed by a speech from the black woman who led the raid, and under whose inspiration it was originated and conducted. For sound sense and real native eloquence, her address would do honor to any man, and it created a great sensation.

And now a word of this woman—this black heroine—this fugitive slave. She is now called "Moses," having inherited the name, for the many daring feats she has accomplished in behalf of the bondmen and the many slaves she has set free. She was formerly a slave in Virginia—she determined upon "freedom or death" and escaped to Canada. She there planned the deliverance of all her kindred, and made nine successful trips to different slave states, effecting the escape of over 180 slaves and their successful establishment in Canada. Since the rebellion she has devoted herself to her great work of delivering the bondmen, with an energy and sagacity that cannot be exceeded. Many and many times she has penetrated the enemy's lines and discovered their situation and condition, and escaped without injury, but not without extreme hazard. True, she is but a woman, and a "nigger" at that, but in patriotism, sagacity, energy, ability and all that elevates human character, she is head and shoulders above all the copperheads in the land, and above many who vaunt their patriotism and boast their philanthropy, swaggering of their superiority because of the cuticle in which their Creator condescended to envelop them.

Source

"From Florida: Colonel Montgomery's Raid," *Wisconsin State Journal*, Madison, WI, 20 June 1863, reprinted in Jean Humez, *Harriet Tubman: The Life and the Life Stories* (Madison: University of Wisconsin Press, 2003), 288–290.

CONFLICT WITH TRAIN CONDUCTOR
OCTOBER 1865

In mid-October of 1865, Tubman took a train from Philadelphia to New York, leaving her work in hospitals and orphanages in the Washington, D.C., area to return to her family in Auburn, New York. She possessed a half-fare ticket because of her wartime service and sat in a regular car, but the conductor on the Camden & South Amboy train ordered her to a smoking car. Martha Coffin Wright narrated the ensuing tussle in this letter to Marianne Pelham Mott; Martha, Lucretia Mott's younger sister; and Marianne, Lucretia Mott's daughter-in-law, were among Tubman's friends who tried to help her seek justice in this civil rights case. Tubman, however, ultimately decided not to sue the train company, but many of her peers like Sojourner Truth successfully prosecuted conductors who refused them service.

––––––

Harriet Tubman was here yesterday—it was quite dark & wet, when she left, but she didn't kear for that—she'd as lief go in de dark as de light—How dreadful it was for that wicked conductor to drag her out into the smoking car & hurt her so seriously, disabling her left arm, perhaps for the Winter— She still has the misery in her Shoulder & side & carries her hand in a sling—It took three of them to drag her out after first trying to wrench her finger and then her arm—She told the man he was a copperhead scoundrel, for which he choked her—she was on the 11 o'cl (p. m.) train between Cambden & South Amboy—She told him she didn't thank any body to call her cullud pusson—She wd he called [her] black or Negro—She was as proud of being a black woman as he was of being white—

It was not tho't best to publish the circumstances till they found whether something cd be got from the Company—D. told her that she could sue the company here, at her home, and he wd write to Mr. Phillips' son-in-law, at the A. S. Office, and enquire whether the witness advertised for, had been found, but if not, her own testimony, & her Drs. wd be sufficient [insert over line: "he has written '——Donalley Esq.'"]—She shewed me her documents, and told me what Sister L. and Thomas gave her.—She said there was to be a letter sent to me for her, this week, from Mr. Phillips or his son-in-law. So she is coming again—

Source

Martha Coffin Wright to Marianne Pelham Mott, 7 November 1865, reprinted in Jean Humez, *Harriet Tubman: The Life and the Life Stories* (Madison: University of Wisconsin Press, 2003), 292.

HARRIET TUBMAN'S MARRIAGE TO NELSON DAVIS MARCH 18, 1869

Harriet Tubman married Nelson Davis at the Central Presbyterian Church in Auburn, New York, a predominantly white congregation. The fact that she and Davis were married at a white church with Auburn's black and white elite in attendance indicates the esteem the community held for Tubman. Tubman's marriage also signifies one of the most important benefits of freedom in the Reconstruction era: legal and public recognition of marriage vows.

———

There is no more tyrannical master than custom. Cruel masters formerly domineered over slaves, politicians once in power put the screws to unfortunate wights [sic] not so lucky; kings at will strike off the heads of devoted subjects, but custom rules with a still stronger hand. None so poor but what will honor its call, and none so rich that dare defy its mandates. We never were more forcibly impressed with this fact than last evening in attending a wedding in high life at Central Church where the bride and groom were billed to appear at 6:30 p.m., and just as the clock struck seven the manly form of the groom darkened the door. Undoubtedly emulating the example of preceding brides and grooms, they were ready, but there was [sic] a few things which detained them at the last moment. Before a large and very select audience, Harriet Tubman, the heroine of many a thrilling incident by fire and flood, the emancipator of a large number of her race and the faithful Union Scout and Spy, took unto herself a husband and made one

William Nelson a happy man, (at least that is the supposition.) Both born slaves, as they grew in years and knowledge recognized the glory of freedom, still later in the eventful struggle they fled from bondage, until finally, by the blessing of Divine Providence, they stood there, last evening, Free, and were joined as man and wife. The audience was large, consisting of the friends of the parties and a large number of first families in the city. Ladies and gentlemen who were interested in Harriet, and who for years had advised and assisted her, came to see her married. After the ceremony Rev. Mr. Fowler made some very touching and happy allusions to their past trials and apparently plain sailing the parties now had when the ceremony ended amid the congratulations of the assembly. We tender our congratulations to the happy bride and groom, and may they never see a less happy moment than when Shimer, that prince of good fellow, spurred on by a prominent Democratic politician of the Third Ward, rushed frantically forward, and in an excited manner congratulated them on the happy event.

SOURCE

Auburn Morning News, 19 March 1869, transcription from Earl Conrad Collection, Schomburg Center for Research in Black Culture, New York Public Library, copy courtesy of Kate Clifford Larson.

Tubman Honored at Founding Convention of the National Association of Colored Women July 20–22, 1896

Tubman attended the first convention of the NACW and was honored by its members in numerous ways. First, a sketch of Tubman during the war (reprinted on front cover) was featured on the convention program; second, Rosetta Douglass-Sprague, Frederick Douglass's daughter, identified Tubman as one of the race's most "heroic women"; third, Tubman spoke and sang to the group; and finally, she was chosen to introduce Ida B. Wells Barnett's baby to the crowd, who was then deemed "the baby of the Federation." Tubman's notoriety among her peers and the rising generation of black women activists is evident throughout the document.

July 20, 1896. Morning Session.

The first Annual Convention of the National Federation of Afro-American Women convened in the 19th Street Baptist Church, Washington, D.C., on the above date, Mrs. Booker T. Washington of Tuskegee, Ala., President in the chair, assisted by Mrs. Mary H. Dickerson of Newport, R.I., First Vice-President. . . .

Rev. (Walter H.) Brooks delivered a pleasant address of welcome, declaring that when the best women of the land unite in one mighty company all their force of character, their intelligence and their active services, to lift up and ennoble the womanhood, a brighter and better day was dawning.

Mrs. Rosetta Douglass-Sprague, only daughter of the late Frederick Douglass, responded in behalf of the Afro-American women of the United States.

"From the log cabins of the South have come forth some of our most heroic women, whose words, acts and deeds are a stimulus to us at this hour. We have such women by the score, women in whose hearts philanthropic impulses have burned with ardor; whose love for mankind was second only to their love for God. Women who have suffered death rather than be robbed of their virtue. Women who have endured untold misery for the betterment of the condition of their brothers and sisters.

"While the white race have chronicled deeds of heroism and acts of mercy of the women of pioneer and other days, so we are pleased to note in the personality of such women as Phyllis Wheatley, Margaret Garner, Sojourner Truth and our venerable friend, Harriet Tubman, sterling qualities of head, heart and hand, that hold no insignificant place in the annals of heroic womanhood.

"Our wants are numerous. We want homes in which purity can be taught, not hovels that are police-court feeders; we want industrial schools where labor of all kinds is taught, enabling our boys and girls to become skilled in the trades; we want the dram shops closed; we want the pool rooms and the gambling dens of every variety swept out of existence; we want reform schools for our girls in such cities where the conscience of the white Christian is not elastic enough to take in the Negro child.

"These and many more are the wants we desire gratified. Your words of welcome, your gracious greeting, cheering us on in our endeavor," said Mrs. Sprague, "is an inspiration for us to work with a will and a determination worthy of our cause.

"Our progress depends in the united strength of both men and women—the women alone nor the men alone cannot do the work.

"We have so fully realized that fact by witnessing the work of our men with the women in the rear. This is indeed the women's era, and we are coming."

JULY 20, 1896. EVENING SESSION, 8:15 P.M.

The meeting was called to order by the President, who introduced Mrs. Victoria Earle Mathews of New York City as the Chairman of the evening. Mrs. Mathews gave a vivid account of the work accomplished by the National Federation during the past year, also an account of her visit through the South, which was received with applause by the large audience. . . .

Miss S. Cole and Mr. Jas. T. Walker rendered vocal solos, after which Mother Harriet was introduced to the audience by Mrs. Mathews, who referred briefly to the great services that Mrs. Tubman had rendered to her race.

When Mrs. Mathews retired to take the chair of the presiding officer, and Mrs. Tubman stood alone on the front of the rostrum, the audience, which not only filled every seat, but also much of the standing room in the aisles, rose as one person and greeted her with the waving of handkerchiefs and the clapping of hands. This was kept up for at least a minute, and Mrs. Tubman was much affected by the hearty reception given her.

When the applause had somewhat subsided, Mrs. Tubman acknowledged the compliment paid her in appropriate words, and at the request of some of the leading officers of the Convention related a little of her war experience. Despite the weight of advancing years, Mrs. Tubman is the possessor of a strong and musical voice, which last evening penetrated every portion of the large auditorium in which the Convention was held, and a war melody which she sang was fully as attractively rendered as were any of the other vocal selections of the evening. . . . After the benediction by Rev. Crummell, the meeting adjourned.

July 21, 1896. Afternoon Session. 2 p.m.

Mrs. Mathews stated that both Committees [Committee from the National League and Committee of the National Federation] had agreed upon the name of the new organization [National Association of Colored Women]. Mrs. Fanny Jackson Coppins, Philadelphia, thought the present name of the Federation too long, and that as the race was known in the census as colored people she did not admire the name Afro-American, but colored.

Mrs. Mathews, New York City, replied by permission of the chair, that her preference would always be for Afro-American as the name meant so much to the Negro in America. . . . She was not a colored American, but an Afro-American.

Evening Session. 8 p.m.

The evening session was called to order by the President, Mrs. Booker T. Washington. The meeting was opened with Devotional Exercises, after which Mrs. Fanny Jackson Coppins, Philadelphia, spoke of "The Necessity of a Course of Training for the Elevation and Improvement of Domestic Service." . . .

By request, Mother Tubman gave one of her characteristic songs, which thrilled the audience. Mrs. Mathews announced that the Committee on Union had agreed upon a basis of union, and that the two Committees appointed by the two "national bodies" now existed as a Committee of the whole, and that they would elect the officers of the new organization Wednesday. . . .

July 22, 1896. Morning Session.

Reports from six clubs were then read, after which Mrs. Thurman of Michigan made a motion that Baby Barnett be the first Honorary Member of the Federation (Carried).

Suggested by Mrs. B. K. Bruce that as Mother Tubman was the oldest member, that she introduce Baby Barnett to the audience.

Motion, Mrs. Thurman, that Baby Barnett be hereafter known as the Baby of the Federation. (Carried.)

Afternoon Session. 2:30 p.m.

The meeting was called to order by the President ... Miss Jenny Dean of Manassas Industrial School gave an interesting account of her work. . . .

Mother Tubman spoke of "More Homes for our Aged Ones," and her remarks were listened to attentively, after which Mrs. T. H. Lyles of St. Paul, Minn., pledged $25.00 to the Tubman Home. . . .

Evening Session. 8:15 p.m.

The convention was opened with a chorus of one hundred voices, Prof. J. T. Layton, Director. . . .

"Our Country Women and Children" was the interesting topic of which Miss Georgia Washington of Central Alabama, a graduate of Hampton Institute, Virginia, read a paper. She referred particularly to the situation of the colored women at Mount Meigs, a village near Montgomery, Ala., where a school has been established for Afro-Americans. "Country women," she said, "are suffering for the help and for the influence of her more educated sister of the North and other sections."

A chorus by the pupils of the Girls High School was rendered after which Mrs. Lucy B. Thurman, National Superintendent of the W.C.T.U. work among Afro-Americans, made an earnest appeal for a contribution to assist in defraying the expenses of Mother Harriet Tubman during her visit in Washington.

Mrs. Thurman appointed Mrs. Victoria Earle Mathews, Mrs. B. K. Bruce, Mrs. Rosetta Douglass Sprague, Mrs. T. J. Lyles, Miss L. C. Anthony, Mrs. Ida B. Wells Barnett, Miss Jenny Dean and Miss Georgia Washington to wait upon the audience. The contribution netted $27.42.

Source

National Association of Colored Women's Clubs, Official Minutes, 1902, reprinted in Jean Humez, *Harriet Tubman: The Life and the Life Stories* (Madison: University of Wisconsin Press, 2003), 306–310.

THE PRESS AMPLIFIES THE MYTH
OF HARRIET TUBMAN
JULY 31, 1909

Evidence of the myths surrounding Tubman abound in this short article from a Minnesota paper. The story offers exaggerated claims that Tubman single-handedly led "3,000 slaves" out of bondage and falsely reports that the state of Maryland advertised an award of $52,000 (approximately $1.4 million today) for her capture. The paper deems her "the greatest woman the United States ever produced."

It is proposed to found at Auburn, New York, an industrial school as a memorial to Harriet Tubman Davis, who still resides in that city at the age of about ninety. The school is to be under the auspices of the A.M.E. Zion church. Mrs. Davis well deserves such a memorial for she was one of the most remarkable women that any race ever produced. She was such an efficient conductor on the underground railroad, that Maryland offered $52,000 for her arrest. She was a friend of Seward, Garrison, John Brown, Gerrit Smith, and Lincoln. She personally conducted 3,000 slaves from the South to freedom. She was a trusted spy for Major General David Hunter during the rebel-lion. Though "unattached," congress granted her a pension. Judged by her works, she was the greatest woman the United States ever produced.

SOURCE

The Appeal, Saint Paul, MN, 31 July 1909, *Chronicling America: Historic American Newspapers*, Lib. of Congress, http://chroniclingamerica.loc.gov/lccn/sn83016810/1909-07-31/ed-1/seq-4/.

FRANKLIN B. SANBORN'S MEMORIAL
TO HARRIET TUBMAN
MARCH 19, 1913

Franklin Sanborn published the first biographical sketch of Tubman in 1863, and in this article fifty years later, he memorializes her. One of her few contemporaries still living (he died four years later), Sanborn notes her friendships with white allies like John Brown and Ednah Dow Cheney and adds that "Miss Anne Whiting" tried unsuccessfully to teach Tubman to read. Even in this laudatory portrait from a longtime friend, however, prejudices about African Americans emerge in the midst of compliments.

Brutus in Shakespeare's play of "Julius Caesar," hearing in battle of the untimely death of Cassius, says to his loyal Romans: "Friends,—'tis impossible that ever Rome should breed his fellow; I do owe more tears to this dead man than you shall see me pay."

Something like this might I say of Araminta Ross, who became by marriage successively Mrs. Tubman and Mrs. Davis; but whose career was shaped by herself and her Lord, and scarcely influenced at all by her marriages, which were only special instances of her general plan of life,—to exist for the benefit of others, to whom she devoted magnificent powers, ever in readiness to serve the cause of humanity, as she understood it. As I was the first scribe who ever drew from her the story of her life and ancestry [which has been singularly exaggerated by lovers of the marvelous], I will repeat here the facts given by me in a Boston newspaper, 50 years ago, July 17, 1863, when she was in the service of the Union army against the enslavers of her race, who were then fighting to destroy our free Republic, in which she was born a slave near Cambridge, on the Eastern Shore of Maryland, not earlier than 1820, nor later than 1821. . . .

I first met her at a boarding-house in Boston, probably in the summer of 1858, when she had become acquainted with John Brown, and was aiding him in his scheme to raise colored soldiers for his small band of men who were to lessen the value of slaves in Virginia, as she had done in Maryland. For, although I could never count more than 150 slaves brought away from Maryland under her direct lead, yet her example and incitement may have led to the escape of 150 more. I calculate the average market value of the human cattle she led off at $750 a head, as things stood in the 10 years 1849–1859, when her work was done; that means $100,000; and if as many more escaped through her example, another $100,000 may be set down. . . .

She visited me at Concord, in all, four or five times, and always came first to me there. I took her to Emerson's house; but she was never a guest there for more than a day at a time. She was more with Miss Anne Whiting, who vainly tried to teach her to read; she was with the Alcotts, the Brookses, with Mrs. Horace Mann; but her whole stay in Concord, in 30 years, could not have exceeded a fortnight. The Stearnses, Cheneys and others introduced her to Gov. Andrew in 1861, who gave her passes to the South, where my good friend, Elbridge Gerry Dudley, then at the Sea Islands, 1862–3, gave her the means of becoming acquainted with Gens. Hunter and Saxton, Col. Shaw and Col. Montgomery of Kansas. Under his command she did her best service in S. Carolina; but her direct way of interpreting orders, and Montgomery's soldierly way of acting under general orders, offended the more fastidious Col. Higginson, and led to some censures of both Montgomery and Harriet.

Harriet was by no means faultless; she was ignorant, partial,—could never see any fault in her friends; if money was given her, she would give it away, often to the undeserving; her soul was generous, her judgment defective, but never perverse. She was the type of her race, loyal to the death, secretive as the grave, but never with hatred in her heart for her worst oppressors. "With malice toward none, with charity for all," describes her as it hardly describes the most generous white person. Mercy and patience, those two qualities which the blacks display in excess, accompanied with deceit and indifference in moral matters, were Harriet's outstanding qualities; together with a courage and self-sacrifice the martyrs and angels might envy. Many have died and will die who have used greater faculties; none who have consecrated what they had to the cause of the poor with greater zeal or a truer heart.

SOURCE

Franklin B. Sanborn, "Concerning Harriet Tubman and Fugitive Slaves," *Springfield [Mass.] Republican*, 19 March 1913, reprinted in Jean Humez, *Harriet Tubman: The Life and the Life Stories* (Madison: University of Wisconsin Press, 2003), 320–323.

S.S. Harriet Tubman Announced
March 21, 1942

Memorials of Tubman persisted into the mid-twentieth century, when during World War II, the S.S. Harriet Tubman became the first navy vessel to be named after a black woman. Tubman joined famous black men like Frederick Douglass and Toussaint L'Ouverture who were all deemed "outstanding Negro(s) of the western hemisphere" by the navy commission.

———

WASHINGTON—The selection of a name for the thirteenth Liberty ship to honor an outstanding Negro of the western hemisphere was announced this week by the Maritime Commission. The SS HARRIET TUBMAN will be the first ship to be named in honor of a Negro woman. It has not yet been officially assigned to a shipyard, but efforts are being made to have it built at the Bethlehem-Fairfield shipyard in Baltimore, since she was a native of Maryland.

Harriet Tubman was born in slavery about 1815 and when she was 25 escaped from her master's plantation in Maryland to New England, where she joined with Garrison, Brown and other abolitionists to become an active promoter of the "underground railway." She first rescued her parents and during two decades before the Civil War made repeated journeys into the South, taking over 400 or more of her race to the North and into Canada.

During the war she served with Massachusetts troops as a scout and guided Col. James Montgomery and his men in their memorable expedition into South Carolina. At the close of the war, through the help of Secretary of State William H. Seward, she was able to make her home in Auburn, N.Y., where she soon become engaged in philanthropic service in behalf of the poor and aged of her people. Her efforts led to the foundation of the Harriet Tubman Home for Indigent Aged Negroes. She died in Auburn in 1913.

Other Liberty ships named for Negroes include the SS Booker T. Washington, George Washington Carver, Paul Laurence Dunbar, Frederick Douglass, John Merrick, Robert L. Vann James Weldon Johnson, John Hope, John H. Murphy, Robert S. Abbott, Edward Savoy and Toussaint L'Ouverture.

The Navy Department has named a naval vessel, the Destroyer Escort Leonard Roy Harmon, in honor of a Negro messman who received the Navy Cross posthumously for heroic conduct in Guadalcanal.

Source

"SS Harriet Tubman to Memorialize Abolitionist," 15 April 1944, *The Chicago Defender (National edition) (1921–1967)*, reprinted at http://search.proquest.com/docview/492600297?accountid=14676.

BIBLIOGRAPHY

PRINTED PRIMARY SOURCES

Anonymous, "The Anti-Slavery Alphabet." Philadelphia: Merrihew and Thompson, 1847. Reprinted at http://www.gutenberg.org/files/16081/16081-h/16081-h.htm.

Bradford, Sarah H. *Harriet, the Moses of Her People*. New York: J.J. Little & Co., 1901.

——. *Scenes in the Life of Harriet Tubman*. Auburn, NY: W.J. Moses, 1869.

Grainger, James. *The Sugar Cane: A Poem in Four Books*. London: R. and J. Dodsley, 1764.

Higginson, Thomas Wentworth. *Army Life in a Black Regiment*. Boston: Fields, Osgood, and Co., 1870.

Johnson, Charles F. *The Long Roll; Being a Journal of the Civil War, as set down during the years 1861–1863*. East Aurora, NY: The Roycrofters, 1911.

McGuire, Judith White Brockenbrough. *Diary of a Southern Refugee, During the War, By a Lady of Virginia*. Richmond, VA: J.W. Randolph & English Publishers, 1889.

Pearson, Elizabeth Ware, ed. *Letters from Port Royal: Written at the Time of the Civil War*. Boston, MA: W.B. Clarke Co., 1906.

Reid, Richard M., ed. *Practicing Medicine in a Black Regiment: The Civil War Diary of Burt G. Wilder, 55th Massachusetts*. Amherst: University of Massachusetts Press, 2010.

Sanborn, Franklin. *The Life and Letters of John Brown: Liberator of Kansas, and Martyr of Virginia*. Boston: Roberts Brothers, 1891.

Scott, Robert N., ed. *War of the Rebellion: A Compilation of the Official Records of the Union and Confederate Armies*, Series 1-Volume XIV. Washington, D.C.: Government Printing Office, 1885.

Siebert, Wilbur H. *The Underground Railroad in Slavery and Freedom*. New York: The MacMillan Company, 1898.

Still, William. *The Underground Railroad: Authentic Narratives and First-Hand Accounts*. New York: Dover Publications, 2007; first published by Porter & Coates, 1872.

SECONDARY SOURCES

Abrahamson, James. *The Men of Secession and Civil War, 1859–1861*. Wilmington, DE: Scholarly Resources, 2000.

Allen, Thomas B. *Harriet Tubman, Secret Agent: How Daring Slaves and Free Blacks Spied for the Union During the Civil War*. New York: National Geographic Society, 2006.

Ambrose, Douglas. "Of Stations and Relations: Proslavery Christianity in Early National Virginia." In *Religion and the Antebellum Debate Over Slavery*, edited by John R. McKivigan and Mitchell Snay, 35–67. Athens: University of Georgia Press, 1998.

Baker, Jean H. *James Buchanan*. New York: Times Books, 2004.

Berkin, Carol. *First Generations: Women in Colonial America*. New York: MacMillan, 1997.

Berlin, Ira. *Generations of Captivity: A History of African-American Slaves*. Cambridge: Harvard University Press, 2003.

——. "Who Freed the Slaves?: Emancipation and Its Meaning." In *Union and Emancipation: Essays on Politics and Race in the Civil War Era*, edited by David Blight and Brooks Simpson, 105–122. Kent, OH: Kent State University Press, 1997.

Berlin, Ira, Joseph P. Reidy, and Leslie Rowland, eds. *Freedom's Soldiers: The Black Military Experience in the Civil War*. Cambridge: Cambridge University Press, 1998.

Berry, Daina Ramey and Deleso A. Alford, eds. *Enslaved Women in America: An Encyclopedia*. Santa Barbara, CA: ABC-CLIO, 2012.

Blackett, Richard. *Making Freedom: The Underground Railroad and the Politics of Slavery*. Chapel Hill: The University of North Carolina Press, 2013.

Blackwell, Marilyn S. and Kristen T. Oertel, *Frontier Feminist: Clarina Howard Nichols and the Politics of Motherhood*. Lawrence: University Press of Kansas, 2010.

Blight, David. *American Oracle: The Civil War in the Civil Rights Era*. Cambridge, MA: Belknap/Harvard, 2011.

——. *Race and Reunion: The Civil War in American Memory*. Cambridge: Belknap/Harvard University Press, 2001.

——. *A Slave No More: Two Men Who Escaped to Freedom*. Boston: Houghton, Mifflin, Harcourt, 2007.

Bordewich, Fergus. *Bound for Canaan: The Epic Story of the Underground Railroad, America's First Civil Rights Movement*. New York: Harper Collins, 2005.

Borritt, Gabor, ed. *Slavery, Resistance, and Freedom*. New York: Oxford University Press, 2007.

Boster, Dea H. *African American Slavery and Disability: Bodies, Property, and Power in the Antebellum South, 1830–1860*. New York: Routledge, 2013.

Bowman, Shearer David. *At the Precipice: Americans North and South during the Secession Crisis*. Chapel Hill: University of North Carolina Press, 2010.

Breen, Patrick H. "Contested Communion: The Limits of White Solidarity in Nat Turner's Virginia." *Journal of the Early Republic* 27, No. 4 (Winter 2007): 685–703.

Broyld, Dann J. "Harriet Tubman: Transnationalism and the Land of a Queen in the Late Antebellum," *Meridians: Feminism, Race, and Transnationalism* 12, No. 2 (2014): 78–98.

Bryant, Christopher A. "Stopping Time: The Pro-Slavery and 'Irrevocable' Thirteenth Amendment," *Harvard Journal of Law and Public Policy* 26, No. 2 (2003): 501.

Budiansky,Stephen. *The Bloody Shirt: Terror after Appomattox*. New York: Penguin, 2008,.

Burke, Diane Mutti. *On Slavery's Border: Missouri's Small Slaveholding Households*. Athens: University of Georgia Press, 2011.

Calarco, Tom. *People of the Underground Railroad: A Biographical Dictionary*. Westport, CT: Greenwood Press, 2008.

Camp, Stephanie. *Enslaved Women and Everyday Resistance in the Plantation South*. Chapel Hill: The University of North Carolina Press, 2004.

Cary, Brycchan. *From Peace to Freedom: Quaker Rhetoric and the Birth of American Antislavery, 1657–1761*. New York: Yale University Press, 2012.

Cimbala, Paul. *Under the Guardianship of the Bureau: The Freedmen's Bureau and the Reconstruction of Georgia, 1865–1870*. Athens: University of Georgia Press, 1997.

Clinton, Catherine. *Harriet Tubman: The Road to Freedom*. Boston: Back Bay Books, 2004.

Collier-Thomas, Bettye. *Jesus, Jobs, and Justice: African American Women and Religion*. New York: Knopf, 2010.

Conrad, Earl. *Harriet Tubman*. Washington, D.C.: Associated Publishers, 1943.

Douglass, Frederick. *Life and Times of Frederick Douglass from 1817 to 1882*. London: Christian Age Office, 1882.

——. *Narrative of the Life of Frederick Douglass*. New York: Bedford/St. Martin's, 2003, 1845.

Downs, Jim. *Sick from Freedom: African-American Illness and Suffering during the Civil War and Reconstruction*. New York: Oxford University Press, 2012.

Du Bois, W.E.B. *Black Reconstruction in America*. New York: Atheneum, 1992, 1935.

Dudden, Faye E. *Fighting Chance: The Struggle over Woman Suffrage and Black Suffrage in Reconstruction America*. New York: Oxford University Press, 2011.

Earle, Jonathan and Diane Mutti Burke, eds. *Bleeding Kansas and Bleeding Missouri: The Long Civil War on the Border*. Lawrence: University Press of Kansas, 2013.

Edwards, Rebecca. *Angels in the Machinery: Gender in American Party Politics from the Civil War to the Progressive Era*. New York: Oxford University Press, 1997.

Emberton, Carole. *Beyond Redemption: Race, Violence, and the American South after the Civil War*. Chicago: University of Chicago Press, 2013.

Etcheson, Nicole. *Bleeding Kansas: Contested Liberty in the Civil War Era*. Lawrence: University Press of Kansas, 2004.

Fahs, Alice and Joan Waugh, eds. *The Memory of the Civil War in American Culture*. Chapel Hill: The University of North Carolina Press, 2004.

Faulkner, Carol. *Lucretia Mott's Heresy: Abolition and Women's Rights in Nineteenth-Century America*. Philadelphia: University of Pennsylvania Press, 2011.

——. *Women's Radical Reconstruction: The Freedmen's Aid Movement*. Philadelphia: University of Pennsylvania Press, 2004.

Fields, Barbara Jeanne. *Slavery and Freedom on the Middle Ground: Maryland during the Nineteenth Century*. New Haven: Yale University Press, 1985.

Finkelman, Paul. *His Soul Goes Marching On: Responses to John Brown and the Harpers Ferry Raid*. Charlottesville, VA: University Press of Virginia, 1995.

——. *An Imperfect Union: Slavery, Federalism, and Comity*. Union, NJ: The Lawbook Exchange, 2000.

——. "Lincoln, Emancipation and the Limits of Constitutional Change." *Supreme Court Review* (2008): 349–387.

——. *Slavery and the Founders: Race and Liberty in the Age of Jefferson*, 3rd ed. New York: M.E. Sharpe, 2014.

——. "The Long Road to Dignity: The Wrong of Segregation and What the Civil Rights Act of 1964 Had to Change," *Louisiana Law Review* 74 (2014): 1045–1046, 1048, 1050.

Finkelman, Paul and Donald Kennon, eds. *Congress and the Crisis of the 1850s*. Athens: Ohio University Press, 2012.

Finseth, Ian Frederick, ed. *The Underground Railroad: Authentic Narratives and First-Hand Accounts*. New York: Dover Publications, 2007.

Foner, Eric. *Forever Free: The Story of Emancipation and Reconstruction*. New York: Vintage, 2005.

——. *Gateway to Freedom: The Hidden History of the Underground Railroad*. New York: Norton, 2015.

——. *Reconstruction: America's Unfinished Revolution, 1863–1877*. New York: Harper and Row, 1988.

——. "Rooted in Reconstruction," *The Nation* 287, No. 18 (November 2008): 30.

——. *The Life and Writings of Frederick Douglass: Reconstruction and After*. New York: International Publishers, 1950.

Foner, Philip S., ed. *Frederick Douglass on Women's Rights*. New York: Da Capo Press, 1992.

Footner, Geoffrey. *Tidewater Triumph: The Development and Worldwide Success of the Chesapeake Bay Pilot Schooner*. Centerville, MD: Tidewater Publishers, 1998.

Forbes, Ella. *African American Women during the Civil War*. New York: Routledge, 1998.

Ford, Bridget. "Black Spiritual Defiance and the Politics of Slavery in Antebellum Louisville." *The Journal of Southern History* 78, No. 1 (2012): 69–106.

Franklin, John Hope and Loren Schweninger, eds. *Runaway Slaves: Rebels on the Plantation*. New York: Oxford University Press, 1999.

Frazier, Harriet C. *Slavery and Crime in Missouri, 1773–1865.* Jefferson, NC: McFarland and Co., 2009.

Frost, Jerry William. *The Quaker Origins of Antislavery.* Norwood, PA: Norwood Editions, 1980.

Gara, Larry. *The Liberty Line: The Legend of the Underground Railroad.* Lexington: University of Kentucky Press, 1961.

Gienapp, William E. *The Origins of the Republican Party, 1852–56.* New York: Oxford University Press, 1987.

Giesberg, Judith Ann. *Army at Home: Women and the Civil War on the Northern Home Front.* Chapel Hill: The University of North Carolina Press, 2009.

——. *Civil War Sisterhood: The U.S. Sanitary Commission and Women's Politics in Transition.* Boston: Northeastern University Press, 2000.

Gilpin, Blakeslee. *John Brown Still Lives! America's Long Reckoning with Violence, Equality and Change.* Chapel Hill: University of North Carolina Press, 2011.

Glasrud, Bruce A. and Pitre, Merline, eds. *Black Women in Texas History.* College Station: Texas A & M University Press, 2008.

Glatthaar, Joseph. "Black Glory: The African-American Role in Union History." In *Why the Confederacy Lost*, edited by Gabor S. Borritt, 133–162. New York: Oxford University Press, 1992.

——. *Forged in Battle: The Civil War Alliance of Black Soldiers and White Officers* New York: The Free Press, 1990.

Glymph, Thavolia. *Out of the House of Bondage: The Transformation of the Plantation Household.* New York: Cambridge University Press, 2008.

Gomez, Michael. *Exchanging Our Country Marks: The Transformation of African Identities in the Colonial and Antebellum South.* Chapel Hill: University of North Carolina Press, 1998.

Gordon, Ann, ed. *The Selected Letters of Elizabeth Cady Stanton and Susan B. Anthony.* New Brunswick: Rutgers University Press, 2013.

Gordon, Ann and Bettye Collier-Thomas, eds. *African American Women and the Vote, 1837–1965.* Amherst: University of Massachusetts Press, 1997.

Gordon-Reed, Annette. *The Hemingses of Monticello: An American Family.* New York: Norton, 2008.

Gustafson, Melanie Susan. *Women and the Republican Party, 1854–1924.* Urbana: University of Illinois Press, 2001.

Hagedorn, Ann. *Beyond the River: The Untold Story of the Heroes of the Underground Railroad.* New York: Simon and Schuster, 2002.

Hamm, Thomas D. *The Quakers in America.* New York: Columbia University Press, 2003.

Hankins, Barry. *The Second Great Awakening and the Transcendentalists.* Westport, CT: Greenwood Press, 2004.

Harrold, Stanley. *Border War: Fighting over Slavery before the Civil War.* Chapel Hill: The University of North Carolina Press, 2010.

——. *Subversives: Antislavery Community in Washington, D.C., 1828–1865.* Baton Rouge: Louisiana State University Press, 2003.

——. *The Rise of Aggressive Abolitionism: Addresses to the Slaves.* Lexington: University of Kentucky Press, 2004.

Hobson, Janell. "Harriet Tubman: A Legacy of Resistance." Meridians: Feminism, Race, Transnationalism 12, No. 22 (2014): 1–8.

Holzer, Harold. *Lincoln President-Elect: Abraham Lincoln and the Great Secession Winter.* New York: Simon & Schuster, 2008.

Horton, Lois E. *Harriet Tubman and the Fight for Freedom: A Brief History with Documents.* New York: Bedford/St. Martin's, 2013.

Humez, Jean. *Harriet Tubman: The Life and the Life Stories.* Madison, WI: The University of Wisconsin Press, 2003.

Humphreys, Margaret. *Marrow of Tragedy: The Health Crisis of the American Civil War.* Baltimore: Johns Hopkins University Press, 2013.

Janney, Carolyn. *Remembering the Civil War: Reunion and the Limits of Reconciliation.* Chapel Hill: The University of North Carolina Press, 2013.

Jenkins, Wilbert L. *Seizing the New Day: African Americans in Post-Civil War Charleston.* Bloomington: Indiana University Press, 1998.

Jones, Jacqueline. *Labor of Love, Labor of Sorrow: Black Women, Work, and the Family, from Slavery to the Present.* New York: Basic Books, 1985.

Jones, Kelly Houston. "'A Rough, Saucy Set Of Hands To Manage': Slave Resistance in Arkansas." *Arkansas Historical Quarterly* 71, No. 1 (2012): 1–21.

Jordan, Ryan P. *Slavery and the Meetinghouse: The Quakers and the Abolitionist Dilemma, 1820–1865.* Bloomington: Indiana University Press, 2007.

Kaiser, Mary Farmer. *Freedwomen and the Freedmen's Bureau: Race, Gender, and Public Policy in the Age of Emancipation.* New York: Fordham University Press, 2010.

Keith, LeAnna. *The Colfax Massacre: The Untold Story of Black Power, White Terror, and the Death of Reconstruction.* New York: Oxford University Press, 2008.

King, Wilma. *Stolen Childhood: Slave Youth in Nineteenth Century America.* Bloomington: Indiana University Press, 2011.

Landsberg, Allison. *Prosthetic Memory: The Transformation of American Remembrance in the Age of Mass Culture.* New York: Columbia University Press, 2004.

Lansana, Quraysh Ali. *They Shall Run: Harriet Tubman Poems.* Chicago: Third World Press, 2004.

Larson, Kate Clifford. *Bound for the Promised Land: Harriet Tubman, Portrait of an American Hero.* New York: Ballantine, 2004.

Libby, David J. *Slavery and Frontier Mississippi, 1720–1835.* Oxford: University Press of Mississippi, 2004.

Lupton, John A. "Abraham Lincoln and the Corwin Amendment." *Illinois Periodicals Online.* http://www.lib.niu.edu/2006/ih060934.html.

Marszalek, John F. *Lincoln and the Military.* Carbondale, IL: Southern Illinois University Press, 2014.

May, Vivian M. "Under-Theorized and Under-Taught: Re-examining Harriet Tubman's Place in Women's Studies," Meridians: Feminism, Race, Transnationalism 12, No. 22 (2014): 28–49.

McCandless, Peter. *Slavery, Disease, and Suffering in the Southern Low Country.* Cambridge: Cambridge University Press, 2011.

McGlone, Robert E. *John Brown's War Against Slavery.* New York: Cambridge University Press, 2009.

McGowan, James A. *Station Master on the Underground Railroad: The Life and Letters of Thomas Garrett.* Jefferson, NC: McFarland, 2005.

McNair, Glenn. *Criminal Injustice: Slaves and Free Blacks in Georgia's Criminal Justice System.* Charlottesville: University of Virginia Press, 2009.

Meier, Michael T. "Lorenzo Thomas and the Recruitment of Blacks." In *Black Soldiers in Blue: African American Troops in the Civil War Era,* edited by John David Smith, 249–275. Chapel Hill: The University of North Carolina Press, 2002.

Middleton, Stephen, ed. *Black Congressmen during Reconstruction: A Documentary Sourcebook* Westport, CT: Greenwood Press, 2002.

Moreau, Joseph. *Schoolbook Nation: Conflicts Over American History Textbooks from the Civil War to the Present.* Ann Arbor: University of Michigan, 2003.

Morgan, Jennifer. *Laboring Women: Reproduction and Gender in New World Slavery.* Philadelphia: University of Pennsylvania Press, 2004.

Morgan, Philip D. "Slave Life in Piedmont Virginia." In *Colonial Chesapeake Society,* edited by Lois Green Carr, Philip D. Morgan, and Jean B. Russo 433–484. Chapel Hill: University of North Carolina Press, 1988.

Morris, Thomas D. *Free Men All: The Personal Liberty Laws of the North.* Baltimore: Johns Hopkins University Press, 1974.

——. *Southern Slavery and the Law: 1619–1860.* Chapel Hill: University of North Carolina Press, 1996.

Mutti Burke, Diane. *On Slavery's Border: Missouri's Small-Slaveholding Households.* Athens: University of Georgia Press, 2010.

Oertel, Kristen. *Bleeding Borders: Race, Gender, and Violence in Pre-Civil War Kansas.* Baton Rouge: Louisiana State University Press, 2009.

——. "'Nigger-loving Fanatics' and 'Villains of the Blackest Dye'": Racialized Manhood and the Sectional Debates" In *Bleeding Kansas and Bleeding Missouri: The Long Civil War on the Border,* edited by Jonathan Earle and Diane Mutti Burke, 65–80. Lawrence: University Press of Kansas, 2013.

Painter, Nell Irvin. *Sojourner Truth: A Life, A Symbol.* New York: Norton, 1996.

Patton, Venetria K. *Women in Chains: The Legacy of Slavery in Black Women's Fiction.* Albany: State University of New York Press, 2000.

Petry, Ann. *Harriet Tubman: Conductor on the Underground Railroad.* New York: Harper Collins, 1996, 1955.

Phillips, Christopher. *Freedom's Port: The African American Community of Baltimore.* Urbana: University of Illinois Press, 1997.

Raboteau, Albert. *Slave Religion: The "Invisible Institution" in the Antebellum South.* New York: Oxford University Press, 2004, 1978.

Re, Richard M. and Re, Christopher M. "Voting and Vice: Criminal Disenfranchisement and the Reconstruction Amendments," *The Yale Law Journal* 121, No. 7 (May 2012): 1584.

Redkey, Edwin S. *A Grand Army of Black Men: Letters from African-American Soldiers in the Union Army, 1861–1865.* New York: Cambridge University Press, 1992.

——. "Brave, Black Volunteers: Profile of the Fifty-fourth Massachusetts Regiment." In *Hope and Glory: Essays on the Legacy of the Fifty-Fourth Massachusetts Regiment,* edited by Donald Yacavone, 21–34. Amherst: University of Massachusetts Press, 2001.

Reynolds, David. *John Brown, Abolitionist: The Man Who Killed Slavery, Sparked the Civil War, and Seeded Civil Rights.* New York: Random House, 2005.

Schechter, Patricia A. *Ida B. Wells-Barnett and American Reform, 1880–1930.* Chapel Hill: The University of North Carolina Press, 2001.

Schroeder, Alan and Jerry Pinkney. *Minty: A Story of Young Harriet Tubman.* New York: Puffin Books, 2000, 1996.

Scott, James. *Domination and the Arts of Resistance: Hidden Transcripts.* New Haven: Yale University Press, 1990.

Scully, Randolph Ferguson. "'I Come Here Before You Did and I Shall Not Go Away': Race, Gender, and Evangelical Community on the Eve of Nat Turner's Rebellion." *Journal of the Early Republic* 27, No. 4 (Winter 2007): 661–684.

Sernett, Milton C. *Harriet Tubman: Myth, Memory, and History.* Durham, NC: Duke University Press, 2007.

Smith, John David, ed. *Black Soldiers in Blue: African American Troops in the Civil War Era* Chapel Hill: The University of North Carolina Press, 2002.

Snay, Mitchell. *Gospel of Disunion: Religion and Separatism in the Antebellum South.* Chapel Hill: University of North Carolina Press, 1997.

Sneider, Allison L. *Suffragists in an Imperial Age: U.S. Expansion and the Woman Question, 1870–1929.* New York: Oxford University Press, 2008.

Snyder, Terri L. "Suicide, Slavery, and Memory in North America." *The Journal of American History* 39 (June 2010): 39–62.

——. "'To Seeke for Justice': Gender, Servitude, and Household Government in the Early Modern Chesapeake." In *Early Modern Virginia: Reconsidering the Old Dominion,* edited by Douglas Bradburn and John C. Coombs, 128–157. Charlottesville: University of Virginia Press, 2011.

Sommerville, Dianne Miller. *Rape and Race in the Nineteenth-Century South.* Chapel Hill: University of North Carolina Press, 2004.

Sparks, Randy J. "'To Rend the Body of Christ': Proslavery Ideology and Religious Schism from a Mississippi Perspective." In *Religion and the Antebellum Debate Over Slavery,* edited by John R. McKivigan and Mitchell Snay, 273–295. Athens: University of Georgia Press, 1998.

Stampp, Kenneth. *The Peculiar Institution: Slavery in the Ante-Bellum South*. New York: Knopf, 1956.

Stanton, Lucia C. *"Those Who Labor for My Happiness": Slavery at Thomas Jefferson's Monticello*. Charlottesville: University of Virginia Press, 2012.

Sweet, James. *Recreating Africa: Culture, Kinship, and Religion in the Afro-Portuguese World*. Chapel Hill: University of North Carolina Press, 2003.

Taylor, Nikki Marie. *Frontiers of Freedom: Cincinnati's Black Community*. Athens, OH: Ohio University Press, 2005.

Venet, Wendy Hamand. *A Strong-Minded Woman: The Life of Mary Livermore*. Amherst: University of Massachusetts Press, 2005.

Wang, Xi. *The Trial of Democracy: Black Suffrage and Northern Republicans, 1860–1910*. Athens: University of Georgia Press, 1997.

Waugh, Joan. *On the Brink of Civil War: The Compromise of 1850 and How It Changed the Course of American History*. Wilmington, DE: Scholarly Resources, 2003.

Westwood, Howard. *Black Troops, White Commanders, and Freedmen during the American Civil War*. Carbondale, IL: Southern Illinois University Press, 2008.

White, Deborah Gray. *Ar'n't I a Woman: Female Slaves in the Plantation South*. New York: Norton, 1999.

——. *Too Heavy a Load: Black Women in Defense of Themselves, 1894–1944*. New York: Norton, 1999.

Wiencek, Henry. "The Dark Side of Thomas Jefferson." *Smithsonian* 43, No. 6 (2012). http://www.smithsonianmag.com/history/the-dark-side-of-thomas-jefferson-35976004/.

Wilson, Keith P. *Campfires of Freedom: The Camp Life of Black Soldiers during the Civil War*. Kent, OH: Kent State University Press, 2002.

Wood, Betty. *Women's Work, Men's Work: The Informal Slave Economies of Lowcountry Georgia*. Athens: University of Georgia Press, 1995.

Wunder, John R. and Joann M. Ross. *The Nebraska-Kansas Act of 1854*. Lincoln: The University of Nebraska Press, 2008.

Yacavone, Donald, ed., *Freedom's Journey: African American Voices of the Civil War*. Chicago: Lawrence Hill Books, 2004.

INDEX

Note: HT = Harriet Tubman